The Tyndale Old Testament Commentaries

General Editor:

PROFESSOR D. J. WISEMAN, O.B.E., M.A., D.LIT., F.B.A., F.S.A.

PSALMS 1–72

TO MY WIFE
Psalm 13:6

PSALMS 1—72

AN INTRODUCTION AND COMMENTARY ON BOOKS I AND II OF THE PSALMS

by

THE REV. DEREK KIDNER, M.A., A.R.C.M.

formerly Warden of Tyndale House, Cambridge

INTER-VARSITY PRESS
LEICESTER, ENGLAND
DOWNERS GROVE, ILLINOIS, U.S.A.

Inter-Varsity Press
38 De Montfort Street, Leicester LE1 7GP, England
Box 1400, Downers Grove, Illinois 60515 U.S.A.

*Inter-Varsity Press, England, is the publishing division of the Universities and
Colleges Christian Fellowship (formerly the Inter-Varsity Fellowship), a student
movement linking Christian Unions in universities and colleges throughout the United
Kingdom and the Republic of Ireland, and a member movement of the International
Fellowship of Evangelical Students. For information about local and national
activities write to UCCF, 38 De Montfort Street, Leicester, LE1 7GP.*

*InterVarsity Press, U.S.A., is the book-publishing division of Inter-Varsity
Christian Fellowship, a student movement active on campus at hundreds of
universities, colleges and schools of nursing. For information about local and regional
activities, write IVCF, 233 Langdon St., Madison, WI 53703.*

*Distributed in Canada through InterVarsity Press, 860 Denison St., Unit 3,
Markham, Ontario L3R 4H1, Canada.*

*Text set in Great Britain
Printed in the United States of America*

*UK ISBN 0-85111-627-2 (hardback)
UK ISBN 0-85111-828-3 (paperback)
Library of Congress Catalog Card Number: 75-23852
USA ISBN 0-87784-868-8 (hardback)
USA ISBN 0-87784-264-7 (paperback)
USA ISBN 0-87784-880-7 (set of Tyndale Old Testament Commentaries, hardback)
USA ISBN 0-87784-280-9 (set of Tyndale Old Testament Commentaries, paperback)*

21	20	19	18	17	16	15	14	13	12	11	10	9	8
96	95	94	93	92	91	90	89	88	87	86	85	84	

GENERAL PREFACE

THE welcome accorded to the volumes already published in the *Tyndale Old Testament Commentaries* and, not least, to the first to have appeared in the series, *Proverbs* by the Rev. Derek Kidner, encouraged us to invite him to write two volumes on the *Psalms*, of which this is the first. God's people have always been characterized by their use of hymns and songs of various types in their worship, so the Psalms remain a pivotal book for Old Testament study which has a continuing relevance today.

This volume continues the aim of this series, which is to provide the student of the Bible who has no specialized training in biblical theology, history and languages with a handy, up-to-date commentary on each book. While the primary emphasis is on exegesis, major critical questions have not been overlooked where they are essential to the understanding of the text. The length and variety of some books such as the Psalms, preclude any exhaustive treatment within the number of pages allocated. Enough is given us, however, to stimulate devotional thought both for the public preacher and the private student.

While all are united in their belief in the divine inspiration, essential trustworthiness and practical relevance of the sacred writings, individual authors have freely made their own contributions. No detailed uniformity of method has been imposed in the handling of books of such varied subject-matter, form and style as the Old Testament.

For economy in comment Mr Kidner has, in this volume, made primary reference to the Revised Standard Version, with permission, and it is assumed that the reader will usually have this at hand. In a day of many commentaries and translations some, like that provided by Professor M. Dahood in his *Psalms* (Anchor Bible), lean heavily in their interpretation of the Hebrew text on the basis of the Ugaritic literature, the understanding of which is still often disputed. Mr Kidner makes reference to this new approach only at some points to avoid burdening the general reader with overmuch detail often of a negative nature.

Interest in the meaning and message of the Old Testament

continues undiminished and it is hoped that this series will thus further the systematic study of the revelation of God and His will and ways as seen in these records. It is the prayer of the editor and publisher, as of the authors, that these books will help many to understand, and to respond to, the Word of God today.

D. J. WISEMAN

CONTENTS

CHIEF ABBREVIATIONS

Anderson	*The Book of Psalms* by A. A. Anderson (*New Century Bible*, Oliphants), 1972.
ANET	*Ancient Near Eastern Texts* by J. B. Pritchard, ²1955.
AV	English Authorized Version (King James), 1611.
BASOR	*Bulletin of the American Schools of Oriental Research.*
BDB	*Hebrew-English Lexicon of the Old Testament* by F. Brown, S. R. Driver and C. A. Briggs, 1907.
BH	*Biblia Hebraica* edited by R. Kittel and P. Kahle, ⁷1951.
Bib.	*Biblica.*
Briggs	*Psalms* by C. A. and E. G. Briggs (*International Critical Commentary*, T. & T. Clark), 1906–07.
Childs	*Memory and Tradition in Israel* by B. S. Childs (*SBT* 37, SCM Press), 1962.
Dahood	*Psalms* by M. J. Dahood (*Anchor Bible*, Doubleday), 1966–70.
Delitzsch	*Psalms* by F. Delitzsch, ⁴1883.
Eaton	*Psalms* by J. H. Eaton (*Torch Bible Commentaries*, SCM Press), 1967.
ET	*Expository Times.*
EV	English versions.
Gelineau	*The Psalms: A New Translation* arranged for singing to the psalmody of Joseph Gelineau (Fontana), 1963.
G-K	*Hebrew Grammar* by W. Gesenius, edited by E. Kautzsch and A. E. Cowley, ²1910.
HTR	*Harvard Theological Review.*
HUCA	*Hebrew Union College Annual.*
JB	Jerusalem Bible, 1966.
JBL	*Journal of Biblical Literature.*
JSS	*Journal of Semitic Studies.*
JTS	*Journal of Theological Studies.*
K-B	*Lexicon in Veteris Testamenti Libros* by L. Koehler and W. Baumgartner, 1953.
Keet	*A Study of the Psalms of Ascents* by C. C. Keet (Mitre), 1969.

Kirkpatrick	*Psalms* by A. F. Kirkpatrick (*Cambridge Bible for Schools and Colleges*, CUP), 1891–1901.
Kissane	*Psalms* by E. J. Kissane (Browne and Nolan), 1953–54.
LXX	The Septuagint (pre-Christian Greek version of the Old Testament).
mg.	margin.
Mowinckel	*The Psalms in Israel's Worship* by S. Mowinckel (Blackwell), 1962.
MT	Massoretic Text.
NBC	*The New Bible Commentary Revised* edited by D. Guthrie, J. A. Motyer, A. M. Stibbs and D. J. Wiseman (IVP), 1970.
NBD	*The New Bible Dictionary* edited by J. D. Douglas *et al.* (IVP), 1962.
NEB	The New English Bible, 1970.
OTS	*Oudtestamentische Studiën.*
PBV	Prayer Book Version, 1662.
Perowne	*The Psalms* by J. S. Perowne (G. Bell), 1864.
RP	The Revised Psalter (SPCK), 1964.
RSV	American Revised Standard Version, 1952.
RV	English Revised Version, 1881.
SBT	*Studies in Biblical Theology* (SCM Press).
Syr.	The Peshitta (Syriac version of the Old Testament).
Targ.	The Targum (Aramaic version of the Old Testament).
TB	*Tyndale Bulletin.*
TEV	Today's English Version: the Psalms, 1970.
TRP	*The Text of the Revised Psalter.* Notes by D. W. Thomas (SPCK), 1963.
VT	*Vetus Testamentum.*
Vulg.	The Vulgate (Jerome's Latin version of the Bible).
Weiser	*Psalms* by A. Weiser (*Old Testament Library*, SCM Press), 1962.
ZAW	*Zeitschrift für die alttestamentliche Wissenschaft.*

INTRODUCTION

I. HEBREW POETRY

THE Old Testament repeatedly breaks out into poetry. Even its narratives are graced here and there with a couplet or a longer sequence of verse to make some memorable point (*cf.*, *e.g.*, Gn. 2–4 in any modern version), and its prophecies predominantly take this form. While the Psalms are the main body of poems in Scripture, and were given (with Job and Proverbs) a distinctive system of accents by the Massoretes[1] to mark the fact, they are themselves surrounded by poetry and rooted in a long and popular poetic tradition.

By its suppleness of form, Hebrew poetry lent itself well to this widespread use. A proverbial saying, a riddle, an orator's appeal, a prayer, a thanksgiving, to mention only a few varieties of speech, could all slip into its rhythms almost effortlessly, for its metre was not parcelled out in 'feet' or in a prescribed arrangement of strong and weak syllables, but heard in the sound of, say, three or four stresses in a short sentence or phrase, matched by an answering line of about the same length. The lighter syllables interspersed with the stronger were of no fixed number, and the tally of strong beats in a line could itself be varied with some freedom within a single poem. There was room and to spare for spontaneity.

A hint of these rhythms can be felt at times even in translation, when our words happen to correspond roughly with the Hebrew. In the latter, while there are sometimes lines of two stresses, or of four or even more, the commonest rhythm is 3:3, which comes through in, *e.g.*, the RSV of Psalm 26:2,

> Próve me, O Lórd, and trý me;
> tést my héart and my mínd.

The next psalm to this, Psalm 27, is mostly in a 3:2 rhythm,

---

[1] These were the Jewish custodians of the text, *c.* 500–1000 AD. The Massoretic Text, abbreviated here as MT, is the standard Hebrew text of the Old Testament. For further details see *NBD*, article 'Text and Versions', I, II.

which again has left its mark on the translation. *E.g.*, in verse 1,

> The Lórd is my líght and my salvátion;
> whóm shall I féar?

This pattern of 3:2 is often referred to as *qînâ* (lament), because its falling cadence, with its suggestion of finality, made it a favourite measure for elegies (as in the book of Lamentations) and for lamentings (*e.g.* Is. 14:12ff.); but this finality could equally express joy and confidence, as Psalm 27 fully demonstrates.

The flexibility found within the single line of verse extends to the larger units as well. What we have called a couplet (or, in Albright's term, a bicolon) can build up at times to the higher climax of a triplet, or tricolon, as in Psalm 92:9 (Heb. 10):

> For, lo, thy enemies, O Lord,
>   for, lo, thy enemies shall perish;
> all evildoers shall be scattered.[1]

Similarly in the poem as a whole it is the exception rather than the rule to find stanzas of equal length or even of any clear definition. Sometimes, to be sure, a refrain will map out a distinct design, as in Psalms 42–43 where this is carried through with some intricacy, and sometimes an acrostic will create its own framework (most elaborately in Ps. 119); but mostly the movement of the thought is free to form whatever pattern it most naturally would adopt.

But the fundamental characteristic of this poetry was not its external forms or rhythms, but its way of matching or echoing one thought with another. This has been described as thought-rhyme, but more often as 'parallelism', a term introduced by Bishop Robert Lowth in the eighteenth century.[2]

---

[1] The victory songs of Moses and Deborah have some stirring examples of this (*e.g.* Ex. 15:8,11; Jdg. 5:21), and it was a feature of early Canaanite poetry. See W. F. Albright, *Yahweh and the Gods of Canaan* (Athlone Press, 1968), pp. 4ff. An Ugaritic hymn to Baal contains lines almost identical with Ps. 92:9, above.

[2] See Lecture XIX in his *Lectures on the Sacred Poetry of the Hebrews*, first published in Latin in 1753. Lowth's analysis still commands wide respect, although further refinements have been suggested (see the next footnote) and the appeal of plain repetition, as well as parallelism, in early poetry has been emphasized by the literature discovered at Ugarit. For some recent modifications and criticisms of Lowth's categories, see S. Gevirtz, *Patterns in the Early Poetry of Israel* (Chicago University Press, 1963); and W. Whallon, *Formula, Character, and Context* (Harvard University Press, 1969).

It is recognizable at once in such a couplet as Psalm 103:10, where the two lines are synonymous:

> He does not deal with us according to our sins,
> nor requite us according to our iniquities.

In this form of parallelism the second line (or sometimes a second verse) simply reinforces the first, so that its content is enriched and the total effect becomes spacious and impressive. The nuances of difference between the synonyms should not be over-pressed; they are in double harness rather than in competition. So, *e.g.*, 'man' and 'the son of man' in Psalm 8:4, or 'my soul' and 'my flesh' in 63:1, are paired rather than contrasted.

Synonyms alone, however, would be tedious, and the form has many variations. The 'climactic parallelism' of, *e.g.*, Psalm 93:3, or of 92:9 quoted above, shows the powerful effect of letting the second line, like a second wave, mount higher than the first, perhaps to be outstripped in turn by a third. In various other ways the regularity of the matching lines can be modified, so that the second, for instance, enlarges on a single feature of the first, as in 145:18—

> The Lord is near to all who call upon him,
> to all who call upon him in truth

—or else perhaps is its complement or counterpart, as in 63:8, rather than its echo:

> My soul clings to thee;
> thy right hand upholds me.

This last example has something in common with Lowth's second category, 'antithetic parallelism', on which less needs to be said. It is most familiar to us from the sayings of Proverbs 10ff., and most characteristic of the didactic psalms; *e.g.* 37:21:

> The wicked borrows, and cannot pay back,
> but the righteous is generous and gives.

To these two classes, synonymous and antithetic, Lowth added a third, which he named 'synthetic or constructive parallelism', where 'the sentences answer to each other . . . merely by the form of construction'. He assigned to this category everything which fell outside the first two groups, and

3

in this he has been followed by various modern exponents (subject in most cases to the addition of one or two sub-categories).[1] But some of Lowth's most telling examples might well be classed as virtually synonymous parallels (*e.g.* Pss. 19:7ff.; 62:11a), and for the rest it would seem better to discard the term 'parallelism' and merely speak of couplets or bicola, in the many cases where the thought and diction move straight on to the second line of a pair, without a backward glance.

A final point deserves emphasis, and this too was one of Lowth's observations. It is the striking fact that this type of poetry loses less than perhaps any other in the process of translation. In many literatures the appeal of a poem lies chiefly in verbal felicities and associations, or in metrical subtleties, which tend to fail of their effect even in a related language. The programme-notes of any *Lieder* recital are enough to prove the point! But the poetry of the Psalms has a broad simplicity of rhythm and imagery which survives transplanting into almost any soil. Above all, the fact that its parallelisms are those of sense rather than of sound allows it to reproduce its chief effects with very little loss of either force or beauty. It is well fitted by God's providence to invite 'all the earth' to 'sing the glory of his name'.

II. THE STRUCTURE OF THE PSALTER

Most modern versions mark out the division of the Psalter into its five 'books', which respectively begin at Psalms 1, 42, 73, 90 and 107. The basis of this is to be found in the Psalter itself, which crowns each of these groups with a doxology. The Septuagint (abbreviated as LXX), translated in the third or second century BC, witnesses to the antiquity of these landmarks, and earlier still the Chronicler quotes the one which concludes Book IV (1 Ch. 16:35f.).[2]

---

[1] *E.g.* Briggs (pp. xxxiv ff.) gives specimens of (a) 'emblematic' parallelism, where the synonyms grow elaborate, as in 129:5–8; (b) 'stairlike' (*cf.* the climactic parallelism referred to above, but embracing also the more gradual progression from key-word to key-word in, *e.g.*, 25:1–7); (c) 'introverted', following the chiastic pattern a.b.b'.a'. (as in 30:8–10, where 8 corresponds to 10, and 9a to 9b).

[2] For a different interpretation of the significance of this, see Mowinckel, II, pp. 193ff.

There are other pointers beside these to the components of the collection and to the stages of its growth. One of the most noticeable is the postscript to Book II: 'The prayers of David, the son of Jesse, are ended' (72:20). This at once raises the question why eighteen further psalms of David should be found after this point, and a dozen psalms by other authors before it; to which the most likely answer is that a self-contained compilation once ended here, to which other psalm-books, with their own selections of material, were later added. But within the unit itself (1–72) there are signs that the two books which compose it were used at first independently of one another. For example, two psalms in Book II (53 and 70) are almost exact duplicates of material in Book I; also in Book II the term Elohim (God) largely replaces the name Yahweh (the Lord)—a difference of customary religious language which is comparable to the preferences and aversions found in our own circles, where one group tends to speak of 'God' and another of 'the Lord', or one generation uses 'Thou' in worship and another 'You'. Just as the wording of a hymn will vary a little from one collection to another, to suit the needs of different Christian groups, so, it seems, did the wording of the psalms, leaving traces of the little collections which were eventually brought together for the use of all Israel. The differing use of divine names continues as between blocks of material in the remaining psalms, in that Elohim tends to predominate in 73–83, but Yahweh in the rest of Book III, *i.e.* in 84–89; after which, in Books IV and V, Yahweh is used almost without variation.[1] No doubt some of these distinctions reflect the personal preferences of the authors; but others are evidently editorial, adapting an existing psalm to the language of its users. *E.g.*, in Psalms 84f., 87f., of Book III, which come from the same group of temple singers as 42–49 in Book II, the preference of Book II for 'Elohim' has disappeared.

We have mentioned 'blocks of material', and these provide some further glimpses of the history of the Psalter. Book II opens with a group of psalms (42–49) attributed to the sons

[1] S. R. Driver, *Introduction to the Literature of the Old Testament* (T. & T. Clark, ⁷1896), p. 371, gives the following statistics: Bk I, Yahweh **272**, Elohim (unqualified) 15; Bk II, E 164, Y 30; Bk III, Pss. 73–83, E 36, Y 13; Pss. 84–89, Y 31, E 7; Bk IV, Y only; Bk V, Y only (except in 144:9; also in Ps. 108 which is drawn from Pss. 57 and 60).

of Korah, a hereditary guild of temple officials. Book III, as we have seen, contains four more of their psalms, but they are preceded by psalms of Asaph (73–83),[1] a musician who was founder of another of the temple guilds. These two bodies of musicians, then, each had their special stock of material. But among the collected psalms of David, Asaph and Korah (and including three Davidic psalms from Bk V) we find fifty-five which are earmarked for 'the choirmaster' (if that is the right translation[2]). This suggests that at some stage the over-all director of temple music had his own compilation, a forerunner of the complete Psalter or a specialized selection from it.

Books IV and V have some other clusters, mostly linked by their subjects or uses rather than their authorship. Such are 93–100, on the world-wide kingship of the Lord; 113–118, the 'Egyptian Hallel' ('praise') sung on Passover night; 120–134, 'Songs of Ascents' (*i.e.* of pilgrimage?[3]) which were part of the 'Great Hallel', 120–136; and a final Hallel consisting of 146–150 which all begin and end with Hallelujah. There are also two sets of Davidic psalms, 108–110 and 138–145.

Last of all, perhaps, the collection was prefaced by Psalm 1, which has no title or author's name, unlike most of the psalms in Book I.

The picture that emerges is a mixture of order and informality of arrangement, which invites but also defeats the attempt to account for every detail of its final form. There is some chronological progression, with David most in evidence in the first half, and a clear allusion to the captivity towards the close of Book V (Ps. 137). But David reappears in the next psalm (138), and by contrast, the fall of Jerusalem has been lamented as far back as Psalm 74. Progress of theological or cultic thought is no easier to demonstrate. While there has been no lack of theories, which tend to reflect the thought-forms of successive ages (*e.g.* Gregory of Nyssa saw in the five books five steps to moral perfection, somewhat as Athanasius interpreted the fifteen Psalms of Ascent; in a

[1] The Asaph group has a solitary forerunner in Bk II, *i.e.*, Ps. 50. Ewald was perhaps the first to point out that by transferring 42–50 to follow 72, the psalms of David, Korah (first group) and Asaph would come in straight sequence.

[2] See p. 40.   [3] See p. 43.

different vein Delitzsch found a series of catchwords linking one psalm to the next throughout the 150), any scheme which discovers a logical necessity in the position of every psalm probably throws more light on the subtlety of its proponent than on the pattern of the Psalter. Its structure is perhaps best compared with that of a cathedral built and perfected over a matter of centuries, in a harmonious variety of styles, rather than a palace displaying the formal symmetry of a single and all-embracing plan.

III. SOME TRENDS IN THE MODERN STUDY OF THE PSALMS

Few areas of the Old Testament have proved more fascinating to scholars in recent years than the Psalms. After Wellhausen, critical opinion had seemed likely to remain agreed that the Psalter was a product of Israel's post-exilic maturity, when the teaching of the prophets and the collapse of the monarchy had combined to give new prominence to individual piety. As late as 1922 John Skinner could speak of Jeremiah as in some sense 'the first of the psalmists',[1] in that his unheeded prophecy had driven him to wrestle with God and discover in the process the realm of personal communion. The office of a prophet was soon to disappear, along with the establishment which it had criticized and exhorted; soon a new kind of voice would be heard, addressing God rather than man, and 'a new spiritual type—the Old Testament saint'[2]—would come into view with the poets of the Psalter.

But a fresh approach to psalm studies had been pioneered by H. Gunkel as far back as 1904, which was to force a reappraisal of the provenance and function of the psalms, which other scholars would carry far beyond the originator's first thoughts. Gunkel's method was first to seek out the living context of the psalms, looking into the songs and poems to be found elsewhere in the Bible and in contemporary cultures; and secondly to classify the material by its form rather than its content, somewhat after the botanizing method of Linnaeus (an analogy which Gunkel himself employed[3]). One of the

[1] J. Skinner, *Prophecy and Religion* (CUP, 1922), p. 222.
[2] *Ibid.*, p. 223.
[3] *Cf.* H. Gunkel, *The Psalms* (Facet Books, B.S. 19, Fortress Press, Philadelphia, 1967), p. 5, footnote. This is a translation by T. Horner of Gunkel's article on the Psalms in *Religion im Geschichte und Gegenwart* ([1]1909; [2]1930).

points that emerged from this was the close similarity of the Psalter's main types of material to the hymns, laments, thanksgivings, prayers, and pieces for royal occasions, which arose out of the various situations found in the rest of the Old Testament. Gunkel concluded that 'this poetry, which belongs to worship, is as old as worship itself, and springs from the same age as the national saga, justice, the Torah, and all other treasures of the national life.'[1] Jeremiah therefore (to return to Skinner's example), so far from being the originator of the psalm of personal supplication, was taking up and developing a form that was already well established.[2]

For all this, Gunkel still considered that most of the material in the Psalter was post-exilic, but written still in the idiom created by the old rituals, although they were outgrown and religion had 'come of age'—for this celebrated metaphor was his, a generation before it was Bonhoeffer's. It was the conservatism of religious habit, he considered, which left the stamp of the old cultic patterns on the new spiritual material, so that the private suppliant used language that had been designed to serve the king, or spoke of his troubles and their cure as if they were the assaults of sickness and the rites of expiation.

It was Mowinckel, in his series of monographs, *Psalmenstudien, I–VI* (1921–24), who carried this line of study nearer to its true conclusion, by refusing the artificiality of detaching the psalms from the rituals that had supposedly shaped them. Gunkel, he pointed out, had shared the prejudice of his age against cultic religion, and so had stopped halfway along the path he had opened up. We must accept what the psalms imply, and not only see them as, in the main, 'real cult psalms composed for . . . the actual services in the Temple',[3] but 'must try to form as complete and vivid a picture as possible of the old Israelite and Jewish cult and its many situations and acts'.[4] Psalms and liturgy must illuminate each other.

One startling result of this approach was the re-dating of the psalms. Their golden age was now held to be the monarchy, even if it was still too much to ascribe more than one or two

[1] 'The Poetry of the Psalter', in *Old Testament Essays*, ed. D. C. Simpson (Griffin, London, 1927), p. 136.

[2] *Ibid.*, p. 135.

[3] Mowinckel, I, p. xxiii.

[4] *Ibid.*, p. 35.

to David himself. Even more notable, however, was the emergence of a new picture of Israelite worship, constructed not so much from the data of the laws (which Mowinckel considered 'one-sided and fragmentary') as from 'hints', as he puts it, 'in the psalms themselves',[1] with supporting evidence from other oriental cults.

Following this lead, different scholars have discerned different festivals as the major sources of the psalms. Mowinckel himself saw the feast of Ingathering and Tabernacles, at the turn of the year, as the chief of these, celebrating God's epiphany and enthronement with a ritual so elaborate that it gave rise to more than forty psalms. Here the drama of creation was enacted, with a ritual battle against the sea and its monsters (*cf.*, *e.g.*, Ps. 89:9f.), like the battles in Canaanite and Babylonian myths. In due course Yahweh, His presence symbolized by the ark, would ascend Mount Zion in procession, there to be challenged, admitted (24:7ff.) and finally acclaimed with the cry, 'The Lord has become king!' (*e.g.* 93:1). As king, He would confirm His covenant with Israel and the house of David, admonish them to keep His laws (81:8ff.; 95:8ff.), and, like Marduk fixing the fate of the coming year, He would 'judge the world with righteousness' (96:13); in other words He would set events on their right course and assign to the nations their destinies.

All this activity was, in Mowinckel's view, concerned with the here and now, not the distant future. Annually this great day, the Day of the Lord, would be looked to as the time of restoring all things in readiness for the coming year; but gradually these hopes, unfulfilled, would be projected to a future age. So, out of this very festival, Israel's eschatology was brought to birth.

Reactions to Mowinckel have varied, predictably enough, between an eagerness which would outrun him in his own direction, and a cautious appraisal which would question or modify much of his position. But on the whole he has won considerable acceptance: every commentator must reckon with him, and if the first question now asked about a given psalm tends to be Gunkel's enquiry as to the group in which to place it, the second is likely to be Mowinckel's, namely, 'to which cultic occasion must this psalm group have belonged,

---

[1] *Ibid.*, p. 36.

and what has the congregation experienced or felt on that occasion?'[1]

A rather exaggerated response to the new methods came from a British group of scholars who came to be known as the Myth and Ritual school (from the title of a symposium edited in 1933 by S. H. Hooke), and from a number of Scandinavians, notably Engnell and Widengren, who assiduously pursued the idea of a cultic pattern common to the ancient Near-East. Scarcely a feature of the Babylonian *akitu* festival or of Canaanite fertility rites failed to betray to them its presence in the psalms. Not content with Mowinckel's suggestion that Yahweh inherited the Jebusite cultus of 'Elyon the Most High, some scholars convinced themselves that He celebrated an annual marriage with Anath[2] and a ritual death and resurrection like that of Tammuz,[3] in all of which His part was acted by the king. This was not only the view of the Scandinavians Widengren and Hvidberg; T. H. Robinson expressed it (in an imperturbably matter-of-fact style) in the words: 'The divine marriage followed, consummated in the sacred hut, and this was succeeded by the death of Jahweh. After a period of lamentation He was restored to life, and, with His consort, was led to His home in the Temple, there to reign until the changes of the year brought back again the festal season.'[4]

Other scholars, with a stronger appreciation of Yahweh as the living God, saw the king's role as playing the part not of Yahweh Himself but of His adopted son, and reconstructed the cultic drama as a double sequence of conflict and victory: first the Creator's quelling of His cosmic foes, to reassert His kingship and renew the earth; then the Davidic king's struggle with the kings of the earth and the power of death, in which he was humiliated and all but engulfed (*cf.* 18:4f.), to be rescued in the nick of time.

An attractive feature of this approach was its liberation of the Psalter from its association with ecclesiastical decorum.

[1] Mowinckel, I, p. 32. For criticisms of his approach, see below, pp. 13–18; 45f.

[2] T. H. Robinson, 'Hebrew Myths', in *Myth and Ritual*, ed. S. H. Hooke (Oxford, 1933), pp. 185f.

[3] *Cf.* G. Widengren in *Myth, Ritual and Kingship*, ed. S. H. Hooke (Oxford, 1958), pp. 190ff.

[4] *Myth and Ritual*, pp. 188f.

To picture a cultic drama of battles, processions and homage-shouts is at least to find the psalms coming alive with some of the colour and excitement which are implied in their allusions to clapping and lamenting, dancing and prostration. In an imaginative reconstruction of the New Year festival, for instance, one writer pictures the gradual extinguishing of the torches, the divesting of the king of his royal attire, and, with the onset of total darkness, the king lying prostrate at the feet of his enemies, where he cries out to Yahweh the words of Psalm 89: *How long, O Lord? Wilt thou hide thyself for ever? . . . Remember, O Lord, how thy servant is scorned . . .* 'At last, when the atmosphere has become almost unbearable in its intensity, Yahweh *does* come to deliver his people. He comes at dawn, symbolized by the sun, the supreme source of light and life, and is victorious . . .'[1]

This is gripping and memorable, even if it raises the question, How are we to know whether any of it happened this way?

We will return to this: but meanwhile we can note a second attraction of this cult-dramatic conception. It brought together certain Old Testament themes which might otherwise have seemed unrelated or arbitrary. For one thing, it bridged the gulf between the king and the suffering Servant. Here was one way of seeing the two offices united meaningfully in one person. For another, its presentation of the king as 'sacral', a unique mediator between God and His people, of whom he was (on this view) the embodiment and representative, made a context for Messianic prophecy. If the king's anointing made him a person apart, with a crucial role to fulfil in relation to God and man, some of the exalted Messianic titles would begin to appear less violently inappropriate to the Messiah's predecessors, even though they were still too magnificent to fit any king in his own person.

But this very concept of sacral kingship is precarious, and has come under attack from many quarters. It is doubtful whether it would have suggested itself to biblical scholars from the bare scriptural evidence without the prompting of comparative anthropology.[2] This is at best a dubious source,

---

[1] D. Anders-Richards, *The Drama of the Psalms* (Darton, Longman & Todd, 1968), p. 41.

[2] *Cf.* Widengren's remarks on the influence of Frazer on the Myth and Ritual School, and of Grönbech on Pedersen and Mowinckel. See *Myth, Ritual and Kingship*, pp. 152, 154.

as C. R. North implied when he criticized Mowinckel's method of 'working inwards from the wide circle of a primitive and general Semitic *Umwelt*, instead of outwards from the centre of the prophetic consciousness';[1] and in this particular area even the idea of a common Near-Eastern pattern of kingship or of worship is contradicted by the evidence, as several scholars have pointed out.

By itself, the biblical material shows two aspects of the king, with a certain tension between them which the theory of sacral kingship resolves too easily. On the one hand various royal psalms (in particular Pss. 2, 45, 110) use language for the king which gives him a seemingly divine status as God's 'son' (2:7) or even as God incarnate (45:6, lit.); and in the narratives his person is sacred, as the Lord's Anointed. There were also times when he presided as priest (*cf.* 2 Sa. 6:12ff.; 1 Ki. 8). On the other hand there is no description of the king's supposed combat and deliverance at an annual festival, on which so much of his people's welfare is alleged to have hung. And it is surely significant, as M. Noth points out,[2] that in Israel kingship arrived only late on the scene, and aroused mixed feelings among the faithful when it did. The king's known activities as priest, referred to above, belonged to quite exceptional occasions; he was warned away from any assumption of a general right to this area (1 Sa. 13:8ff.; 2 Ch. 26:18).

We can hardly do better than follow the New Testament's handling of this paradox, which is not to play down either side of it (*e.g.* by emending the texts or easing the translations), but to let it push us towards the unique solution it was to receive in Jesus Christ. Several passages treat it in this way. One is our Lord's pressing of the paradox of Psalm 110: David's Lord, David's son; another is Peter's use of the same oracle and of Psalm 16, to contrast the incorruption and the heavenly throne of which David spoke with the tomb which he himself was to occupy; yet another is the string of testimonies from the psalms in Hebrews 1, familiar to many as the Epistle for Christmas Day, where full value is given to such expressions as 'Thou art my Son' and 'Thy throne, O

---

[1] *ZAW* 50 (1932), p. 35, cited by A. R. Johnson in *Myth, Ritual and Kingship*, p. 224.
[2] M. Noth, 'God, King and Nation', in *The Laws in the Pentateuch, and Other Essays* (English Edition, Oliver & Boyd, 1966), pp. 161ff.

God, is for ever'.[1] This involves, to be sure, a frankly super-naturalist view of these oracles; but it is hard to see why it should be thought improper for the Holy Spirit to inspire prophecies on the central subject of all revelation.

We have been looking at the more extreme followers—or, in some cases, out-distancers—of Mowinckel. At the other extreme there are those who disagree with him entirely, or at certain crucial points. An example of the latter is R. de Vaux, who returns a decided negative to the question, 'Was there a New Year Feast (in Old Testament times)?' and a 'No'—or at the least 'Not Proven'—to the question, 'Was there a feast of the Enthronement of Yahweh?' He agrees with those who find it a serious objection that no connection between the kingship of Yahweh and the Feast of Tabernacles is found explicitly in Scripture (the one exception that is claimed, Zc. 14:16, he dismisses as fortuitous, since the whole chapter is about Yahweh's coming reign). The cry, *Yahweh mālak*, in Psalm 93:1, *etc.* is simply a loyal acclamation, 'The Lord is King'; it is not a formula of enthronement. The psalms which contain it are psalms in praise of Yahweh's reign, not announcements of His accession.[2] As for the Day of the Lord, which to Mowinckel meant originally the day of the same festival, de Vaux agrees with those who, like von Rad, see it as a battle-day, since war, not divine kingship, is the invariable context of the Day of the Lord in the Old Testament.[3]

Among commentators, some have followed Mowinckel's example in treating one festival as the pre-eminent influence, but have identified it differently. H.-J. Kraus argues for a feast that celebrated the choice of Zion and the house of David, but not (until after the Exile) the enthronement of Yahweh.[4] And A. Weiser regards a festival of the Covenant as the seed-bed of almost the entire Psalter. Weiser's position is hailed by Mowinckel as broadly in agreement with his

---

[1] This subject is treated more fully in Section IV, below, pp. 18ff. ('The Messianic Hope').

[2] R. de Vaux, *Ancient Israel* (Darton, Longman & Todd, 1961), pp. 502–506.

[3] R. de Vaux, *op. cit.*, p. 264; G. von Rad, *Old Testament Theology*, II (Oliver & Boyd, 1965), p. 123n.

[4] Mowinckel discusses Kraus's theory of this in *The Psalms in Israel's Worship*, II, pp. 230f.

own, although Weiser himself would not concur with this, since he regards History and Law as the twin pillars of the covenant-renewal.[1] But since the whole scheme of salvation was enacted in the festal week, as Weiser sees it, there is inevitably much common ground between him and Mowinckel.

More important than these agreements and disagreements, however, is the concept of *actualization* which is bound up with the cultic understanding of the psalms. The cult-drama, it is held, was far more than a teaching aid. It brought the events it enacted into the present moment. In a religion dominated by magic this would have implied an automatic unleashing of power for good or ill, but in the religion of the Old Testament it confronted the worshipper with God and His acts, inviting an immediate response of faith. The Exodus and Sinai, cultically re-lived, were no longer buried in the past; they became for the believer his own salvation and his own glimpse of the theophany. 'I have seen thee in the sanctuary.' God could address the present congregation, not merely refer to their forefathers, as those who have 'made a covenant with me by sacrifice' (50:5); and in the enthronement ritual (for Weiser accepts this, even with its postulated Babylonian background) the cry 'The Lord is become King' embraces, as he puts it, 'the whole past, however remote, and includes the consummation of the Kingdom of God at the end of time'.[2]

Yet as soon as one asks in what sense the Exodus deliverance was experienced by the worshipper in a later age, one is confronted by the once-for-all finality of that event. It could only be re-experienced either by analogy (as when a man might view some present predicament as the equivalent of Israel's plight in Egypt) or else by a sense of continuity, in that one was an inheritor of the salvation which began its course at the Red Sea. But this act of mental translation destroys the immediacy which is implied to be the essence of a cultic event. Only in this somewhat oblique sense does it seem proper to speak of 'actualization' in the Israelite cult. Even so, it had an important part to play in emphasizing the fact that God is not the God of the dead but of the living, and that His acts have 'the dynamic characteristic' (as Brevard

[1] Weiser, p. 32.
[2] *Ibid.*, p. 618.

S. Childs has put it) 'of refusing to be relegated to the past'.[1] This is expressed with Hebraic directness when Moses says to the new generation at the end of the forty years in the wilderness, 'Not with our fathers did the Lord make this covenant, but with us, who are all of us here alive this day' (Dt. 5:3). Yet that very setting, in the wilderness, should warn us against taking the vivid language with wooden literalism. It was one way of confronting the new generation with the continuing covenant and with the living God; but it was not the only way. The same point could be made by quite other means: not by telescoping past and present but by holding them firmly apart. This is the method of Psalm 95, which deals with the same set of events. The 'today' of this passage is set in contrast to 'the day at Massah'; the present scene in contrast to 'the wilderness'; the present generation in contrast to the one that put God to the proof.

So the festivals in Israel (in my view) were not the means, *ex opere operato*, of annihilating time or of renewing the potency of the past: they were kept 'that you may *remember* the day when you came out of . . . Egypt', and '*remember* that you were a slave in Egypt' (Dt. 16:3, 12), and 'that your generations may *know* that I made the people . . . dwell in booths when I brought them out of . . . Egypt' (Lv. 23:43). This is the language of conscious, rational response, not mystical experience. And in case we should think this an accident of language, it is borne out by the altered form in which the Passover was to be kept after the unrepeatable first occasion. The festival was henceforth unmistakably a commemoration— not a means of making a past event 'effective in the present' (to quote an exposition of it in a modern ecumenical statement[2])—for never again was the protective blood to be daubed on the lintel and doorposts. That feature had been the crux of the Passover in Egypt; its abolition was as eloquent as the cry, 'It is finished!'

Enough has been said to show that the Old Testament's exposition of a cultic occasion can differ very sharply from the findings of comparative religion. And this emphasizes the difficulty of controlling an interpretation in the absence of a

[1] Childs, p. 88.
[2] The Anglican/Roman Catholic Agreed Statement on the Eucharist (1972), item II, which argues from the Passover, so understood, to the Eucharist.

biblical comment to settle the point. How does one distinguish a vivid figure of speech from a cultic act? Not, surely, by enquiring whether in Babylon or Ugarit the words were cultically acted out, for their gods were many, and visible, and sexual, and hungry; susceptible to magic, and revealed by omens. One might borrow their language, but it would suffer a sea-change. To 'see the face of God' the Israelite would need no eyes, to consult Him, no divination.

How formative, again, was the cult? There is a very wide difference between the answer of such as Engnell, that even the 'individual laments' were set-pieces from the cultic death of Yahweh, and the answer of Westermann, for example, that the native element of the psalms was 'not the isolation of a cultic milieu, but rather the heart of the chosen people's life whence it radiated into every area'.[1] The various positions between these extremes tend to be argued from rather arbitrary premises. It is rare to find a set of criteria for distinguishing cultic from non-cultic psalms, such as Szörényi's list of external and internal indications (summarized in D. J. A. Clines' valuable survey of Psalm Research[2]); and even this sober and reasonable list rejects the evidence offered by the psalm titles.

At this point we are faced again with the almost head-on clash between modern opinion and the testimony of the text itself—for the titles are part of that text, appearing in the Hebrew Bible as verse 1, or as part of it, wherever they occur. Many of these superscriptions witness explicitly to the function of their psalms in the cult: 'A Psalm for the thank offering' (100); 'A prayer of one afflicted, when he is faint and pours out his complaint before the Lord' (102); 'A Song for the Sabbath' (92); and so on. Others imply it by ascribing their material to the levitical singers, chiefly Asaph and the sons of Korah.

But seventy-three psalms, comprising nearly half the Psalter, are introduced with the formula 'Of David'; and fourteen of these are linked to episodes in his career, mostly from his days of persecution. At their face value, then, these are

---

[1] C. Westermann, *Isaiah 40–66* (SCM Press, 1969), p. 8. *Cf.* his *The Praise of God in the Psalms* (Epworth, 1966), p. 155.
[2] 'Psalm Research since 1955: I. The Psalms and the Cult', *Tyndale Bulletin* 18 (1967), p. 107. (I have no first-hand knowledge of Szörényi's works.)

psalms straight from life: from the battlefield or 'the cave', not from the sanctuary or the cultic drama. But the musical directions and the allusions to 'the choirmaster' (as this term is usually translated[1]) show that they were collected, and where necessary adapted, for use in worship. This is the opposite direction of flow (that is, from life to cult) from what is pictured by most modern scholars. It is intrinsically no less probable than its antithesis, and it is rejected for no compelling reasons. Gunkel, for example, generalizes from the history of religions that 'psalms . . . composed for the cultus are, on the whole, older than those which the pious poet composed for his own use', He adds, for good measure, that in Protestant hymnody 'the "chorale" is older than the "spiritual song"'.[2] Mowinckel is not at quite such a loss for arguments, but he relies, like Gunkel, mostly on generalizations. E.g., as examples of discrepancies between the psalms and the times of David, he points to the approving attitudes in the early monarchy to animal sacrifices and to wealth and power (forgetting perhaps the famous rebuke of Samuel to Saul in 1 Sa. 15:22, and the fact that David knew poverty and persecution). For a fuller discussion see vi. b (pp. 33ff.) and vii (pp. 43f.).

It may seem unnecessary to attach much importance to the 'small print' of the psalms (as it appears in our English Bibles, if it appears at all). But apart from the unwisdom of dismissing part of our data unheard, there remains the fact that any document which is known to be from life makes a different impact on the reader from one that is commissioned to meet a standard type of need. If we are intended to share the heart-searchings of a man as exceptional and as sorely tried as David, we shall be the poorer if we insist on treating his works as anonymous and divorced from his eventful life. To revert to Gunkel's simile, if we give ourselves too much to 'botanizing' among the psalms, we need not be surprised if we are left with little more than a row of specimens.

Perhaps this is unconsciously corroborated by Mowinckel himself, from whom we read the revealing words: 'What strikes us in the biblical psalms is the uniformity and formality which characterize most of them. One is often so like another

[1] See vi. c. 3, below, p. 40.
[2] H. Gunkel, *The Psalms: a form-critical Introduction* (Fortress Press, 1967), p. 5.

that they are difficult to differentiate.'[1] Although he makes this the ground of his type-analysis, it is possible that the analysis has fed back something of its own formality to the material as he sees it. Approached without this apparatus, but with the information which the psalms and their headings supply, each poem (in the experience of at least one student of them) emerges with its own strong individuality. To turn from the close study of one psalm to the next is to be faced with, so to speak, a new personality, in an encounter which requires some effort of readjustment.

If, in conclusion, we may change the metaphor, it may be fair to say that the Psalter, taken on its own terms, is not so much a liturgical library, storing up standard literature for cultic requirements, as a hospitable house, well lived in, where most things can be found and borrowed after some searching, and whose first occupants have left on it everywhere the imprint of their experiences and the stamp of their characters.

IV. THE MESSIANIC HOPE

Christianity shares with traditional Judaism the conviction that many passages in the psalms are Messianic: that is, predictions or foreshadowings of the Christ. Here we shall look first at the content of the passages interpreted by the New Testament in this way, and then at the extent of Messianic material beyond these quoted parts of the Psalter.

First, then, the *content* of the Messianic hope. Confining ourselves to those psalms, about fifteen in number, which the New Testament cites in this connection, we can find at least the following aspects of the One who was to come.

a. The anointed King

The Psalter loses little time in introducing the figure of the king, who will play so large a part in it. As early as Psalm 2 it presents him in terms which leave the limitations of local kingship far behind. The psalm would serve well enough (and doubtless did) as a regular enthronement anthem for a new king, when its language would be construed as courtly rhetoric, treating the modest empire of David as though it were the world. But there is more than rhetoric here. The

---

[1] Mowinckel, I, p. 30.

poem draws out the logic of the fact that the Davidic king reigns on behalf of God, whose throne is in the heavens (2:4). The uttermost parts of the earth are therefore his by right, and will be his in fact. Full weight, too, is given to his double title, the Lord's *anointed* and His *son*. On the second of these we shall speak separately; meanwhile the first of them introduces us at once to the word *māšiaḥ*, whose Aramaic form was transliterated in Greek texts as *messias* or translated as *christos*, whence we have 'Messiah' and 'Christ'.

Anointing implied consecration[1] to high office, not only investing the anointed person with a holy status (so that, *e.g.*, to do violence to him would be sacrilege[2]), but also empowering him for his task (*cf.* 89:20ff.), since the outward rite was consummated, at its best, by the gift of the Spirit. Such was Saul's anointing (1 Sa. 10:1, 6), and David's (1 Sa. 16:13); such also was that of the Servant of the Lord, if this is the right term for the figure described in Isaiah 61:1ff., with whom Jesus identified Himself. Anointing was the initiating rite for both priests and kings, and on one occasion at least, for a prophet (1 Ki. 19:16).

The king was therefore much more than a leader. Although some schools of thought have exaggerated his sacredness, as though he were the nation's mediator between earth and heaven, it remains true that his people's fortunes were bound up with him, and something of the glory of God seen in him. David's prowess, as much as his office, may have won him the title 'the lamp of Israel' (2 Sa. 21:17); but an undistinguished successor of his was still 'the breath of our nostrils, the Lord's anointed' (La. 4:20); and twice the king is prayed for in the psalms as 'our shield' (84:9; 89:18). As for divine honours, the language of sonship in Psalm 2, of co-regency with God in Psalm 110, and of Godhead itself in Psalm 45, which we discuss below, was understood, we may suppose, as terminology not to be pressed (until the New Testament insisted that it should be), yet as not entirely inappropriate. Meanwhile the painful inadequacies of the actual kings helped to raise men's eyes towards One to come. The Targum's addition to Psalm 72:1 is but one instance of this, where 'the king' becomes 'king Messiah'.

---

[1] *E.g.* Lv. 8:12, '. . . and anointed (Aaron), to consecrate him'.
[2] *E.g.* 'How is it you were not afraid . . . to destroy the Lord's anointed?' (2 Sa. 1:14). *Cf.* 'Touch not my anointed ones' (Ps. 105:15).

b. '*My son*'

This is the language of Psalm 2:7, a verse much quoted in the
New Testament. Approaching it within the Old Testament
we find two great landmarks on the way to it, in the statement
'Israel is my son, my firstborn' (Ex. 4:22, RV) and the promise
to David concerning his heir to the throne, 'I will be his
father, and he shall be my son' (2 Sa. 7:14). This pledge
referred initially to Solomon, as the rest of that sentence and
the succeeding verse made plain; but it was coupled with the
promise of an unending dynasty. So in each new reign it is
likely that the king's enthronement was the occasion when he
entered formally into this inheritance (and was possibly
presented with such a 'decree' as that of Psalm 2:7, where
see comment), thereby to become the supreme expression of
his people's sonship and their status as God's firstborn in the
world (*cf*. 89:27 with Dt. 28:1).

But Psalm 2 offers him the whole earth, and seems to
couple the Lord and His anointed as Father and Son in more
than mere name. The impression that this is no ordinary son
of David, and this language no mere *Hofstil* (courtly address),
is confirmed by Psalm 110 where, as our Lord pointed out,
David himself salutes One who is his sovereign, set at God's
right hand. Hebrews 1:13 draws out a further contrast by
asking 'To what angel has he ever said, "Sit at my right
hand . . ."?' On this, F. F. Bruce aptly comments: 'The
most exalted angels are those whose privilege it is to "stand
in the presence of God" like Gabriel (Lk. 1:19), but none of
them has ever been invited to sit before Him, still less to sit
in the place of unique honour at His right hand.'[1] Once
again, in addressing the king as Son, the Old Testament has
introduced a theme which, undeveloped, suits its immediate
context, but outgrows it utterly as its implications fully
unfold.

The New Testament, revealing God's only-begotten Son as
co-eternal with the Father, refers the 'today' of Psalm 2:7
to the incarnate Son's resurrection, when, like a king at his
crowning, He was 'designated Son of God in power' (Rom.
1:4; *cf*. Acts 13:33).

---

[1] F. F. Bruce, *The Epistle to the Hebrews* (*New London Commentary*, Marshall,
Morgan & Scott, 1964), p. 24.

c. 'God'

By avoiding the obvious translation of Psalm 45:6, the RSV and NEB have weakened the impact of a text which, plainly translated, says to the king, 'Thy throne, O God, is for ever and ever' (AV, RV, *cf.* JB). Even the pre-Christian LXX made no attempt to turn the force of this, and its vast implications are put beyond doubt in Hebrews 1:8, which contrasts this way of speaking to the Son with what is said to the angels. It is perhaps the boldest Messianic oracle in the Psalter; but it is not alone. The same chapter of Hebrews finds references to Christ in two other sayings which speak immediately of God. One of these is Psalm 97:7 ('all gods (or angels) bow down before him'), where the context is a theophany. The comment of Hebrews 1:6 implies that when God manifests Himself on earth He does so in the person of His Son. The second reference is to Psalm 102:25–27 (Heb. 26–28), which is quoted in Hebrews 1:10–12 as God's address to One whom He entitles 'Lord',[1] and to whom He ascribes eternity and the creating of the universe. The LXX's vocalization of Psalm 102:23f. supports the Epistle in its inference that the speaker is indeed God Himself.[2] So startling an exegesis of the psalm must have been too dazzling to contemplate, until events, in the coming of Christ, accustomed the eyes of believers to the full glory of the truth.

In case we should ascribe these bold interpretations to the bias of one Epistle, we may add to this list the exposition of Psalm 68:18 in Ephesians 4:8–11, where the description of *God's* ascent of 'the high mount', leading captivity captive, is seen to be fulfilled in *Christ's* ascension into heaven. The New Testament once again unveils the hidden light of the Old.

d. 'Thy servant'

This is not a distinctive title in the Psalter, although David tends to use it when he is in distress (*e.g.* 69:17; 86:2, 4, 16), and the expression 'the servant of the Lord' occurs in the

---

[1] Heb. 1:10 runs straight on from verses 8f., thus: 'But of the Son he says, "Thy throne, O God, is for ever . . ." And "Thou, Lord, didst found the earth . . ." '

[2] See the comment on this passage in Vol. Two. On its use in Heb. 1:10–12 see especially F. F. Bruce, *op. cit.*, pp. 21–23, to which I am much indebted here.

headings of two Davidic psalms (18 and 36). We use it here as a convenient pointer to the role of the innocent sufferer, which strongly colours the portrait in which Jesus recognized Himself in the Psalter.

Most of our Lord's references to the psalms are in fact to this element in them; indeed the tragic Psalm 69 is the New Testament's largest quarry of quotations and allusions to Christ in the whole collection, six or seven different verses or phrases being drawn from it to interpret His cross and passion. From this psalm and its companions (notably 22, 35, 40, 41, 109, 118) the Gospels, Acts and Epistles find their most telling words to highlight such matters as His reforming zeal (69:9a), His deliberate self-offering (40:6-8), His experience of isolation (69:8), betrayal, hatred and rejection (41:9; 69:4; 35:19; 118:22), His suffering of reproach (69:9b), mockery (22:7f.; 69:21), stripping (22:18) and, it may be, nailing (22:16). They treat many of these explicitly as prophecies fulfilled; indeed Peter tells us that in Psalm 16 David, 'being a prophet, . . . foresaw and spoke of the resurrection of the Christ' (Acts 2:30f.). In Acts 1:16-20 and Romans 11:9f. the apostles also show us predictions of the fate of Judas (109:8; *cf.* 69:25) and of unbelieving Israel (69:22f.). Jesus Himself, on the cross, found words in the psalms for His darkest hour and for His last breath (22:1; 31:5).

e. Other terms

There are a few other expressions whose Messianic content unfolds with the coming of Christ.

1. The high calling of *man*, or, in the parallel term, *the son of man* (8:4), is contrasted in Hebrews 2:5ff. with humanity's failure to attain to it, but is shown to be fulfilled in Jesus, who is the Man *par excellence*—a truth about Him which complements His title of 'God' in Psalm 45, discussed above.[1]

2. Psalm 110:4 designates the warrior-king, who is enthroned at God's right hand, 'a *priest* for ever'. This is the only such reference in the Psalter, but in Zechariah the crowning of the high priest Joshua, who is also addressed with a

---

[1] Psalm 80:17 uses similar terms to those of 8:4, but is speaking of Israel. It is therefore Messianic only in the sense that Christ was the true Israel and the true Vine. But the Targum interpreted the parallel verse 15b (deleted by RSV, *etc.*) as Messianic, although the New Testament does not make use of it.

Messianic oracle (Zc. 6:11ff.), dramatically confirmed this side of the Messiah's calling. The psalm refers back to Melchi-zedek, the archetypal priest-king encountered in Genesis 14:18ff., and the relevance of every detail of that narrative to the high-priesthood of Christ is expounded in Hebrews 7, which itself leads on to the fuller discussion of priesthood and sacrifice in Hebrews 8–10. So the single sentence in Psalm 110, which is quoted in Hebrews 5:6, is the germ of one of the great themes of that Epistle, and consequently the means of showing how the earthly priesthood of the Old Testament was destined to be superseded by the heavenly priesthood of Christ. Our understanding of the relationship of the old order to the new would have been unimaginably poorer without this verse and its exposition.

3. 'The *stone* which the builders rejected' (118:22) was identified by our Lord as referring to Himself; and His words were reinforced by His accepting the crowd's Hosannas and the 'Blessed is he who comes . . .'—acclamations drawn from this psalm. But He opened up new vistas by relating this 'stone' oracle to two more (Lk. 20:18), and referring both of them to Himself. In its first context the stone on which men fall and are broken is no less than the 'Lord of hosts', as the Jewish audience would be well aware;[1] and the stone which will grind what it falls upon to powder is the stone 'cut out without hands' in Nebuchadnezzar's dream: *i.e.*, the kingdom to end all kingdoms.[2]

So Jesus took a psalm in which a persecuted Israel appears to be personified, and He not only treated the portrait as His own, and the persecutors as His unbelieving people, but identified Himself with God the Rock of Israel on the one hand, and with the kingdom (the stone which became a great mountain) on the other. He is thus the cornerstone not only in that He binds His church together, but in that He unites heaven and earth in His own Person.

Our second main concern is to enquire into the *extent* of the Messianic element in the Psalter.

We have seen that the New Testament draws material of this kind from some fifteen psalms. But a closer look at the

---

[1] The same use of Is. 8:13–15 is made in 1 Pet. 2:8, reinforced by 3:14b,15, whose allusion to Is. 8:13 is clearer in AV, RV than in RSV.
[2] Dn. 2:34f. (AV, RV), 44.

way these are handled will suggest that they are regarded as samples of a much larger corpus. It would scarcely seem too much to infer from this treatment that wherever David or the Davidic king appears in the Psalter (except where he is confessing failure to live up to his calling), he foreshadows in some degree the Messiah.

This seems to be implied, for instance, in the New Testament's attitude to Psalm 18 (= 2 Sa. 22), which is the personal testimony of David. It is quoted twice in the Epistles with reference to Christ, and in each case it is the manner of quotation, even more than the matter, which is significant for our present purpose. Hebrews 2:13 quotes verse 2 (in the LXX wording of 2 Sa. 22:3): 'I will put my trust in him'; and Romans 15:9 quotes verse 49 (LXX): 'Therefore I will praise thee among the Gentiles, and sing to thy name.' The special interest of these phrases for us is their *lack* of special interest. They do not force us, by some striking claim or paradox, to look for a supernatural figure to fulfil them: they fit David perfectly. Verse 2 in fact seems almost too basic a response to be distinctive of the Messiah, and indeed it is quoted to prove the very point that he is one of us, 'made like his brethren in every respect' (Heb. 2:17; *cf.* verse 11). But this would have no force unless the writer already assumed that his readers would hear the words of David as the words also of the Messiah. The same phenomenon appears in verse 49 as used in Romans 15. The fact that neither of these authors troubles to state, let alone to argue, that the psalm is Messianic suggests that the New Testament takes it for granted that Davidic and royal psalms have this added dimension. This tallies with the similar handling of the psalms in the preaching of Peter and in the Gospels.

If we enquire how this arose we are confronted not with a merely rabbinic tradition (which could be mistaken), but with our Lord Himself. When 'he opened their minds to understand the scriptures' (Lk. 24:45), it was with special reference to their Messianic content. 'Thus it is written, that the Christ should suffer and on the third day rise from the dead, and that repentance and forgiveness of sins should be preached in his name to all nations.' Although Luke 24 gives few details of this instruction, the rest of the New Testament shows how the apostles unanimously understood it; and the proof that they had not *mis*understood it can be found in His own teaching.

His words, like theirs, reveal the assumption that what was Davidic in the psalms was Messianic, not only where the reference was overt, as in the oracle 'The Lord says to my Lord' (110:1), but where it initially spoke of David's personal vicissitudes, as in Psalm 41:9 and 69:4 (=35:19), cited in John 13:18 and 15:25 as scriptures awaiting fulfilment—not merely as apt and familiar sayings. Quite evidently He would have said of David what He said of Moses: 'he wrote of me.'

We seem to be justified in saying of David and his fellow-psalmists what was said of Moses and his generation: 'these things happened to them *typikōs*', or significantly. We see the Davidic king *vis-à-vis* the nations, whom he is to subdue (2:9), *vis-à-vis* his people, whom he guides 'by the skilfulness of his hands' (78:72, AV), or his bride whose beauty he will 'greatly desire' (45:11), or his God whose authority he wields (110:2). We see David the man after God's own heart (as in, say, Pss. 16, 18 or 40), and the suffering David whose schooling was danger, hatred and ingratitude, who was betrayed by some of his closest friends and by his dearest son.

David does not emerge faultless from the Psalter, any more than from the records. When he asserts his righteousness (18:20ff.) it is only relative, for he is a forgiven man (32:1) who has greatly sinned (51). But as the perfect kingdom is foreshadowed by a limited and imperfect one, so the perfect Man is typified by a sinner whose sufferings, faith, sovereignty and sonship He utterly transcends.

The special quality of the Psalter's Messianic prophecy, then, is that it is lived out, as well as spoken out. There are one or two purely prophetic oracles, *e.g.* 2:7; 110:1, and much use is made of them in the New Testament; but still more is made of the prayers and praises that arose straight out of life, from situations such as Christ Himself would experience, though in a bigger context and at a deeper level as the embodiment and completion of Israel, of kingship, of man and of sacrifice, and as the incarnation of God.

V. CRIES FOR VENGEANCE

The sudden transitions in the psalms from humble devotion to fiery imprecation create an embarrassing problem for the Christian, who is assured that all Scripture is inspired and profitable, but equally that he himself is to bless those who

curse him. Our approach to this problem will be to pay attention to the substance of these outbursts before looking at the
tone of them, and to the New Testament's use of them before
finally discussing their relevance to us.

a. Their substance

We may summarize this as the plea that justice shall be done,
and the right be vindicated. This is a concern which the New
Testament warmly upholds. The parable of the unjust judge,
for instance, reiterates the word 'vindicate' with a persistence
worthy of the widow herself, and does so not only in the story
(where it might be merely incidental) but in the application:
'And will not God vindicate his elect? . . . he will vindicate
them speedily' (Lk. 18:1–8). This word, it should be understood, implies stronger judicial action than the clearing of a
person's name; its primary associations are with retribution.

The gospel, to be sure, radically redirects our concern, as
we shall emphasize, but it does so partly by introducing the
new situation created by the cross, and partly by clarifying
what was barely visible at an earlier stage: the life to come.
To get fully in tune with the psalmists on this issue we should
have to suspend our consciousness of having a gospel to impart
(which affects our attitude to fellow-sinners) and our assurance
of a final righting of wrongs (which affects our attitude to
present anomalies). Without these certainties, only a cynic
could feel no impatience to see justice triumphant and evil
men broken; and these authors were no cynics. It would
be better, in fact, to speak of their attuning our ears to the gospel
than of our adjusting to their situation, for we cannot truly
hear its answers until we have felt the force of their questions.

I have argued elsewhere[1] that the history of David, their
chief spokesman, gives proof enough that his passion for justice
was genuine, not a cover for vindictiveness. There have been
few men more capable of generosity under personal attack,
as he proved by his attitudes to Saul and Absalom, to say
nothing of Shimei;[2] and no ruler was more deeply stirred to

[1] D. Kidner, *Hard Sayings* (IVP, 1972), pp. 15–17.

[2] 2 Sa. 16:11; 19:16–23. David later changed his mind, keeping only the
letter of his promise (1 Ki. 2:8f.). He may have seen in Shimei a threat to
the already threatened Solomon (whose decision to put him under house-
arrest tends to confirm this: 1 Ki. 2:36). But if David in fact lapsed from
his former magnanimity, it was still a lapse, not a habit, and as uncharacter-
istic of him as his treachery towards Uriah.

anger by cruel and unscrupulous actions, even when they appeared to favour his cause. What he asked of God was no more—and could certainly be no less—than the verdict and intervention which a victim of injustice could expect from him, David himself, as king of Israel. The more seriously he took his ideal of kingship from God—

> When one rules justly over men,
> ruling in the fear of God—

(to quote from his 'last words'[1]), the more unthinkable it was that he should slander Him by underrating His abhorrence of evil.

b. *Their tone*

The tone and spirit of these cries range from the plaintive to the ferocious. Hatred is sometimes met by hatred, cruelty by cruelty. 'Let there be none to extend kindness to him, nor any to pity his fatherless children!' (109:12). 'O daughter of Babylon . . . Happy shall he be who takes your little ones and dashes them against the rock!' (137:8f).

It is only fair to point out that the words wrung from these sufferers as they plead their case are a measure of the deeds which provoked them. Those deeds were not wrung from anyone: they were the brutal response to love (109:4) and to pathetic weakness (137). To say that they were inexcusable is as inadequate as it is true. It needs saying with passion.

Here we should notice that invective has its own rhetoric, in which horror may be piled on horror more to express the speaker's sense of outrage than to spell out the penalties he literally intends. This can be seen quite clearly in the curse which Jeremiah elaborated with savage eloquence against the man who brought his father congratulations on his birth instead of murdering the pregnant mother![2] Such immoderate language has an air of irresponsibility which cries out for criticism, yet it would be a mistake to wish it away. It has as valid a function in this kind of context as hyperbole has in the realm of description: a vividness of communication which is beyond the reach of cautious literalism.

This brings us close to the heart of the matter, which is

---

[1] 2 Sa. 23:1,3.
[2] Je. 20:15–17.

that the psalms have among other roles in Scripture one which is peculiarly their own: to touch and kindle us rather than simply to address us. The passages on which we may be tempted to sit in judgment have the shocking immediacy of a scream, to startle us into feeling something of the desperation which produced them. This is revelation in a much more indirect but more intimate than most other forms. Without it we should have less embarrassment but still less conception of the 'dark places of the earth' which are 'full of the habitations of cruelty',[1] a cruelty which can bring faithful men to breaking-point.

The comparison with Jeremiah can perhaps be pushed further, to take in the fact that his cries are not presented to us in the void. In the context of his life they emerge as a stage in his struggle to come to terms with his calling—a struggle which deepened him and enlightens us. More explicitly, God's answers to him mingle encouragement and rebuke.[2] It is the same with Job: he has darkened counsel with 'words without knowledge', yet 'spoken . . . what is right' (Jb. 38:2; 42:7). In short, God reads the whole message: not only the words but the man and the situation, as Job's comforters failed to do. He is less shockable than we—or, more accurately, shocked or moved by different things, since He looks on the heart, and since He is afflicted in all our afflictions.

Jeremiah and Job teach us to take together question and answer, and the surface of a saying with the depth beneath it, as inseparable parts of the inspired revelation. But we must take care not to insist on our own answers. Jeremiah's petulance, for example, was rebuked in 12:5, but the substance of his prayer for retribution was upheld (11:20–23; 12:7ff.), where we no doubt would have disallowed it. Similarly the psalms receive endorsements in Scripture which sometimes take us by surprise. This leads to our next section.

c. Their New Testament use

Our Lord, at the beginning of His ministry, made a pointed omission from an Old Testament passage, by closing the book before the phrase 'the day of vengeance of our God' (Is. 61:1f.; Lk. 4:18–20). This, taken with His teaching on

---

[1] Ps. 74:20, AV.
[2] *E.g.* Je. 12:5; 15:19.

repaying evil with good, might suggest His discarding of the whole concept of judgment; but it soon becomes clear that matters are not as simple as this. He has come with salvation, yet its very approach brings judgment all the closer. The 'wicked husbandmen' in the parable are brought to a final, and as it turns out, a fatal decision when the son of the house confronts them; the small towns of Galilee, having had their taste of heaven, now face a deeper hell than Sodom's.

This paradox has its bearing on the psalms of imprecation. The psalmists in their eagerness for judgment call on God to hasten it; the gospel by contrast shows God's eagerness to save, but reveals new depths and immensities of judgment which are its corollary. 'Now they have no excuse for their sin.'

In its quotations and echoes of the Psalter on this theme the New Testament sometimes speaks with less severity than its source, sometimes with more, but never with mere personal rancour. We shall return to this in the final section; meanwhile we can note, as samples, that God's wrath and the Messiah's 'rod of iron', which are prominent in Psalm 2, are prominent in Revelation;[1] that the 'day of his wrath' (110:5) finds its echo in Romans 2:5, and the anger called down on those 'who do not know' God (79:6) is confirmed in 2 Thessalonians 1:8 (where, however, the offence is clarified as refusal to acknowledge Him, not mere ignorance).

Occasionally the New Testament breaks off a quotation at the point where retribution is threatened in the Psalter, but this is usually for reasons of relevance rather than any reservations of doctrine. For example in John 10:34 the point at issue has been fully made with the words 'I said, you are gods'; nothing would be gained by completing the quotation: ' . . . nevertheless, you shall die like men' (Ps. 82:7). Much the same is true of 1 Peter 3:12, quoting only half of Psalm 34:16. Again, in Romans 3:19 the phrase, 'that every mouth may be stopped', concludes the case against man which has been built up in the previous chapters, so that he falls silent. There is no need here of the sanctions which loom up behind Psalm 63:11. On the other hand the silence is significant in John 13:18, where our Lord quotes Psalm 41:9 on the friend 'who

---

[1] *Cf., e.g.,* 'the wrath of the Lamb', Rev. 6:16. For the 'rod of iron' see Rev. 2:27; 12:5; 19:15.

ate my bread' and 'lifted his heel against me', but forbears to pray, as David prayed, for the opportunity to requite him. He has something better to offer him.

At the same time there is 'sorer punishment' revealed in the New Testament than in the psalms, simply because the whole scale of human destiny has come into sight. This is very clear from a comparison of Psalm 6:8 with Matthew 7:23, where the words 'Depart from me, all you workers of evil' are transformed from a cry of relief by David into a sentence of death by Christ. The principle is the same: truth and lies cannot live together. 'Outside' will be 'every one who loves and practises falsehood'.[1] But it is one thing to be driven off by David; quite another by Christ, to the final exclusion which is also the climax of almost every parable in the Gospels.

The New Testament, then, so far from minimizing the role of judgment, increases its gravity at the same time as it removes it from the sphere of private reprisal. This is well illustrated by its use of two of the most heated outbursts of the Psalter, in Psalms 69 and 109. Each of them is treated as prophecy, and taken to be the sentence of God on invincible impenitence. Peter quotes Psalms 69:25[2] and 109:8 of Judas, in the spirit of our Lord's sorrowful but unquestioning references to his perdition. Paul has a similar tenderness for Israel (for whom he could wish himself accursed) when he sees them inheriting the doom of Psalm 69:22f.: 'Let their feast become a snare . . . let their eyes be darkened . . . and bend their backs for ever' (Rom. 11:9f.)—but he clearly regards the clause 'for ever' as revocable if they will repent, as indeed he expects them to do. So we gain the additional insight into these maledictions, that for all their appearance of implacability they are to be taken as conditional, as indeed the prophets' oracles were.[3] Their full force was for the obdurate; upon repentance they would become 'a curse that is causeless', which, as Proverbs 26:2 assures us, 'does not alight'.

d. *Their present relevance*

As a preliminary to this question there are two further elements in the New Testament to take into account, however briefly.

[1] Rev. 22: 15; *cf.* also Ps. 5:6.
[2] Jesus likewise alludes to this verse, it seems, in His lament for Jerusalem, Mt. 23:37f. There is only grief here.
[3] See Je. 18:7–10; Jon. 3:4,10.

The first is the plea of God's elect for vindication, mentioned already in the first section; a plea which our Lord accepts in Luke 18:7f., and which is echoed in the martyrs' cry in Revelation 6:10: 'How long before thou wilt judge and avenge our blood on those who dwell upon the earth?' What seems to be meant in both cases is the accusing *fact* of innocent blood, 'crying' like Abel's 'from the ground' to God.[1] It can hardly mean the conscious prayer of the martyrs, for in reality the example of Stephen set the tone for his successors (as his Master's did for him), ending the old tradition of indignant protest (*cf.* 2 Ch. 24:22; Je. 18:23). But Stephen's prayer for his enemies could be answered only through their repentance, as indeed it was in the case of Saul. Otherwise, in the sight of heaven this blood would still be on their heads. Even the atoning blood of Christ, although 'it speaks more graciously than the blood of Abel', becomes damning evidence against those who abuse it.[2]

The second element is the occasional equivalent of cursing in the New Testament. The Lord Himself led the way with His acted and spoken oracles of judgment on unfruitful Israel (Mk. 11:14; 12:9) and on unfaithful churches (Rev. 2f.). In the age of the apostles, if the fate of Ananias and Sapphira was not actually invoked, the temporary blinding of Elymas was; so too was the handing over of the Corinthian offender to Satan (1 Cor. 5:5). The future requital of Alexander the coppersmith is stated in terms of Psalm 62:12 in 2 Timothy 4:14 (but note the prayer of verse 16). What is common to all these cases is concern for the welfare of the kingdom or of the offender himself (including Alexander, it may be, while there was yet hope of repentance: 1 Tim. 1:20). The personal interests of those who call down these judgments have nothing of the prominence which they appear to have in the psalms. The fewness of these prayers or oracles of judgment, and the absence of bitterness, are proof enough of the new thing that has happened; but their presence at all in the New Testament confirms its continuity with the Old.

We conclude, then, that it is not open to us to renounce or ignore the psalmists, part of whose function in God's economy was to make *articulate* the cry of 'all the righteous blood shed on earth' (to borrow our Lord's phrase). But equally it is not

---

[1] Gn. 4:10; *cf.* Mt. 23:35; Heb. 12:24; see also Nu. 35:33.
[2] Heb. 10:26–31; 12:24; Mt. 23:37.

open to us simply to occupy the ground on which they stood. Between our day and theirs, our calling and theirs, stands the cross. We are ministers of reconciliation, and this is a day of good tidings.

To the question, Can a Christian use these cries for vengeance as his own? the short answer must surely be No; no more than he should echo the curses of Jeremiah or the protests of Job. He may of course translate them into affirmations of God's judgment, and into denunciations of 'the spiritual hosts of wickedness' which are the real enemy. As for the men of flesh and blood who 'live as enemies of the cross of Christ' or who make themselves our enemies, our instructions are to pray not against them but for them; to turn them from the power of Satan to God; to repay their evil with good; and to choose none of their ways. 'As men in need, who may yet be rescued, they are to be loved and sought; as men who have injured us, they must be forgiven. But as men to follow or to cultivate'—and here the psalms and the New Testament speak with one voice—'they are to be rejected utterly, as are the principalities and powers behind them.'[1]

If these passages in the psalms open our eyes to the depths and just deserts of evil, and to the dangers of borrowing its weapons, they have done their work. To say that theirs is not the last word on the subject is no reproach: more work first needed to be done. That work and final word belonged to Christ, and we are its inheritors.

VI. TITLES AND TECHNICAL TERMS

a. Their authenticity and antiquity

The notes reproduced in small print in most of our versions,[2] at the head of all but a few of the psalms, are part of the canonical text of the Hebrew Bible (unlike the marginal notes added by the Massoretes) and are included in its numbering of the verses. Hence in most psalms which bear a title the verse-numbers in the Hebrew text are out of step with ours. The New Testament not only treats these headings as holy writ, but following our Lord's example it is prepared to build its arguments on one or another of the notes of author-

---

[1] D. Kidner, *Hard Sayings* (IVP, 1972), p. 17.
[2] The NEB omits them altogether.

ship which form part of them (Mk. 12:35–37; Acts 2:29ff., 34ff.; 13:35–37). We need look no further than this for their authentication; but some of the criticisms brought against them will be discussed in section *b*, below.

As regards their antiquity, two main facts emerge from the terms they use. First, that they are editorial, using the third person for any comments they make (*e.g.*, 'when he fled from Absalom his son', Ps. 3), and are therefore later than the psalms themselves. But secondly, they are old enough for their technical terms to have become already largely meaningless to the Jews of the second or third century BC who translated the Psalter into Greek. This leaves a period of several centuries in which they could have been written, but it is the time during which most of the Old Testament was in the making. Similar psalm-notes occur in canonical books outside the Psalter: *e.g.* 2 Samuel 22:1 (*cf.* Ps. 18, title); Isaiah 38:9, 21f.; Habakkuk 3:1, 19b. The second and third of these examples also raise the question whether some of the material found at the head of certain psalms may not in fact be concluding notes rather than titles. This will be discussed later, under the heading 'Liturgical Notes' (below, *c.* 3).

b. Notes of authors

David. Seventy-three psalms, nearly half the Psalter, have the note *leḏāwīḏ*, '(belonging) to David'. Hence the collection as a whole tended to be termed simply 'David' (Heb. 4:7, RV). While the preposition *le* has a variety of meanings (*cf.* the note 'to' or 'for' the choirmaster, in RSV, JB; or AV's title of Pss. 72 and 127, 'A Psalm for Solomon'), there can be little doubt that in this context and in analogous ones it has the genitive sense, and is a genitive of authorship. This is clear from the expanded title of Psalm 18, which goes on to say 'who addressed the words of this song to the Lord. . . . He said:' (and here follows the poem itself). It is also clear from the New Testament, which sees in this phrase the David of history, whose 'tomb is with us', as Peter could remark, 'to this day' (Acts 2:29). For good measure, the Old Testament preserves other poems of David,[1] and knows him as 'the sweet psalmist of Israel' (2 Sa. 23:1) and an inventor of musical instruments (Am. 6:5).

[1] See his lament for Saul and Jonathan, 2 Sa. 1:17–27, and his 'last words', 2 Sa. 23:1–7.

His authorship of the psalms that bear his name has been challenged on various grounds. The commonest critical opinion is that while David may indeed have been a poet, we cannot tell which if any of the psalms he wrote. Some early critics tried to settle the question on aesthetic grounds, judging certain poems to be unworthy of his genius if he were the author of the lament for Saul or of Psalm 18 (=2 Sa. 22). Others have applied theological criteria (was Ps. 139 conceivable in his day?), or spiritual criteria (was the rough warrior capable of such faith and love?), or historical (did even David have so wide a range of experience?—and what of the allusions to the temple, which was not yet built?[1]), or linguistic (has Ps. 139 too many Aramaisms for a man of Judah?), or even textual (does LXX's attribution of Pss. 93–99 and seven other psalms to David, in addition to the MT's attributions, point to an excessive editorial freedom?).

Some of these objections are arbitrary and simplistic; none is adequate to the task of proving a general negative, even though some isolated questions remain unanswered.[2] But the modern study of the psalms in the Gunkel–Mowinckel tradition has largely by-passed these points of detail by its insistence on seeing the Psalter in a cultic rather than a personal or historical setting. (On this, see section III, above, pp. 7–18.) By asking what recurrent situation a given psalm was composed to meet, this school of thought tends to answer with Mowinckel that the psalms entitled *ledāwīd* were composed *for the use of* the davidic king, the '*David*' of the time being, in his capacity as embodiment and representative of Israel, for whom he speaks in most occurrences of the 'I' and 'me' of the Psalter. On this view it was by a misunderstanding that the editors of the Psalter saw David as an author, and

---

[1] See on 5:7.

[2] Ps. 139 poses perhaps the hardest of these problems, not by its theology (which is never datable) but by its various touches of provincial dialect, associated more with the north than with David's native south. Conceivably it could owe these to its finding a home at first on the outskirts of Israel (was it composed by David on campaign?) and being brought into the main collection only late in the process of compilation, as its presence in Bk V suggests. See the section on 'The Structure of the Psalter' (above, II) for other evidence that the worshippers' local variations of speech left their mark on the language of the psalms. This suggestion is offered more as a reminder of our ignorance than as a confident answer.

consequently added the biographical notes which introduce some of the psalms.[1] On this question see section VII below, pp. 43ff.

Solomon. Psalms 72 and 127, where see comments.

The sons of Korah. Twelve psalms (42–49, 84f., 87f.) are ascribed to this Levitical family, descendants of the rebel leader of that name, whose children were spared—to our great gain—when he died for his rebellion (Nu. 26:10f.). One part of this family became the temple doorkeepers and guardians (1 Ch. 9:17ff.; *cf.* Ps. 84:10?), another part the singers and musicians of the temple choir founded under David by Heman, whose fellow-Levites Asaph and Jeduthun (or Ethan) directed the choirs drawn from the other two clans of that tribe (1 Ch. 6:31, 33, 39, 44).

Asaph. Another twelve psalms have this ascription: 50, 73–83. See the paragraph above for Asaph's relation to his colleagues; see also 1 Chronicles 16:5; 2 Chronicles 29:30. In the headings, his name evidently stands for his choir in at least some instances, since such laments as 74 and 79 tell of disasters witnessed by no contemporary of David.

Heman the Ezrahite. Psalm 88. Heman was the founder of the choir known as 'the sons of Korah' (see above), and was famed for his wisdom (1 Ki. 4:31). Ezrahite is evidently an equivalent of Zerahite, a clan of Judah (1 Ch. 2:6), although Heman was also a Levite, with Ephraimite connections (1 Ch. 6:33; *cf.* 1 Sa. 1:1). These links, possibly adoptive, between Levi and other tribes, if the Heman of 1 Chronicles 2:6 is rightly identified with the Korahite founder, are not unparalleled: *cf.* Judges 17:7 and the subsequent affiliations of the Levite in question.

Ethan the Ezrahite. Psalm 89. Ethan is probably identical with **Jeduthun,** who founded one of the three choirs (*cf.* 1 Ch. 15:19; 2 Ch. 5:12). Ethan shared with Heman a reputation for wisdom, and membership of the same Judahite clan (see on Heman, above).

---

[1] Mowinckel, I, pp. 77f.

35

Psalms 39, 62, 77 have the name Jeduthun in their titles; see the comment on the first of these.

Moses. Psalm 90. Few commentators accept the authorship of this psalm, so stated, yet few deny the unusual and majestic qualities which can be pointed out in support of it. Against Mosaic authorship Mowinckel chiefly argues from the outlook of the psalm, finding it too individualistic and too unambitious to have issued from the milieu of a primitive and youthful people bent on conquest. Others diagnose signs of a long national history in the opening verse, and sense the mood of Isaiah 40 in the comparison of human life to grass and in the plea that punishment has already lasted long enough.

The last argument is double-edged, since the psalm could equally have influenced the prophecy as the prophecy the psalm. Again the long memory is not simply Israel's but man's, for the psalm is primarily about humanity before God. As positive indications, it has been pointed out by commentators of various shades of opinion that the psalm has distinct echoes of early Genesis, in the Creation and Fall, and in the apparent allusion to the longevity of the antediluvians[1] (which are not common themes in the Old Testament); also that it has affinities to the language of the Song and the Blessing of Moses (Dt. 32 and 33),[2] and a wistfulness of mood which is very appropriate to the circumstances of a doomed generation in the wilderness. Even the individualism of the psalm has its counterpart in Deuteronomy, where it is small consolation to Moses that the nation will enter the land if he himself may not (Dt. 3:23ff.).

c. Technical terms

The endless explanations offered for these are a confession of our uncertainty. For a fuller discussion, see any of the larger commentaries.

1. Interjections

Selah. This occurs 71 times (and a further three times in Hab. 3), predominantly in Books I–III of the Psalter. Probably it is the signal for an interlude (*cf.* LXX) or change of musical accompaniment. It is usually thought to come from a root

[1] *Cf.* Anderson, II, p. 651.
[2] *Cf.* Briggs, II, p. 272.

sll, to lift up (*cf.* 68:4, Heb. 5), *i.e.*, perhaps, to strike up with the instruments or voices; but a root *slh*, supposedly corresponding to an Aramaic verb 'to bend', *i.e.* bow down, has alternatively been suggested.[1] Other possibilities are that the vowels indicate the response *neṣaḥ*, 'for ever' (*cf.* Targ.) to be interjected at this point (sometimes, however, with dubious relevance); or that the consonants of Selah are an acrostic signifying either 'change of voices' or 'repeat from the beginning'[2] The first interpretation probably remains the best.

Higgaion. In Psalm 9:16 (Heb. 17) this word follows Selah as a detached note, but it is found in 19:14 (15) and 92:3 (4) within the sentences ('the *meditation* of my heart', 'the *melody* of the lyre'). The related verb is usually taken to mean 'murmur' and thence 'meditate' (see on 2:1); consequently as a musical direction it may perhaps indicate the quieter instruments. Eerdmans however holds that it never refers to instrumental music (in spite of 92:3, which he reinterprets) but rather to the recital of Scripture, accompanied or unaccompanied.[3] His interpretation creates difficulties in some contexts, and it would seem better to retain the idea of meditation or of quiet music.

2. *Classifications*

Psalm (*mizmor*) and **Song** (*šîr*) are not completely distinguishable to us, but the former probably implied by its name that it was sung to an instrumental accompaniment. L. Delekat cites Ecclesiasticus 44:5 to support his view that a psalm was a composed piece, designed for a particular occasion, whereas a song (*šîr*) was something more generally known and sung (the word can be used of a secular as well as a religious song), and not necessarily accompanied. The double title, where it occurs, would then indicate a formal poem by David or Asaph, *etc.*, which had become by its popularity virtually an institution.[4]

---

[1] B. D. Eerdmans, *The Hebrew Book of Psalms* (*OTS* 4, 1947), pp. 85, 89, citing the description in the Mishnah of the daily sacrifice, where at each pause in the psalm trumpets were blown and the people prostrated themselves.

[2] *Cf.* K-B.

[3] B. D. Eerdmans, *op. cit.*, pp. 79f.

[4] L. Delekat, 'Probleme der Psalmenüberschriften', *ZAW* 76 (1964), 281f.

Shiggaion (Ps. 7; *cf.* the plural, 'according to Shigionoth', Hab. 3:1) seems to be derived from a verb 'to err' or 'wander'; but neither of these psalms is penitential. Kirkpatrick therefore applied this to the poetic form, as being wild and ecstatic.[1] Eerdmans draws attention to Arabic and Assyrian verbs denoting a stirring of the emotions.[2]

Miktam (Pss. 16, 56–60; all Davidic) is another obscure title. AV mg.'s 'A golden psalm' is too precariously linked to the noun *keṭem*, gold. A sounder derivation, perhaps, is from an assumed cognate verb to the Akkadian *katamu*, 'to cover'. Mowinckel infers atonement from this; but these psalms are concerned with insecurity rather than sin. Eerdmans makes the attractive suggestion that in view of the perils named in several of the titles, the 'covering' is that of the lips in secrecy, and so the heading should be translated 'A silent prayer'. 'In none of these cases David could have recited a prayer in the usual way.'[3]

Maskil (thirteen psalms,[4] mostly in Bks II and III). This is the participle of a verb meaning to make wise or prudent, or to have success or skill. The LXX translates it '(a psalm) of understanding'. While there are some explicit references to imparting wisdom (*e.g.* 32:8; 78:1), not many of this group are 'teaching psalms', and conversely there are obvious candidates for such a title which are not given it (*e.g.* Pss. 1, 37, *etc.*). From the other senses of the verb the meanings 'efficacious psalm' and 'skilful psalm' have been suggested; the former implying that it was part of a ritual for securing help for an enterprise, and the latter that it was an example of fine writing or was matched to elaborate music. Once again, we do not yet know the answer.

A Prayer (five psalms[5]); **A Praise** (Ps. 145). The plurals of these could serve as titles for entire collections of psalms: see note on 72:20.

---

[1] Kirkpatrick, p. xx.
[2] B. D. Eerdmans, *op. cit.*, p. 77.
[3] *Ibid.*, p. 75.
[4] Pss. 32, 42, 44, 45, 52–55, 74, 78, 88, 89, 142.
[5] Pss. 17, 86, 90, 102, 142.

3. *Liturgical notes*

An independent example of such notes and directives can be found outside the Psalter, at Habakkuk 3:19b. Since in this case it follows the psalm, it has been argued that in the Psalter as well the equivalent material may have originally done the same, and that apart from the classifying title ('Psalm', 'Song', *etc.*) and the author's name and explanatory details, the liturgical notes refer back to the preceding psalm.[1] For possible supporting examples see below on 'According to Lilies' and on 'The Dove on Far-off Terebinths'; also the introductions to Psalms 30 and 88, and the footnote to 48:14. Against these, however, see below on 'The Hind of the Dawn'; see also on 148:14.[2] On the whole, the evidence for such editorial misplacements is too inconclusive to upset the prevailing lay-out of the headings; but if in exceptional cases a psalm was annotated originally in the manner of Habakkuk 3:19, it is not unreasonable to suppose that its conclusion might have become joined to the next psalm by force of editorial habit.

To turn to the meaning of this material, the most general view is that some of the obscure phrases are the names of tunes or types of music to be used (*cf.* RV, RSV, JB), identified by the opening or most characteristic words of familiar songs. This may sound suspiciously modern and western,[3] and can be only a tentative opinion; yet we find melodic modes named and sharply differentiated from one another as far back as Plato in the fourth century BC,[4] and melodic instruments—which breed melodies—mentioned in the Psalter (*e.g.* oboe and flute, *ḥālîl* and *'ûgāb*). We can also find many allusions in the Old Testament to popular songs, a vintagers' catch-phrase in a psalm-heading (see below, on 'Do Not Destroy', p. 43), and, for what it is worth, a comparison by Clement of Alexandria (*c.* 200 AD) between the way of sing-

---

[1] J. W. Thirtle, *The Titles of the Psalms* (Frowde, 1904), *passim*.
[2] *Cf.* R. A. F. MacKenzie, 'Ps. 148: 14b,c: Conclusion or Title?', *Bib.* 51[2] (1970), pp. 221–224.
[3] *Cf.* the criticisms by Eerdmans, *op. cit.*, p. 51; Delekat, *art. cit.*, p. 291; Mowinckel, I, pp. 8f.; II, p. 213n.
[4] *Republic*, Bk III (Everyman Edition, p. 81). Some of these are recognizable not only in Christian liturgical music but in medieval Jewish prayer modes, an independent development from what was evidently a common ancient Near-Eastern musical stock. See Example 300, *New Oxford History of Music*, I (OUP, 1957), p. 323.

ing the Hebrew psalms and a Greek banqueting-song.[1]

Sometimes, however, these phrases can be seen as pointers to some aspect of the subject-matter or use of the psalm, since the preposition translated 'according to' can also mean 'about', 'over', *etc.* Each must be taken on its own evidence.

To the choirmaster (*lamᵉnaṣṣēaḥ*) is a note attached to fifty-five psalms, and also to the psalm of Habakkuk (Hab. 3:19b). The Hebrew root means to excel, and thence to superintend. The familiar translation, which is as reasonable as any, suggests that for the choirmaster there was compiled a collection of psalms drawn from the separate sources and choirs, possibly for special occasions, possibly as a stage towards making the complete Psalter.

The ancient versions, however, translated it in various other ways, connecting it with the Hebrew for 'evermore' (*cf.* LXX, 'to the end') or 'victor' (*e.g.* Jerome) or 'praise' (Targ.); and there is no lack of modern suggestions. Mowinckel arrives at the idea of a psalm 'to dispose God to mercy'.[2] Delekat suggests that it might have been originally a response *lāneṣaḥ*, 'evermore' (*cf.* LXX), marking the *end* of a psalm (like an Amen or Hallelujah), but later misinterpreted as a reference to the 'excellent one' who wrote the psalm, who was subsequently identified as David, Asaph, *etc.*[3] Eerdmans argues that the word denotes an overseer of gangs of labourers, who directed the work by rhythmical music, and whose skill was enlisted to keep the processional bearers of the Ark in step.[4]

If the economy of a hypothesis is its strength, the familiar translation has little to fear from its alternatives.

According to The Sheminith (Pss. 6 and 12) is a companion term in 1 Chronicles 15:21 to **According to Alamoth** (Ps. 46; 1 Ch. 15:20). The passage in Chronicles, describing the bringing of the Ark to Jerusalem, tells of eight Levites who were 'to play harps according to Alamoth', and six who were 'to lead with lyres according to the Sheminith'. Alamoth (*ᶜᵃlāmôṯ*) means 'girls'; Sheminith (*šᵉmînîṯ*) means 'eighth'. Although the latter is very enigmatic to us (the eighth string?

---

[1] *Paidagogos*, ii. 4.
[2] Mowinckel, II, p. 212.
[3] L. Delekat, *art. cit.*, pp. 283–286.
[4] B. D. Eerdmans, *op. cit.*, pp. 54–60.

the eighth and crowning ritual act?), the majority opinion is that Alamoth means the treble range, and Sheminith therefore the tenor or bass. But we have no evidence that pitch was reckoned in octaves, a division of intervals which is traditionally ascribed to Pythagoras.[1]

According to The Gittith (Pss. 8, 81, 84). Gath, from which this feminine adjective is derived, means wine-press, and is also the name of a Philistine town. The three main conjectures are therefore that this is a term connected with the vintage (which coincided with the Feast of Tabernacles), or with the Ark's journey from the Gittite's house to Jerusalem (2 Sa. 6.11), or with an instrument (or tune?) which took its name from Gath.

According to Muth-labben (Ps. 9). The phrase '*al-mût labbēn* means 'upon (or about, or according to) death for (or of) the son'. But the ben Asher text and all the ancient versions read the hyphenated words (which are the same as the last two words of 48:14, where see comment) as a single word. The LXX took this to mean 'the secrets of the son'; Aquila made it 'the youth of the son'. Many have suggested that we should read here '(according to) Alamoth . . .', *i.e.*, possibly, 'sung with treble voices by boys' (*cf.* BDB).[2] By re-vocalizing *labbēn* ('for the son') as *lābîn* (to make aware), Delekat translates the phrase 'with prominent treble'.[3]

Reading the title as in RSV, *etc.*, there are many suggestions but no certainty. *E.g.* it is a tune-name; or a reference to a ritual of dying and rising; even (Thirtle) a song on the death of Goliath (who is called '*îš habbēnāyim* in 1 Sa. 17:4). The first of these is the least improbable.

According to The Hind of the Dawn (Ps. 22). This may be a tune-name (see above, p. 39), but is better explained as a glimpse of the theme, and translated (as Eerdmans[4] suggests, agreeing with LXX) 'On the help of (*i.e.*, at) daybreak'. The word '*ayyelet* ('Hind', RSV) is very close to the rare word '*eyālût*, 'help' (19, Heb. 20), and could be vocalized to coincide

---

[1] See E. Werner, *HUCA* 21 (1948), pp. 211–255.
[2] But the singular, lit., 'the son', makes this improbable.
[3] L. Delekat, *art. cit.*, p. 292.
[4] B. D. Eerdmans, *op. cit.*, p. 173.

with it, if it is not indeed a feminine form of *'eyāl* (help), Psalm 88:4 (Heb. 5). So the title draws attention to the deliverance which will light up the final verses of the psalm.

According to Lilies (Pss. 45, 69; *'al-šōšannîm*)
According to Shushan Eduth (Ps. 60; *'al-šûšan 'ēdût*)
According to Lilies. A Testimony (Ps. 80; *'el-šōšannîm 'ēdût*)

The two nouns, *lilies* (or *lily*, Ps. 60) and *testimony* link these titles together. As a tune-name, the allusion to lilies would connect the wedding-psalm 45 appropriately with, *e.g.*, Song of Solomon 2:1; but the rest of these psalms have a sombre note. LXX vocalized this word not as 'lilies' but as 'those who change' (*šeššōnîm?*), and Delekat[1] agrees basically with this, interpreting it as 'those whose situation changes for the worse'. (At Ps. 45 he takes it to refer back to Ps. 44.) The Hebrew consonants allow this in three cases out of the four, but Psalm 60, with the singular, puts it in doubt. In spite of this, Delekat's suggestion goes furthest towards relating the titles to the subject-matter; and the indirect support of LXX strengthens the case.

Testimony (*'ēdût*) could refer in Psalm 60 to God's answering oracle in verses 6–8; but there is no equivalent in Psalm 80. Albright however has pointed out that this word is often used as a synonym for Covenant,[2] and both these psalms make much of this pledged relationship in what they affirm or plead.

At Psalm 80, the words 'of Asaph' are preferably linked with 'A Psalm'.

According to Mahalath (Pss. 53, 88). This could be the name of a tune, or (Mowinckel) an instrument, and it comes twice as a feminine proper name (Gn. 28:9; 2 Ch. 11:18). It is also almost identical with a word for sickness, which would fit Psalm 88, but hardly 53 unless the occasion is a plague sent as a judgment on apostasy. Psalm 88 adds **Leannoth** (*le'annôt*), 'to humble or afflict'.

According to The Dove on Far-off Terebinths (Ps. 56). The RSV takes this to be a tune-name. But the allusion in the

---

[1] L. Delekat, *art. cit.*, pp. 294f.
[2] W. F. Albright, *From the Stone Age to Christianity*[2] (Doubleday, 1957), p. 16.

previous psalm to a dove and to the far distance (55:6f.) can hardly be a coincidence, and raises the question whether such phrases in the 'headings' should rather be read as postscripts (see above, p. 39)—unless, indeed, this is an example of identifying a tune by a well-known phrase of a song, and therefore a direction to sing Psalm 56 to the tune of Psalm 55.

As an added complication, 'terebinths' (*'êlîm*) is read by LXX as 'gods' (*'ēlîm*), but vocalized in MT as 'silence' (*'ēlem*). Mowinckel, accepting the LXX reading, conjectures the sacrifice of a dove, in a ritual which would combine features of the scapegoat and the cleansing of the leper; but there is no secure basis for postulating such a ceremony.

According to Do Not Destroy (Pss. 57–59, 75). This may well be a tune-indication: *cf.* Isaiah 65:8, where the phrase is identified as a popular saying (perhaps a snatch of vintage song), and borrowed to become a reassuring word from God. Yet notice also David's instructions about Saul, 'Destroy him not' (1 Sa. 26:9), and again, as Dahood points out, the prayer of Moses, 'Destroy not thy people' (Dt. 9:26). The latter would chime in with the thought of Isaiah 65:8 and with the note of ultimate trust found in these psalms.

A Song of Ascents (Pss. 120–134). The Mishnah records that fifteen steps led up from the Court of the Women to the Court of the Israelites 'corresponding to the fifteen Songs of Ascents in the Psalms, and upon them the levites used to sing'.[1] But as C. C. Keet points out,[2] there is no record that what they sang there was these psalms, although this is possible and has often been asserted. The most likely reference of the title is to the pilgrimage up to Jerusalem, or the processional ascent of 'the hill of the Lord' (*cf.* Is. 30:29).[3]

VII. DAVIDIC EPISODES IN THE HEADINGS

Fourteen psalms[4] carry headings which connect them with events in David's career. The commentary explores some

[1] Middoth 2: 5, *The Mishnah*, ed. H. Danby (OUP, 1933), p. 593.
[2] Keet, p. 3.
[3] *Cf.* Keet, p. 16. His opening chapter gives an instructive survey of the numerous theories put forward on these psalms.
[4] Pss. 3, 7, 18, 30, 34, 51, 52, 54, 56, 57, 59, 60, 63, 142.

implications of these contexts for the psalms to which they relate; but here we must ask the prior question whether the links are genuine or artificial.

The difficulties which have been felt over these biographical notes are general as well as particular. In general, we may find it hard to understand how a polished work of art, such as the acrostic Psalm 34, could come into being in a life-and-death emergency; or we may notice that the thought of such psalms often ranges further afield than the named situation itself. To both these points it may of course be enough to reply that we are dealing with the products of no ordinary talent, and, further, of divine inspiration, both of which are highly relevant factors; but since God does not gratuitously multiply miracles, the truth may be that it was the nucleus of the psalm—some germinal phrase or sequence—which came to David in the crisis itself, to be developed later as he pondered and re-lived the incident. A further point of growth can occasionally be seen, as in the last two verses of Psalm 51, when David's experience was appropriated as Israel's own, and their prayer or praise grafted on to his—a response which provides an object-lesson to subsequent users of the Psalter.

Turning to particular objections, these are mostly bound up with the rejection of David's personal authorship, which we have already discussed (see on 'David', above, VI. *b*, pp. 33–35ff.). But there are also long-standing criticisms of the biographical notes in themselves.

An example of the older critical approach is S. R. Driver's *Introduction to the Literature of the Old Testament* (7th edition, pp. 376f.). This author's comments are largely subjective: for example, he considers Psalm 34 clearly unsuited to the occasion of David's escape from the king of Gath. For another view of this, see the commentary; but the weakness of the approach is that it merely says in effect, 'In that situation, this is not the psalm one would have composed oneself.' To this (if it is a fair estimate of Driver's objection) the reader can hardly be blamed for replying, 'Exactly; but this is why the psalms live on.' Scarcely less arbitrary is the handling of the title of Psalm 52, where Driver will not allow that Doeg could be the 'rich and powerful man, a persecutor of the righteous', who is portrayed in the psalm; nor can he credit, in that situation, David's serenity at the close. Here again the commentary may clarify some of the details, and expound the faith of David; meanwhile we can point out that Doeg, who was the chief of the king's herdsmen and who further curried favour by wiping out the city of the priests, is hardly misrepresented (as Driver maintains) in this portrait. Even so, the psalm looks beyond the individual to the way of life he represents. Driver's further examples are equally inconclusive; and elsewhere he does his case no service (pp. 375f.) by carefully disproving any connection between Psalm 11 and the revolt of Absalom—a connection which the reader who troubles to check the matter will find to be nowhere mentioned or implied in the psalm or in its title.[1]

Among more recent scholars, Mowinckel dismisses the historical notes as 'typical midrash . . . *i.e.* a learned forming of legends as the result of . . . an unhistorical, speculative exegesis of disconnected details'.[2] But his supporting examples are surprisingly inadequate, consisting mostly of bare assertions and questionable exegesis. *E.g.* he simply asserts that 'actually' Psalm 18 is concerned with a single great battle, not the wars of a lifetime as the title implies. He offers no proof of this. Again, he reads 18:50b[3] as 'explicitly' telling us that the king in question is not David but one of his descendants—an exegesis which fails to reckon with the pivotal promise to David of a dynasty which would be for ever (2 Sa. 7:16), or with the grammatical fact that the verbs of 18:50 are participles, whose time-reference is indeterminate. As for Doeg, Mowinckel even finds fault with the heading of Psalm 52 for saying 'When Doeg came to Saul' instead of 'When David heard that Doeg came to Saul'. He also sees a discrepancy between the psalmist's complaint of 'deceitful words' and Doeg's 'objective truth'—ignoring the damaging context in which Doeg volunteered his information, namely Saul's accusation that David was a traitor whom people were sheltering by their silence (1 Sa. 22:8f.). The only difficulty of any substance which Mowinckel raises against this psalm is its reference to 'the house of God'. On this, see on Psalm 5:7.

An altogether more thoughtful approach is adopted by

[1] The title reads simply 'To the choirmaster. Of David'. The LXX is substantially the same.
[2] Mowinckel, II, pp. 100f.
[3] 'And shows steadfast love to his anointed, to David and his descendants for ever.'

B. S. Childs,[1] who shows that the links between the titles and
the poems are of far more substance and value than Mowinckel
will allow, although he gives reasons for regarding these
editorial notes as 'an extremely late post-exilic phenomenon'
and a product of scholarly and devout study of the Scriptures
rather than of actual historical traditions. If this is so, it is
midrash (research), yet not the fanciful manipulation of
Scripture which that term came to mean in later Judaism.
It is 'part of the biblical tradition itself, and must be taken
seriously as such'.[2]

Childs does not claim more than high probability for his
conclusion on the material's origin, which he treats as a
working hypothesis; and he points out that it leaves certain
problems unsolved. But his article, by showing exegetically
that the narrative notes have a rational relationship to the
contents of the psalms, has the side-effect of demolishing the
main objection to taking them as a genuine historical tradition.

To the present writer, the latter seems the simpler hypothesis,[3] especially as not every item of information can be deduced
from the texts. There would seem to be no reason, for instance,
to introduce the unknown figure of 'Cush a Benjaminite' into
the title of Psalm 7 unless it happened to be a detail passed
down with the psalm itself.

But as we have no direct knowledge of the way in which
these comments came into being, it should perhaps be left an
open question whether some are the product of comparing
scripture with scripture, and others the product of historical
records. What matters is their truth, which there is no valid
reason to doubt, and which finds incidental confirmation in
the light which they throw on the psalms they introduce.[4]

---

[1] B. S. Childs, 'Psalm Titles and Midrashic Exegesis', *JSS* 16[2] (1971),
pp. 137–150.
[2] *Ibid.*, p. 149.
[3] The evidence from LXX's additional Ps. 151 and from the Targum and
Peshitta that biographical notes continued to be added to the Psalms in
late times (*cf.* B.S. Childs, *art. cit.*, p. 143) does not prove anything about
the canonical headings, which could well have been the revered models
for this imitation, especially if they were of known antiquity.
[4] Other aspects of the matter are discussed on pp. 16ff., above.

COMMENTARY

Book I: Psalms 1–41

Psalm 1

The Two Ways

It seems likely that this psalm was specially composed as an introduction to the whole Psalter. Certainly it stands here as a faithful doorkeeper, confronting those who would be in 'the congregation of the righteous' (5) with the basic choice that alone gives reality to worship; with the divine truth (2) that must inform it; and with the ultimate judgment (5, 6) that looms up beyond it.

The tone and themes of the psalm bring to mind the Wisdom writings, especially Proverbs, with their interest in the company a man keeps, in the two ways set before him (*cf.*, *e.g.*, Pr. 2:12ff., 20ff.), and in moral types, notably the scoffers; note too the imagery drawn from nature, and the interest in the logical end of a process. But the wisdom it commends is rooted in the law (2), and the closest parallel to the psalm is found in one of the prophets (Je. 17:5–8); such is the harmony of the different voices of the Old Testament.

1:1–3. The way of life

Preferable to *Blessed*, for which a separate word exists, is 'Happy', or 'The happiness of . . .!'. Such was the Queen of Sheba's exclamation in 1 Kings 10:8, and it is heard twenty-six times in the Psalter.[1] This psalm goes on to show the sober choice that is its basis. The Sermon on the Mount, using the corresponding word in Greek, will go on to expound it still more radically.

Counsel, *way* and *seat* (or 'assembly', or 'dwelling') draw attention to the realms of thinking, behaving and belonging, in which a person's fundamental choice of allegiance is made and carried through; and this is borne out by a hint

---

[1] 1:1; 2:12; 32:1,2; 33:12; 34:8; 40:4; 41:1; 65:4; 84:4,5,12; 89:15; 94:12; 106:3; 112:1; 119:1,2; 127:5; 128:1,2; 137:8,9; 144:15,16; 146:5.

of decisiveness in the tense of the Hebrew verbs (the perfect). It would be reading too much into these verbs to draw a moral from the apparent process of slowing down from walking to sitting, since the journey was in the wrong direction for a start. Yet certainly the three complete phrases show three aspects, indeed three degrees, of departure from God, by portraying conformity to this world at three different levels: accepting its advice, being party to its ways, and adopting the most fatal of its attitudes—for the *scoffers*, if not the most scandalous of sinners, are the farthest from repentance (Pr. 3:34).

2. The three negatives have cleared the way for what is positive, which is their true function and the value of their hard cutting edge. (Even in Eden God gave man a negative, to allow him the privilege of decisive choice.) The mind was the first bastion to defend, in verse 1, and is treated as the key to the whole man. *The law of the Lord* stands opposed to 'the counsel of the wicked' (1), to which it is ultimately the only answer. The psalm is content to develop this one theme, implying that whatever really shapes a man's thinking shapes his life. This is conveniently illustrated also by the next psalm, where the word for 'plot' (2:1b) is the same as for *meditates* here, with results that follow from the very different thoughts that are entertained there. In our verse, the deliberate echo of the charge to Joshua reminds the man of action that the call to think hard about the will of God is not merely for the recluse, but is the secret of achieving anything worth while (*cf. prospers*, here, with Jos. 1:8). *Law* (*tôrâ*) basically means 'direction' or 'instruction'; it can be confined to a single command, or can extend, as here, to Scripture as a whole.

3. With this attractive picture, forming with verse 4 the centrepiece of the psalm, *cf.* the more elaborate passage, Jeremiah 17:5–8. The phrase *its fruit in its season* emphasizes both the distinctiveness and the quiet growth of the product; for the tree is no mere channel, piping the water unchanged from one place to another, but a living organism which absorbs it, to produce in due course something new and delightful, proper to its kind and to its time. The promised immunity of the *leaf* from withering is not independence of the rhythm of the seasons (*cf.* the preceding line, and see on 31:15), but freedom from the crippling damage of drought (*cf.* Je. 17:8b).

1:4, 5. The way of doom

The simile in verse 4 goes as far beyond Jeremiah's contrast of fruitful tree and desert shrub (Je. 17:6) as *the judgment* (5) goes beyond ordinary calamities. And it emphasizes more explicitly what a man *is* than what he sees and feels (*cf.* Je. 17:6a, 8b); hence the unsparing conclusion. *Chaff* is, in such a setting, the ultimate in what is rootless, weightless (*cf.* the 'vain and light persons' of Jdg. 9:4, AV) and useless. The figure is that of winnowing, in which the threshed corn is tossed up for the husks and fragments of straw to blow away, leaving behind only the grain.

Other psalms will point out that the wicked, rather than the righteous, may seem to be the people of substance (*e.g.* 37:35f.). But 'the Day will disclose' the man of straw as surely as the works of straw (*cf.* 1 Cor. 3:12f.). The next verse looks ahead to this.

5. The end has nothing arbitrary about it: note the irreducible contrasts in this verse, whose opening *Therefore* leads inexorably out of what these men have chosen to be (4). Before the Judge they will have, in our similar phrase, not a leg to stand on, and among His people no place. These two aspects of judgment, collapse and expulsion, are portrayed again with immense power in Isaiah 2:10–21.

1:6. The parting of the ways

To 'know' is more than to be informed (as in 139:1–6): it includes to care about, as in 31:7 (Heb. 8), and to own or identify oneself with (*cf.* Pr. 3:6). To *perish* is used in many senses: here for instance of a road or course that comes to nothing or to ruin; elsewhere of hopes or plans frustrated (*e.g.* 112:10; Pr. 11:7), of creatures that get lost (119:176), and of men and achievements that come to grief (2:11; 9:6). The New Testament brings to light the eternal implications which are already contained in it (*e.g.* Jn. 3:16).

So the two ways, and there is no third, part for ever.

Psalm 2

The Lord and His Anointed

Although it has no superscription this psalm is ascribed to David in Acts 4:25, and identified as 'the second psalm' in

Acts 13:33.[1] It is much quoted in the New Testament, both for its high claims for the Person of God's Anointed and for its vision of His universal kingdom. It is unsurpassed for its buoyant, fierce delight in God's dominion and His promise to His King. While it is usually considered a coronation psalm, it seems on closer inspection to recall that occasion (7–9) at a subsequent time of trouble (such as that of 2 Sa. 10). At David's own accession there were no subject-peoples to grow mutinous (3). For Solomon there were plenty, but there were few for any of his successors. A greater, however, than David or Solomon was needed to justify the full fury of these threats and the glory of these promises.

2:1–3. The kings against the King

The psalm plunges straight into its theme, and the initial *Why* sets the tone of its approach, one of astonishment at the senseless rejection of God's rule and ruler. RSV *conspire* misses the note of turbulence caught by other versions, and in 1b it is of interest that *plot* is the verb translated 'meditates' in 1:2 (from the idea of murmuring to oneself or, in a bad sense, muttering). The discontent slowly clarifies into the resolve of verse 3, a typically blind reaction to God's easy yoke and 'cords of compassion' (*cf.* Ho. 11:4). Acts 4:25–28 sees Calvary itself predicted here, with the roles of *kings* and *rulers* fulfilled by, respectively, Herod and Pilate, and those of *nations* and *peoples* by 'the Gentiles and the peoples' (plural, as in the psalm) 'of Israel', united against the Lord's *anointed*, or in Greek, His Christ. That passage points out the quiet sovereignty of God (Acts 4:28), and 1 Corinthians 2:8ff. the obtuseness of man. Every grand alliance against heaven will show, in time, this double pattern.

2:4–6. Divine derision

The New Testament shows the wrath of man harnessed to redemption (see comment above), but also judged, as here. The Lord's *derision* (4) reappears there, in essence, in the confounding of the wise (1 Cor. 1:20) and in heaven's triumph over the arrogant (*e.g.* Col. 2:15; Rev. 11:18; 18:20). But

---

[1] An alternative reading there, naming it the first psalm, reflects the fact that some Heb. MSS treated the second psalm (which lacks a heading) as a continuation of the first.

it becomes very plain that the only laughing matter is the arrogance itself—not the suffering it will cost before it ends.

6. This, with verse 7, is the centrepiece, the answer awaited in verses 1–5 and expounded in 8–12. The *I* is emphatic; the opening is best translated 'But as for me, I have set . . .'. After the bombast of verse 3 this is the neglected voice that has the final say. *Set*, here, is a word specially associated with leaders and their installation in office; hence NEB 'enthroned', JB 'installed'. *Zion, my holy hill,* was almost as late an arrival on the Israelite scene as *my king*; both were authenticated by God's promise (2 Sa. 7: 13ff.). How far-reaching this promise was, the next verse will begin to show.

2:7–9. Divine decree

Now the Lord's Anointed speaks. *The decree* enlarges on the pledge of adoption given to David's heir in 2 Samuel 7:14, 'I will be his father and he shall be my son.' The words here may have been spoken as an oracle by a prophet or read out by the king ('I will tell . . .') in the coronation rite,[1] as the word *today* suggests, to mark the moment when the new sovereign formally took up his inheritance and his titles. The connecting of this announcement with the resurrection, in Acts 13:33 (*cf.* Rom. 1:4), is doubly meaningful against such a background. For any earthly king this form of address could bear only the lightest interpretation, but the New Testament holds us to its full value which excludes the very angels, to leave only one candidate in possession (Heb. 1:5). At Christ's baptism and transfiguration the Father proclaimed Him both Son and Servant in words drawn from this verse and from Isaiah 42:1 (Mt. 3:17; 17:5; 2 Pet. 1:17).

8. Our Lord's post-resurrection charges to the apostles emphasized *the nations* and *the ends of the earth*, pointedly taking up this promise to the newly authenticated king. It has continued to launch missionary ventures whenever its force has come home to the church, whose share in it is confirmed by the New Testament's use of the next verse.

9. Three times the book of Revelation quotes these words, once concerning the victorious Christian (2:27) and twice concerning his Lord (12:5; 19:15). But it follows the LXX

---

[1] Notice the prominence of the Word of God on these occasions: Dt. 17:18; 1 Sa. 10:25; 2 Ki. 11:12.

interpretation of the Hebrew consonants, reading the first verb as 'rule' (lit. 'shepherd') rather than *break*. This gives a wider range to the promise, envisaging an iron discipline in the first place, and, in the second, a final overthrow for the incorrigible (*cf.* Je. 19:10f.). The Christian's present share in subjugating the nations to Christ is finely expressed in 2 Corinthians 10:9ff. The *rod* had the functions of a shepherd's crook in sorting out the flock (Lv. 27:32; Ezk. 20:37) and of a weapon against marauders (*cf.* Ps. 23:4). So it became a symbol of government, translated 'sceptre' in, *e.g.*, Genesis 49:10, and seems more suited to this constructive role, in a kingly context, than to the destruction envisaged in the second line.

2:10-12. The kings are summoned
In view of the foregoing, the mutinous nations of the prologue are offered their only hope, which is submission. But it is an invitation rather than an ultimatum; grace breaks through completely in the closing line.

10. *Be wise* and *be warned* are favourite words of the Wisdom writings. Their presence in this most royal of psalms should remind us not to make these literary categories too rigid. Since 'the ways of the Lord are right' (Ho. 14:9), the Bible never drives a wedge between authority and truth, or between wisdom and obedience.

11, 12. The four Hebrew words that span the verse-division have been a problem to translators from early times, but the general sense is plain, that this is a call to submit to Yahweh and His Anointed with the kiss of homage. *Rejoice with trembling* (AV, RV, LXX, Vulg.) conjures up a startling yet quite appropriate mixture of emotions in face of serving so great a king (*cf.*, *e.g.*, Hab. 3:16, 18). But Dahood's suggestions that *gîl* ('rejoice') can mean 'live' offers an easier translation ('live in trembling') without changing the text. By contrast, 'Kiss his feet' (RSV, JB) is based on the precarious conjecture that the Hebrew terms here for 'rejoice' and 'son' (?) are the scattered fragments of a single word, 'on-his-feet'; and NEB mg. 'kiss the mighty one' evidently makes the assumption that the word *rab* (mighty) has been spelt backwards as *bar* (son). LXX, followed by Vulg., makes matters no clearer with its 'take hold of discipline', which cannot be extracted from our Hebrew text.

The son (AV, RV) is, however, a very doubtful translation, since the definite article is lacking, and 'kiss son' would be as awkward in Hebrew as in English. Further, it is in Aramaic that this word *bar* means 'son'. In Hebrew it means 'pure', and if this (or *bōr*, 'purity') may be taken adverbially it will make the phrase a command to 'kiss sincerely', *i.e.*, 'pay true homage'. This seems the best solution. Although 'the son' is apparently not mentioned in this verse, verses 7ff. have already used the title and left no doubt of its implications.

The NEB's vivid expressions, 'in mid course' and 'flares up in a moment', bring out the urgency of the warning. The quick anger may sound like the touchiness of a despot, but the true comparison is with Christ, whose wrath (like His compassion) blazed up at wrongs which left His contemporaries quite unruffled. This fiery picture is needed alongside that of the one who is 'slow to anger', just as the laughter of verse 4 balances the tears of, *e.g.*, Isaiah 16:9 or 63:9. That is, God's patience is not placidity, any more than His fierce anger is loss of control, His laughter cruelty or His pity sentimentality. When His moment comes for judgment, in any given case, it will be by definition beyond appeasing or postponing.

The final beatitude (*cf.* on 1:1) leaves no doubt of the grace that inspires the call of verses 10ff. What fear and pride interpret as bondage (3) is in fact security and bliss. And there is no *refuge* from Him: only *in him.*

Psalm 3

The Dark Hour

This is the first psalm to bear a title (see Introduction, pp. 32 ff.), and is one of fourteen that are thereby linked with historical episodes, all in the life of David (Pss. 3, 7, 18, 30, 34, 51, 52, 54, 56, 57, 59, 60, 63, 142). His flight from Absalom is recounted in 2 Samuel 15:13ff.

While the title bring a reminder of the king's personal grief ('his son'; *cf.* 2 Sa. 18:33), the psalm itself reveals the larger questions that were pressing upon him: the rising tide of disloyalty (verses 1, 6; *cf.* 2 Sa. 15:13), the rumour that God had withdrawn from him (2; *cf.* 2 Sa. 15:26), and the precarious state of his people (8).

Yet this is also an evening psalm for the ordinary believer, who can reflect that his troubles are nothing beside David's, and David's expectation nothing beside his.

3:1, 2. Human enmity

To be in a minority is itself a test of nerve; more so when the minority is shrinking ('how my enemies have multiplied!' NEB; *cf*. 2 Sa. 15:12f), and the opposition is active (*rising against me*) and accusing—for the thrust of 2b is primarily against David rather than God (*cf*. 2 Sa. 16:8). It was a shaft that went home; but it was salutary, since David, conscience-stricken, threw himself on God's mercy (2 Sa. 16:11f.) and, as the next verses show, on His faithfulness. On *Selah* (2; *cf*. 4, 8), see Introduction, p. 36.

3:3, 4. Divine protection

The terms of verse 3 grow more and more positive, a progress from reassurance to buoyant confidence. *About me* uses a strong preposition, hence NEB 'to cover me'. *My glory* is an expression to ponder: it indicates the honour of serving such a master; perhaps, too, the radiance He imparts (*cf*. 34:5; 2 Cor. 3:13, 18); certainly the comparative unimportance of earthly esteem, always transient and fickle. The sense of *lifter of my head* is well conveyed by NEB 'thou dost raise my head high', in glorious contrast to the picture of dejection (but also of supplication) in 2 Samuel 15:30, 'weeping . . . , barefoot and with his head covered'.

God's *holy hill* (4) was doubly relevant, as the place where God had installed both His king, David himself (with all the promises of 2:6ff.), and His ark, the symbol of His earthly throne (*cf*. 2 Sa. 6:2) and of His covenant. Not Absalom's decrees, but the Lord's, will issue from mount Zion, indeed have been dispatched from there already (lit. 'I cry . . . and he has answered'), to determine David's fortunes. The Christian equivalent of this faith is seen in, *e.g.*, the prayer of Acts 4:23ff. and the language of Hebrews 12:22ff.

3:5, 6. Peace of mind

'For my part'—for the *I* is emphatic, corresponding to the *thou* of verse 3—'I lie down . . . sleep . . . wake': such was his certainty that God had heard him; and so it had in fact turned out. Verse 6 builds on this encouragement: the Hebrew for *ten thousands* is a reminder of the word for 'many' in verses 1 and 2; and although encirclement (6b) now intensifies the threat, he can confidently face the worst.

3:7, 8. Victory and blessing

For David, called to kingship (as we are, Rev. 22:5), refuge is not enough. To settle for less than victory would be a virtual abdication; hence the uncompromising terms of verse 7. Verse 8 attests the basic humility behind it, which recognizes that without the Lord there is no solution or success; that is, none worth having (8b). 'We ask no victories that are not Thine.'[1] So the psalm ends by looking beyond the 'I' and 'me' of all the previous verses, to *thy people* (not even 'my people'), and to *thy blessing*, which goes as far beyond victory as health and fruitfulness go beyond survival. Without this, even a reunited people will lack the breath of life; with it, they can bless the world.

Psalm 4

'Peace! Be Still!'

Evening is the occasion but not the main theme of the psalm, which is concerned with inward peace (8) in a distracting situation. The approach of night, with its temptation to brood on past wrongs (4) and present perils, only challenges David to make his faith explicit and to urge it on others, as a committal of one's cause (4f.) and oneself (3, 8) to a faithful Creator.

Absalom's revolt, which gave rise to Psalm 3, could still be the background here; for David is, as he was then, humiliated (2a) and surrounded by lies (2b), exasperation (4) and gloom (6). But such trials can arise on more occasions than one, and, as the psalm's use in public worship[2] implies, in any person's life.

[1] J. W. Chadwick, 'Eternal Ruler of the ceaseless round'.
[2] On the Psalm Titles, see Introduction, VI, pp. 32ff. On the ascription *to the choirmaster* see p 40.

4:1. Well-founded prayer

The Hebrew word for *in distress*, with its implication of being in a tight corner, has its meaning well brought out in NEB: 'I was hard pressed, and thou didst set me at large'. The present prayer draws strength from the past (*v.*, *e.g.*, Gn. 48:15f., and many other instances). But the phrase *God of my right* is even more steadying, by its appeal to God's character, as upholder of justice, and (by the personal 'my') to His covenant, by which He is the protector of His own. On this, see on Psalm 5:4-6. So the terms in which God is addressed, when they are more than a formality, add their enrichment to the spirit of a prayer and the expectation of its outcome.

4:2, 3. An answer to the fickle

Surrounded by suspicion, David first appeals to people's goodwill and good sense (2): but ultimately the vindication that matters to him is not in their hands but in God's (3).

2. The two halves of the verse throw light on one another, for the humiliations of 2a spring from the 'delusion' (*cf.* JB) and *lies* of 2b. That is, David's authority has been brought into contempt through the false promises and slanders of an enemy. (God Himself knows what this can mean: *cf.* Mal. 1:6. Likewise Paul: Gal. 4:16ff.)

3. Although NEB's phrase is delightful ('the Lord has shown me his marvellous love'), and has some backing from the LXX, it involves three changes in a Hebrew text which already makes sense (as in RSV) and suits the situation—for God's choice of a man, not merely for office or honour but for fellowship (*for himself*), is the ultimate answer to the most wounding of aspersions and discouragements.

4:4, 5. An answer to the hot-heads

If some people's loyalties are too wavering, as above (2), others' are too fierce, settling everything on impulse. *Cf.* Boanerges in Luke 9:54f., and David's supporters in 2 Samuel 1-4; and see James 1:19f. The one can be as damaging, in the long run, as the other.

Be angry could be translated 'Tremble' (JB), but Ephesians 4:26, with LXX, sees anger here, and shows that it need not and should not be sinful. Possibly Paul goes further than David, if our verse is only saying 'sleep on it before you act' (for Paul tells us to banish anger itself before sundown);

yet verse 5 looks humbly to God as one's vindicator. NEB's alteration of 4b is unnecessary, and its footnote misleading: 'to say in one's heart' is a common Hebrew expression for 'to think'.

4:6, 7. An answer to the doleful

Each group of David's friends has its own way of adding to his difficulties, although NEB darkens the scene excessively by translating the prayer of 6b as a further statement, 'the light has fled'.[1] Nevertheless it rightly shows up the *many* as defeatists, like those of 3:2 (introduced with the same Heb. phrase, 'many are saying'). Their words should end with the wistful 6a, if 6b is a prayer. The prayer is David's, and while his friends sigh for better times, he longs and prays for God (6b). The two outlooks are compared in verse 7, which gives a classic contrast between inward and outward joy, the first welling up steadily from God through every discouragement, the second the rare product of a pleasant set of circumstances.

4:8. Well-founded peace

The word *both* is one that usually means 'together', and here seems to imply 'simultaneously'. *Cf.* Gelineau: 'and sleep comes at once'. For the last word of the psalm, one which derives from the root for 'trust', NEB has the best equivalent: 'unafraid'. *Cf.* Proverbs 1:33. This, after all, if it is well-founded, is an even better state than safety.

Psalm 5

Clouded Dawn

The presence of enemies, a shadow seldom absent from David's psalms, is felt here chiefly through the menace of their propaganda (6, 9). This is a morning psalm (3) in five strophes, three of which are turned full-face to God, alternating with two that passionately denounce the enemy to Him. The whole psalm expresses the spirit of the cry in verse 2, 'my King and my God'.

---

[1] An anomaly in the spelling of the verb lends some support to the change, but some ingenuity is needed to sustain it fully, and the traditional understanding of the phrase, with its allusion to the Aaronic Blessing of Nu. 6:26, seems more straightforward.

5:1-3. The morning watch

The word which RSV translates as *groaning* (1) is found else-where only in 39:3 ('as I mused') and is better translated 'my inmost thoughts' (NEB) or 'my sighs' (JB). It is a barely audible self-communing, but there is a growing clarity as it breaks out into a cry for help (2) and then into articulate, disciplined and expectant prayer (2b, 3).

2. The covenant relationship expressed by the repeated 'my', in the phrase *my King and my God*, gives the prayer a firm footing, and the use of the word *King* puts David's own kingship into its right context. He accepts that he is a man under authority, not one who must struggle for his own ends by his own means.

3. The words *a sacrifice* are a translators' assumption, though probably a correct one. The Hebrew has the single word *prepare*, which can be used for setting out in order anything from a feast (23:5) to a case at law (50:21), and therefore perhaps for one's plea to God (AV), or one's self-preparation ('I hold myself in readiness for you', JB); but it is often a priestly term for laying the altar fire and arranging the pieces of the burnt offering (Lv. 1:6f.). The emphasis on *the morning* rather suggests this by its possible allusion to the daily sacrifice at God's threshold, 'where I will meet with you, to speak there to you' (Ex. 29:42). David, it seems, puts his praying into such a context (as in 141:2) to express the assurance of atonement and the total commitment with which he comes before God. But he also comes expectantly. The word *watch* is used of God's prophets posted to report the first sign of His answers: *cf.* Isaiah 21:6, 8; Micah 7:7; Habakkuk 2:1. As at the tent of meeting, God would 'speak there', not only listen.

5:4-6. The Champion of right

The prayer now takes shape as a plea for justice. Note the crescendo from the mild negatives of verse 4 (well translated in NEB) to the expressions of divine wrath in 5b, 6. The very integrity of the Judge, which would be David's undoing if he were under rigorous moral scrutiny, is his refuge under wrongful attack. This emerges openly in Psalm 143:2, where David the plaintiff (as he is in the present psalm) pauses to acknowledge that if God were to try his character instead of his case, he would be undone. This is taken for granted in the psalmists' protestations of innocence. They know that they are in the right *vis-à-vis* their opponents, as disputants in, so to speak, a civil court;[1] and in general relation to God and His law their heart is 'perfect': they are totally committed. To press their language beyond this, in view of, *e.g.*, Psalms 19:12; 32:1-5; 130:3; etc., would be the equivalent of (in NT terms) pressing such a passage as 1 John 3:4ff. into contradicting 1 John 1:8ff.

5:7, 8. The pilgrim spirit

The significance of the words *But I . . . will enter thy house* is sharpened by their proximity to 4b, 'evil can be no guest of thine' (NEB). This is why it must be 'through thy great love' (NEB). It may also be that David is in exile, praying 'that he will bring me back and let me see . . . his habitation' (2 Sa. 15:25), as the expression *toward thy holy temple* could imply. But such words could also be used of prayer offered at the threshold itself (1 Ki. 8:29).

With the ark kept in a mere tent (2 Sa. 7:2), the words *house* and *temple* are surprising on the lips of David. This could indicate that 'of David', in the Psalm titles, is a term used in a special sense (see Introduction, VI. *b*, pp. 34f.); or that the traditional names for God's dwelling lived on from the days of Shiloh (1 Sa. 1:7, 9), as Perowne suggests; or possibly that David's language has been adapted to the use of later worshippers. The second suggestion seems the most cogent. See also on 27:4.

8. The word chosen for *my enemies* perhaps emphasizes their vigilance (*cf.* NEB, but see on 27:11). But the answer to 'my' peril is in the twofold 'thy . . .', with its frank acceptance of a higher standard and a surer aim than one's own. *Cf.* Proverbs 3:6; 4:25; Isaiah 42:16.

> 'The kingdom that I seek
> Is thine; so let the way
> That leads to it be thine,
> Else I must surely stray.'[2]

5:9, 10. The campaign of lies

The 'bloodthirsty and deceitful men' of verse 6 are now exposed and prayed against. With such people all the resources

---

[1] *Cf.* C. S. Lewis, *Reflections on the Psalms* (Bles, 1953), pp. 9-19.
[2] H. Bonar, 'Thy way, not mine, O Lord'.

of speech—*mouth, throat* and *tongue*—combine to achieve (and to conceal) the designs of the heart. The methods are those of the serpent in Eden, and of its minor brood the flatterer and the scandalmonger. *An open sepulchre*, waiting for its occupants, is the grim picture used in Jeremiah 5:16 to name their murderous efficiency in battle II:... and in Romans 3:13 (where the reader finds himself included in the charge) there is probably a hint of the grave's corruption as well.

10. 'Pronounce them guilty' (JB) catches the meaning of the opening plea, which is a single word, the opposite of 'justify'. *Cf.* 34:21f. It is the first of three aspects of judgment in this verse—exposure, collapse, expulsion—for evil is vulnerable to truth, to its own instability and to direct divine action. With regard to the second of these, *i.e.* the rebels' downfall *by their own counsels*, see David's prayer against Ahithophel (2 Sa. 15:31) and its remarkable outcome. Note finally that the motivation of this appeal for judgment is not personal: ultimately the rebellion is not 'against me' but *against thee* (see also on verse 2).

5:11, 12. The sure defence

Although danger is not forgotten (note the defensive words, *refuge* and *shield*), the psalmist now breaks free of his loneliness. He is no longer a man praying on his own, hemmed in by his foes, but is conscious of a whole company who can join him in praise. And by a happy contrast, the last word in the Hebrew, *thou dost cover him* ('compass him', AV, RV), is one whose only other occurrence is in 1 Samuel 23:26, where it describes a hostile force 'closing in' on David, only to find itself quietly deflected by God's encircling, providential care of him.

Psalm 6

Prayers and Tears

This is the first of the seven so-called 'penitential psalms', *viz.* 6, 32, 38, 51, 102, 130, 143. Prayer, by one who is deeply troubled and alarmed, fills the first half of the psalm. The second half, from verse 6, contains no petition: only, at first, weeping, but finally an outburst of defiant faith. The prayers and tears have not been for nothing.

Whatever the original circumstances (the title to Ps. 3 suggests a possible origin), the psalm gives words to those who scarcely have the heart to pray, and brings them within sight of victory.

6:1-5. 'Turn, O Lord'

Not in thy anger, nor . . . in thy wrath are the emphatic phrases of verse 1. This is no general plea against correction and discipline, those favourite themes of the wise (*e.g.* Pr. 3:11, whose nouns mirror the two verbs here); *cf.* Jeremiah 10:23f. But David's conscience is uneasy, and he must appeal to grace to temper the discipline he deserves, whether in sheer mercy or in covenanted love; for these are the nuances of the words used in 2a and 4b. Whether his sense of God's displeasure is the cause (*cf.* 32:3) or the effect of his sickness, he is shaken to the depths (*troubled . . . troubled*; it is the word used in, *e.g.*, Gn. 45:3; Jdg. 20:41) and he fears even for his life. *My bones* and *my soul* are probably not meant as a contrast between the material and the immaterial, but as alternative expressions for the whole man. See the similar but happier parallelism of *bones* and *soul* in 35:9f. The Hebrew for bone can have the sense of '(it)self', as in Exodus 24:10; Ezekiel 24:2 ('very').

The poignant *how long?* is often heard in the Psalms (*e.g.* 13:1; 74:9f.), where we also learn, however, that 'all God's delays are maturings', either of the time, as in Psalm 37, or of the man, as in 119:67.

5. *Remembrance*, in parallel with *praise*, is more than mental recollection: it is recounting God's great deeds in an act of worship: *cf.* 71:15f.; Isaiah 63:7.

Sheol can be pictured in a number of ways: chiefly as a vast sepulchral cavern (*cf.* Ezk. 32:18-32) or stronghold (Pss. 9:13; 107:18; Mt. 16:18); but also as a dark wasteland (Jb. 10:22) or as a beast of prey (*e.g.* Is. 5:14; Jon. 2:2; Hab. 2:5). This is not definitive language, but poetic and evocative; and it is matched by various phrases that highlight the tragedy of death as that which silences a man's worship (as here; *cf.* 30:9; 88:10f.; 115:17; Is. 38:18f.), shatters his plans (146:4), cuts him off from God and man (88:5; Ec. 2:16) and makes an end of him (39:13). These are cries from the heart, that life is all too short, and death implacable and decisive (39:12f.; 49:7ff.; *cf.* Jn. 9:4; Heb. 9:27); they are not denials of God's sovereignty beyond the grave, for in fact Sheol lies open before Him (Pr. 15:11) and He is 'there' (Ps. 139:8). If He no longer 'remembers' the dead (88:5), it is not that He forgets as men forget, but that He brings to an end His saving interventions (88:12; for with God to remember is to act *cf.*, *e.g.*, Gn, 8:1; 30:22).

For the most part, the Old Testament emphasis falls on death as the great leveller (*cf.* Jb. 3:13–19), although sometimes depths beyond depths can be made out, to which tyrants, in particular, are consigned, as in Isaiah 14:13; Ezekiel 32:18ff. But at rare moments the Psalms have glimpses of rescue from Sheol, in terms that suggest resurrection, or a translation like that of Enoch or Elijah (*cf.* 16:10; 17:15; 49:15; 73:24; see comments *in loc.*), and in at least two places in the Old Testament the former of these hopes is spelt out unmistakably (Is. 26:19; Dn. 12:1–3).

6:6, 7. 'My weeping'
Depression and exhaustion as complete as this are beyond self-help or good advice. Even prayer has died away. The *foes* (7) who would normally have roused David only crush his spirit now. If anything is to save him it will owe nothing to his own efforts. Such is the extremity which God is about to transform.

6:8–10. 'The Lord has heard'
The context of our Lord's quotation of *Depart from me . . .* in Matthew 7:23 implies His judgment that David is speaking here as king. This is not merely a hard-pressed sufferer rounding on his tormentors, but a sovereign asserting his power to purge his realm of mischiefmakers,[1] as his kingly vow demanded; *cf.* Psalm 101. He speaks in faith: the victory is yet to come (10), but he already knows that he is answered.

This sudden access of confidence, found in almost every suppliant psalm, is most telling evidence of an answering touch from God, almost as if we saw the singer's face light up in recognition. In subsequent liturgical use God's reassurance

[1] S. Mowinckel, in his early *Psalmenstudien*, argued that throughout the psalms the *workers of evil* were sorcerers thought to have cast a spell on the sufferer, since the word used for evil ('*āwen*) is akin to a word for power. But he later conceded that the term could have a quite general reference: see Mowinckel, II, p. 250.

was possibly conveyed (some have suggested) by a ritual or an oracle, interposed between the petition and the praise; but this is a conjecture, and has little if any bearing on the writing of these psalms, which show the same characteristics whether their titles emphasize their liturgical use (as in, *e.g.*, Pss. 4–6) or the crises from which they sprang (*e.g.* Pss. 3,7, *etc.*). See also on Psalm 12:5, 6.

Psalm 7
A Cry for Justice

Justice will mean salvation, for the two coincide when God tries the case of the oppressed. The psalm moves from the intensely personal plea of a man who is betrayed and hounded, to the conviction that God is judge of all the earth, and that wickedness is self-defeating. So it ends with confidence and praise.

Title
For *Shiggaion* see Introduction, p. 38. Nothing is known of *Cush*; but from Absalom's rebellion it emerged that Benjamin, Saul's tribe, held some bitter enemies of David (2 Sa. 16:5ff.; 20:1ff.). For a list of psalms whose titles allude to David's vicissitudes, see the opening comments on Psalm 3.

7:1, 2. The hunted man
While David's preservation and deliverance were still matters for prayer (1b), his unseen *refuge* was already a fact (as the Heb. tense shows), since it was located in God (1a). That is, he had placed himself in God's hands, and so within God's will, where there is peace (119:165) whatever the outcome.

7:3–5. The oath of innocence
The three *if*-clauses, culminating in the challenge flung down in verse 5, reveal a deeper hurt than persecution, namely slander. Like Job's great protestation (Jb. 31, one of the moral peaks of the Old Testament), David's reply reveals something of his code of honour, as well as the thrust of the accusation (the *this* of verse 3), which alleged that he dealt in bribes and treachery. (Absalom, with admittedly more subtlety, proved how damaging a 'smear campaign'

could be against a David not yet idealized: *cf.* 2 Sa. 15:1–6.)

4. *Friend* here strictly means 'ally'. In the second line NEB and JB have opted[1] for translations which contradict not only the Old Testament's demand of generosity to a personal enemy but also David's known convictions (*cf.*, *e.g.*, Exodus 23:4f.; Leviticus 19:17f.; 1 Samuel 24:10f.; Proverbs 25:21.

7:6–11. The righteous judge

There is great breadth of vision here, revealing a concern for universal justice which was always the motive behind David's personal appeals for vindication. And not only a concern; it is a conviction: judgment is already *appointed* (6; *cf.* Acts 17:31, 'he has fixed a day'). The Hebrew of verse 7 calls on God to 'return' on high (AV, RV), but as this is the prelude to judgment, the very similar word for *take thy seat* may be the right reading. It is one of several passages showing God's exaltation as judge, victor (*cf.* 68:18) and lawgiver (Is. 2:2–4); but the New Testament added a new and startling dimension to the picture, making exaltation a term for the Cross as well as the Throne, and reversing, so to speak, the order and purpose of 7a and 7b (*cf.* Jn. 12:32), until Christ's return as Judge (Mt. 25:31ff.).

My righteousness (8) is not thought of as absolute: it replies to the accusations of verses 3f. (*cf.* on 5:4–6). But David hungers and thirsts for the wider triumph of right; the thought dominates verses 9–11, and the certainty of it springs from the fact that God Himself is far from lukewarm on the matter: indeed His *indignation every day* (11) is more constant than any human zeal, having no tendency to cool down into either compromise or despair.

7:12–16. 'Sin, when it is finished...'

The clause in 12a, *If a man does not repent*,[2] reveals what God

---

[1] Disagreement can arise over (i) the syntax, and (ii) the meaning of the verb, in 4b. (i) The syntax allows, although it does not compel, 4b to be a parenthesis, as in AV, RV (Yea, I have delivered ... mine adversary); *cf.* Gelineau, 'I who saved ...'. (ii) The verb means basically to pull out (*cf.* Lv. 14:40), hence normally to rescue, if its object is a person: *e.g.* Ps. 6:4a (Heb. 5a). RSV *plundered* has the slight support of a related noun (2 Sa. 2:21; Jdg. 14:19) and Syriac verb. But NEB, JB, in agreeing with RSV over the syntax (against AV, RV), and with AV, RV over the verb (against RSV), create a gratuitous conflict between this verse and its wider Old Testament context. JB's footnote, referring to Ex. 21:25, misapplies a *judicial* directive (*cf.* Ex. 21:22, 'as the judges determine') to a personal situation.

[2] NEB loses this phrase in a textual rearrangement.

was waiting for when He seemed merely dilatory (6). How pressing is the need to repent is now implied by the three converging lines of retribution: the wrath of God (12, 13) and the inherent fertility (14) and futility (15f.) of evil. On the first of these, Scripture emphasizes the personal aspect of judgment, in that the sinner must face the living God himself (here pictured as a formidable warrior), not the anonymity of a purely natural process; *cf.*, *e.g.*, Hebrews 10:31; Revelation 6:16.[1] The second picture, of the sinner pregnant with evil (14), has the same hard logic as our Lord's sayings on the bad tree or the evil treasure (Lk. 6:43‑45). The metaphor itself is used in James 1:15 for the growth-cycle of desire–sin–death. The third form of judgment, that of evil coming home to roost (15f.),[2] operates unevenly in the material realm, but inescapably in that of the spirit, in the baleful effect of a wrong attitude on the one who harbours it (*cf.* 1 Jn. 2:11), more disastrous to him than any suffering he inflicts on others.

7:17. Thankful praise
On this change of theme, see the final comment on Psalm 6. *The Most High* ('*elyôn*) is a title seldom found outside the Psalms, but first encountered in the story of Melchizedek and Abram (Gn. 14:18ff.). Canaanite religion gave a similar title to Baal, but Abram, as David does here, claimed it explicitly and only for the Lord. It is specially appropriate as the last word in this psalm, announcing in faith, as an ever-present fact, the exaltation which verses 6f. long to see proclaimed in power.

Psalm 8

Crown of Creation

This psalm is an unsurpassed example of what a hymn should be, celebrating as it does the glory and grace of God, rehearsing who He is and what He has done, and relating us

---

[1] JB may be right, however, in translating verses 12f., 'The enemy may sharpen his sword . . . but the weapons he prepares will kill himself', since the Heb. simply has 'he' as the subject of the verbs (*cf.* RSV mg.), and an emphatic 'for him' at the beginning of verse 13. If so, the thought is parallel to that of 15f.

[2] *Cf.*, *e.g.*, Nu. 32:23; Ps. 9:15; Pr. 26:27; Mt. 26:52.

and our world to Him; all with a masterly economy of words, and in a spirit of mingled joy and awe. It brings to light the unexpectedness of God's ways in the roles He has assigned to the strong and the weak (2), the spectacular and the obscure (3–5), the multitudinous and the few (6 8); but it begins and ends with God Himself, and its overriding theme is 'How excellent is thy name!'

The range of thought takes us not only 'above the heavens' (1) and back to the beginning (3, 6–8) but, as the New Testament points out, on to the very end (see on verse 6). The question 'What is man?' is picked up in three other places in the Old Testament, and the answer of the psalm is expounded in the New as carrying implications which only the incarnation, death and reign of Christ are big enough to satisfy.

8:1, 2. The praise of his glory

This adoration is ardent and intimate, for all its reverence. The God whose glory fills the earth is *our* Lord: we are in covenant with Him. His praise is chanted on high, yet acceptably echoed from the cradle and the nursery. It is the theme of the whole psalm in miniature.

RSV and JB iron out this paradox by running the two verses together (against the punctuation of the Heb. text and of the LXX as quoted by our Lord in Mt. 21:16). If verse 1 is allowed to end with 'Thou whose glory is chanted[1] above the heavens.' (note the full stop), the whole verse then shows its similarity to the great Sanctus of the Seraphim (Is. 6:3), whose cry one to another shook the Temple. So the startling contrast of verse 2 makes the proper impact. With all earth and heaven proclaiming God in verse 1, the rising discord of *foes . . . enemy . . . avenger* presents a challenge which God meets with 'what is weak in the world', the immaterial (*by the mouth*) and the immature. But, as Palm Sunday was to show (Mt. 21:15f.), the free confession of love and trust is a

---

[1] The Heb. consonants allow this sense, reading, with the change of one vowel, *tānâ* ('is [antiphonally?] repeated'); *cf.* Jdg. 5:11; 11:40) for MT's *tenâ* ('O set'). To mean 'Thou who hast set', the verb would have to be emended to *nātattā*. There is some ancient support for this, but no certainty is possible for either of these alternatives. (Dahood, merging and revocalizing two adjacent words, suggests more radically 'I will adore', from *srt*, 'serve, worship', in a postulated energic form of the imperfect.)

devastating answer to the accuser and his arsenal of doubts and slanders.[1]

8:3–8. What is man?

3, 4. Out of this whole array, from stars to sea-creatures, only man can *look* at this scene with the insight to ask such a question, even in doubt; therefore it already points to its answer. Further, man has been taught to say *thy* and *thou* in such a setting: not only to acknowledge a Creator but to converse with Him. From His side, God shows in Isaiah 40:26ff. that the right inference from His ordered heavens is not His remoteness but His eye for detail; and adds in Isaiah 45:18; 51:16 that He planned no meaningless and empty universe, but a home for His family.

David's question can be asked with many nuances. In Psalm 144:3f. it mocks the arrogance of the rebel; in Job 7:17 it is a sufferer's plea for respite; in Job 25:6 it shudders at human sin. But here it has no tinge of pessimism; only astonishment that *thou art mindful* and *thou dost care*. These two exclamations highlight the divine grace implicit in the four that follow (5f.), for all is of God's giving (see also on 9:19f.). *Mindful* has a compassionately purposeful ring, since 'God's remembering always implies his movement toward the object of his memory'[2]; and *care* (lit. 'you attend to') similarly implies His action as well as His concern: *cf.* 'attend(ed) to' in Jeremiah 23:2 in two opposite senses.

5, 6. In the most obvious sense of the Hebrew (as in RV, RSV), verse 5 would seem to allude to the image of God, mentioned in Genesis 1:26 which underlies our verses 6–8. But the LXX takes *God* (*'elōhîm*) in its rarer, generic sense, to mean supernatural beings, *i.e.* 'angels' (*cf.* 1 Sa. 28:13; Ps. 82:1, 6f.), and Hebrews 2:7, 9 follows that translation. *Little* can sometimes mean 'for a little while' in both Hebrew[3] and Greek, which is the sense probably implied in the Epistle.

The New Testament opens up fresh aspects of this passage.

---

[1] For *founded a bulwark* (strength, stronghold), the LXX, cited in Mt. 21:16, has 'perfected praise'. Since the outcome of this praise is the enemy's defeat, as in the Heb., the LXX wording is probably a paraphrase to show what the psalm means by its unusual metaphor of an audible bulwark. *Cf.* 2 Ch. 20:22; Ne. 8:10.

[2] Childs, p. 34.

[3] *E.g.* Jb. 10:20b, RV, NEB.

James 3:7f. points out that man can tame everything but himself, while Hebrews 2:8 in a double comment on our psalm reminds us that while all is 'not yet' subjected to man, our Forerunner is already 'crowned with glory and honour'. Paul looks still further ahead in 1 Corinthians 15:27f. to the fall of the last enemy and the handing back of all delegated power to the Father. As ever, the coming of Christ revealed a whole landscape on the horizon to which the Old Testament was pointing. The New Testament writers had enough confidence in this material (as our Lord had in, *e.g.*, Ps. 110:1 and Ex. 3:6) to win its full depth of meaning from it.

8:9. The praise of his glory

At its return, the refrain will be sung with fresh understanding. It also renews the primary emphasis, which is on God and His grace. For man's dominion over nature, wonderful though it is, takes second place[1] to his calling as servant and worshipper, to whose very children the *name* of the Lord (that is, His glory and goodness: Ex. 33:18f.) has been revealed.

Psalm 9

God: Judge and King

From this point in the Psalter up to Psalm 148 the versions differ over the numbering of the psalms, since the LXX and Vulgate, followed by the Roman church, count Psalms 9 and 10 as a single poem, while the Protestant churches follow the Hebrew reckoning.[2] The absence of a title to Psalm 10 supports the view that it runs on from Psalm 9, and this is strengthened by the presence of a fragmentary acrostic, begun in Psalm 9 and concluded in Psalm 10.[3] But the mood is so changed at 10:1 as to leave the impression that these are in fact two psalms, written as companion pieces to complement one another, concerned as they are with twin realities of a

---

[1] *Cf.* the priorities in Lk. 10:20.

[2] NEB and JB name them '9–10', retaining the familiar numbering, but printing them with no dividing gap.

[3] Ps. 9 has most of the first 11 letters of the 22-letter Heb. alphabet as the initials of alternate verses; but Ps. 10, after beginning with the 12th letter, drops the alphabetic scheme until verses 12–18 where the last four letters appear.

fallen world: the certain triumph of God and the present, if short-lived, triumphing of the wicked.

9:1-12. Vision after victory

The psalm builds up twice to a climax of faith in God's total rule. The first part (verses 1-12) is all affirmation, the fruit of reflection on a great deliverance. The second part (13-20) will be prayer, arising out of suffering.

1, 2. Thankful praise This opening echoes the final verse of Psalm 7, expanding it to name the two chief springs of praise: God's actions and His person (1b, 2a). *Wonderful deeds* (or things) is a single Hebrew word, particularly frequent in the Psalms, used especially of the great redemptive miracles (*e.g.* 106:7, 22), but also of their less obvious counterparts in daily experience (*cf.* 71:17), and of the hidden glories of Scripture (119:18).

3-8. Thine is the kingdom. Where lesser men boast of success and talk of power, David sees God as his rescuer (3) and sings of justice (4). More than this, his thought leaps ahead from his own story (*my enemies, my just cause*, 3f.) to what it prefigures: God's total victory (5f.) and reign of justice, world-wide and everlasting (7f.). The past tenses of verses 5f. are 'prophetic perfects', a feature of the Old Testament: they describe coming events as if they have already happened, so certain is their fulfilment and so clear the vision. But the tenses in 7f. could refer to the future or the present; both are appropriate.

9-12. The Champion of the weak. Verses 9 and 10 are two ways of putting the same thing, first pictorially and then literally. Both are expressed as an exhortation: 'And let the Lord be a stronghold (*cf.* NEB, JB) . . . and let those who know . . .'. *Times of trouble*[1] is an unusual phrase, found only in verse 9 and in 10:1, which strengthens the link between the two psalms (see the opening comments, above). In verse 12

---

[1] BDB identifies *baṣṣārâ* as the singular of a word translated 'drought' in Je. 14:1. Since a stronghold is no refuge from this, the likelier noun (as Dahood suggests) is *ṣārâ*, 'straits', 'distress', plus the preposition *ba*. For the construction, *cf.* Is. 9:2 (Heb.).

there is a further link, in the Hebrew for *he who avenges* (lit. 'seeks', 'requires'), since this is the very thing that the tyrant denies in 10:13b, using the same word. The idea is first expressed in Genesis 9:5; *cf.*, *e.g.*, Deuteronomy 18:19; 2 Chronicles 24:22; Ezekiel 33:6.

13-20. Vision in adversity
Now the psalm mounts up in prayer towards a second but quieter climax, progressing from personal entreaty to confident prophecy, and finally to a bold appeal for action.

13, 14. One man's plight. This is the first hint of distress. It therefore seems that from the outset David has firmly fixed his mind on God and on the glories of the past, the future and the present, not merely as the best antidote to his suffering but as being genuinely more important than his own concerns. Consequently praise continues to mingle with his prayer. *The gates of death* cannot keep him from *the gates of . . . Zion.*

15-18. Justice for the world. The past tenses of verses 15f. could refer to the victories David has already seen (*cf.* 3f.), which verses 17f. recognize as a foretaste of the final rout. But they are more likely to be prophetic perfects (see on 5f.), viewing the end as an accomplished fact. On the combination of the personal and impersonal aspects of judgment, see on Psalm 7:12-16. On *Higgaion. Selah,* see Introduction VI. *c.* 1, pp. 36f.

A revealing nuance in the sentence pronounced on the wicked is that they will 'return' to Sheol (17; *cf.* RV, JB), not merely *depart* there. Death is their native element. On the meaning of *forgotten* (18), see the final comment on Psalm 8:4.

19, 20. Put man in his place! The word for *man*, in both verses, is one which tends to emphasize his frailty. The dignity of man (for whom Ps. 8:4a uses the same word, and Dn. 7:13 the Aramaic equivalent) derives from God, as the verbs of Psalm 8:4-6 make abundantly clear. On his own, man is dust (Gn. 3:19) and a mere breath (Pss. 39:11; 144:4)—to say nothing of his moral state, which is exposed in the companion psalm that follows.

70

Psalm 10
Man: Predator and Prey

On the intimate connection between Psalms 9 and 10, see the opening comments on the former. There the centre of gravity was the judgment to come; here it is the present age, where injustice is rampant.

10:1-11. The tyrant's boast

It is the arrogance of this man, adding Godward insult to manward injury, that dominates this account of him. Perhaps he protests too much: his blasphemy (3b)[1] and his repeated assurances to himself of his impunity (4, 6, 11, 13) betray a basic disquiet. The bold words, '*There is no God*' (4), are bravado, for his inner dialogue contradicts them (verses 11, 13). Yet they are the language of his choices and actions, since *thoughts* in verse 4 means 'schemes', as in verse 2. He is a practising atheist, if hardly a convinced one.

Manward, he has only himself to consider, virtually worshipping his desires (*cf.* 3a with 44:8a) and therefore treating the defenceless as his natural prey (2a, 8–10). One of his chief weapons is the tongue, whose varied techniques of intimidation and confusion are suggested in the long catalogue of verse 7. The pathetic state of his victims is shown in the reiterated word *hapless*, or 'poor wretch' (NEB), found only here (8, 10, 14).[2]

Meanwhile God stands *afar off* (1), and the tyrant is doing nicely, as he would say (5). It is a function of the Psalms to touch the nerve of this problem and keep its pain alive, against the comfort of our familiarity, or indeed complicity, with a corrupt world. There is a hint of an answer in verse 5, in the picture of the earthbound man who is too engrossed at ground level to see what is hanging over him. *Thy judgments* in that verse have a dual sense, as God's rulings or standards, and also His action to enforce them.

---

[1] The word *curses* is lit. 'blesses', either as a euphemism or as the equivalent of 'says farewell to'. It is used similarly in 1 Ki. 21:10; Jb. 1:5. The NEB's emendation is unnecessary.

[2] A probable Egyptian cognate has the sense of 'overwhelmed' or 'demoralized': *cf.* W. G. Simpson in *VT* 19 (1969), pp. 128–131.

10:12–18. The victims' prayer

This prayer is notable for the faith that keeps breaking through.

12–14. The *why* (13, echoing verse 1) is still unanswered; so is the call to God to *arise* (12; cf. 9:19); but the trouble can be faced, for it is not faced alone: *Thou dost see* (14). Verse 14 in fact speaks memorably in faith and about faith: the former in the rising sequence *thou dost see . . . , note . . . , take into thy hands*; and the latter in the phrase, *commits himself* (lit., 'abandons himself') *to thee*, which expresses trust even more completely, because more personally, than the similar[1] saying, 'commit your way to the Lord' (37:5).

15–18. *Break . . . the arm*, which may sound merely brutal, is an expression for the breaking of his power: cf. 44:3. The plea, *seek out his wickedness till thou find none* (*i.e.*, to the last trace), takes up a significant word in this pair of psalms, for the verb 'to seek out' is translated 'avenges' in 9:12 and 'call to account' in 10:13.[2]

As the prayer turns again into affirmation (16–18) it gathers up further themes heard before. Verse 16 looks abroad to *the nations*, as Psalm 9 did, and the psalm ends with the same reminder of puny man, *man who is of the earth* (18), as did its predecessor. Meanwhile, however distant may be the day of justice, one promise is not delayed: *thou wilt strengthen their heart* (17). It is the kind of answer that Paul had to accept, and learnt to value, in 2 Corinthians 12:8–10.

Psalm 11

Panic and Stability

This is a psalm that comes straight from a crisis. It opens with a spirited retort to some demoralizing advice, and goes on to show what is the real scale and pattern of events, and what is more to be prized than safety.

---

[1] But the Heb. uses a different verb.

[2] RV, JB, Gelineau also see this use of it (*i.e.* with God as the subject of 'seek') in 10:4a: cf. RV, 'He will not require it'; but RSV (cf. NEB) gives the more straightforward translation.

11:1–3. Voices of despair

The plea to get away into hiding is still ringing in David's ears as he begins his reply, formulated at first in his advisers' own terms of *refuge*, the true refuge, however, as against the false (*cf.* the same antithesis of *mountains* and *the Lord* in 121:1f.). The advice seems well-meant,[1] like Peter's to our Lord in Matthew 16:22 (*cf.* Acts 21:12), though it could indeed be insincere; *cf.* Nehemiah 6:10–13; Luke 13:31f. Certainly it is persuasive, for there is little defence against the assassin (or slanderer?) of verse 2, while the argument of verse 3 is dispiriting, whichever way it is taken: whether it means that in the prevailing anarchy nothing is worth attempting, or, less probably, that David as the mainstay of his people (*cf.* Is. 19:10, 13) must save his life at all costs. It is hard to know which are the words of David's advisers, after verse 1, and which, if any, are his own reflections (NEB, for example, closes the quotation after verse 2, but RSV after verse 3). In either case they go deep. For an answer David will look up and see the immense realities that overshadow these events.

11:4–7. The forgotten dimension

The feverish scene of verses 1–3 is dwarfed by the Lord, whose name here is emphatic[2] and reiterated. This King is in residence, not in flight: His city 'has foundations' (*cf.* Heb. 11:10), therefore the question of verse 3 can be asked without despair (see also on verse 7). The collapse of what is built on sand may be distressing; it can also be a beginning (Heb. 12:27).

4, 5. The *temple* (or palace; it is the same word) is not an earthly building, as the second line of verse 4 would have shown (*cf.* 18:6, 9) even if Solomon's Temple had been already in existence. Quoting the words of 4a at a later time of crisis, Habakkuk 2:19 underlines their awesomeness with its admonition, 'let all the earth keep silence . . .'

The repetition of *test . . . tests* in 4b, 5a reveals that the initiative is the Lord's, even before the decisive moment of verse 6. His stillness is not inertia but concentra-

---

[1] RSV's slight emendation softens the brusque Heb. text (see RSV mg., *cf.* JB), but can claim some grammatical and textual support.
[2] By its position in the Heb. sentences of verses 4f.

tion,[1] and His patience gives opportunity to both *righteous* and *wicked* (5) to show what they are made of.

6. *Fire*[2] *amd brimstone* (the latter being the old word for sulphur) are an allusion to Genesis 19:24, where they were the means of the overthrow of Sodom. For the phrase is significant and pointed, for Sodom stands in the Bible as a perpetual reminder of sudden and final judgment. *Cf.* the teaching of Luke 17:28–30; 2 Peter 2:6–9.

7. The psalm ends, as it began, with *the Lord*, whose character as *righteous* answers all the fear of 3a and the frustration of 3b. 'The foundations' of righteousness are none other than His nature and will: what He *is* and what He *loves* (7). And if the first line of the psalm showed where the believer's safety lies, the last line shows where his heart should be. God as 'refuge' may be sought from motives that are all too self-regarding; but to *behold his face* is a goal in which only love has any interest. The psalmists knew the experience of seeing God with the inward eye in worship (*e.g.* 27:4; 63:2); but there is little doubt that they were led to look beyond this to an unmediated vision when they would be ransomed and awakened from death 'to behold (His) face in righteousness' (*cf.* 16:8–11; 17:15; 23:6; 49:15; 73:23ff.; 139:18).

Psalm 12

'. . . the easy speeches
That comfort cruel men'[3]

This psalm, on the use and abuse of words, might almost be an expansion of the cry heard in Psalm 11:3, for the situation is full of menace. The pattern is an alternation of prayer—promise—prayer; it contains an assurance of relief, but ends with the conditions still outwardly unchanged.

---

[1] *Behold* (4) suggests gazing intently. Perhaps also *eyelids* implies the thought of screwing up one's eyes to examine something closely (Kirkpatrick). But it may be no more than a use of poetic parallelism, with 'eyelids' as a synonym for 'eyes' in the previous phrase. See also NEB for another possibility: 'he takes their measure at a glance.'

[2] The Heb. text precedes *fire* with 'snares' (consonants *phym*) which RSV and most modern versions assume to be a scribal slip for *coals of* (*phmy*). LXX and Vulg. read the former; Syr. the latter.

[3] G. K. Chesterton, 'O God of earth and altar'.

12:1-4. The power of propaganda

As the psalm opens, it is as though the man of God has looked up to find himself surrounded, and his allies gone.[1] Where another man, in a minority of one, might have re-thought his position, David signals for help. He is not retreating.

2. Empty talk, smooth talk and double talk are here, followed in verses 3f. by the boasters, whose policy sums up that of their fellows: to manipulate the hearer rather than communicate with him, *Lies*, here, are more accurately 'emptiness', a term which embraces falsehood but also its fringe of the insincere[2] and the irresponsible,[3] which cheapen and corrode all human intercourse. See also on verse 8. *Flattering talk* is lit. 'smooth': all the deadlier for the pleasure it gives and the addiction it creates (for its comfort becomes indispensable), as the later history of Israel was to show (Is. 30:10; Jn. 5:44). *A double heart* (lit. 'a heart and a heart') significantly traces the double talk to its source in 'double think'—for the deceiver becomes one of his own victims, with no truth to unite his character.

3, 4. The Bible does not underrate the power of big talk; it is the Lord who must silence it. James 3:5 may have verse 3b in mind, and the Old Testament illustrates the potency of the weapon from beginning to end: from the serpent in Eden to the predicted persecutor whose 'mouth . . . spoke great things' (Dn. 7:20, 25). The New Testament takes up the theme, *e.g.* in 2 Peter 2, Revelation 13. It is not for nothing that the ally of the apocalyptic beast is the false prophet (Rev. 20:10).

12:5, 6. The counter-thrust of truth

This is the first psalm to contain an answering oracle from the Lord; some other examples are Psalms 60, 81, 95. We can only guess at the means by which it came. It is often conjectured that prophets were in attendance at the sanctuary to give God's answer to a prayer as it was uttered. But it seems easier to imagine such an answer as this coming directly to the psalmist; certainly 'the last words of David' consist of

---

[1] NEB unnecessarily turns the *godly* and the *faithful* into abstractions. In the Heb. text they are persons, if we may judge from the first word of the pair.
[2] *E.g.* Ps. 41:6; Ho. 10:4.
[3] *E.g.* Ex. 20:7.

both an oracle, spoken through him, and a personal reflection on it, somewhat in the manner of the present psalm (2 Sa. 23:1-4, 5-7).

The safety for which he longs is a very terse Hebrew phrase, in which *longs* is lit. 'puffs' or 'pants'. It can have a hostile sense (*e.g.* Ezk. 21:31 [Heb. 36]), which accounts for AV, RV; but the construction is simpler in the sense of longing, as understood by RSV, RV mg. and most moderns.

Promises are lit. 'sayings', a quite general term which picks up the thought of not only the pledge just given (5) but the very different words of men in verses 1-4. Here is solid wealth as against empty tokens (2a), and exact truth as against the flattery, equivocation and bombast of verses 2b-4.

A furnace on the ground is more likely to mean 'a crucible of earth' (*cf.* AV), *i.e.* of clay. The objection that the word used for *ground* does not normally mean earth as a material is met by Dahood, who also points out that the preposition (*le*) has at times the sense of 'from' or 'of'.

12:7, 8. The war continues

Protect us is a reading taken from the LXX; the Hebrew pronoun is 'them'. If the Hebrew text is correct it may refer to *the promises*[1] (6), *i.e.* 'keep them'. The next petition, *guard us*, is the reading of the Hebrew[2] as well as the LXX. *Generation* here means 'breed' (JB) or 'circle' (*cf.* 14:5; 24:6; Pr. 30:11-14, Heb.).

The final verse bears closely on the main theme of the psalm, the debasing of the currency of words, although it also has a wider reference. *Vileness* has two areas of meaning: cheapness (*cf.* Je. 15:19; the 'worthless' in contrast to the 'precious') and shameful excess (*cf.* 'gluttonous' in Pr. 23:20; Dt. 21:20). Where the values of 'vain and light persons' (Jdg. 9:4, AV) are glamourized, the blatantly *wicked* will not be slow to seize their chance and 'flaunt themselves' (NEB)—for the Hebrew of verse 8 suggests walking openly about, not merely prowling. The battle of words is no side-issue: a weakness here, and the enemy is in.

---

[1] On the use of a masc. pronoun to refer to a fem. noun, see G-K, 135 o.
[2] On the form of the pronoun here, see G-K, 58 i,k.

Psalm 13
Desolation into Delight

The three pairs of verses climb up from the depths to a fine vantage-point of confidence and hope. If the path is prayer (3f.), the sustaining energy is the faith expressed in verse 5. The prospect from the summit (5) is exhilarating, and the retrospect (6) overwhelming.

13:1, 2. Desolation

Repeated four times, David's *how long* is poignant enough in itself, but its companion phrases analyse the distress, in terms of his relation to God, to himself and to his enemy.

1. No doubt the divine 'forgetting' and 'hiding the face' meant the withholding of practical help (since in the Old Testament God's 'remembering' and 'seeing' are not states of consciousness but preludes to action[1]), but the real hurt of it was personal, if we may judge from David's constant longing to 'behold (God's) face' (11:7; 17:15; *cf.* 27:4, 8; 34:5). The same sense of a friendship that has clouded over is hauntingly expressed in Job 29:1ff.; 30:20ff., and again in Psalm 22:1ff.

2. Within himself, secondly, David is restless—for the Hebrew text of 2a has 'counsel' (*'ēṣôṯ*) as in AV, RV, rather than *pain* (*'aṣṣāḇôṯ*) as conjectured by RSV, *etc.*[2] It is a turmoil of thought (*cf.* 77:3–6) rather than the dull ache of dejection. The third element, his *enemy's* ascendancy, would be dismaying at more than one level: not only as a personal humiliation but as a threat to his kingship (4b) and to his faith in God's justice. David's behaviour at Absalom's revolt is instructive, even if less than perfect, at all these levels, in its personal magnanimity, kingly responsibility, and submissive trust (2 Sa. 15–19).

13:3, 4. Supplication

Whether verse 3 means that illness was the cause or the effect of this low ebb in David's affairs, these two verses show what

[1] For a classical example see Ex. 2:24f., introducing the great events of the exodus. See also the comment on 'mindful' and 'care' in Ps. 8:4.

[2] RSV follows Syr., but LXX (which is older than Syr.) supports the Heb. text.

were the two poles of his world: God, but for whom life would be insupportable, and the enemy, because of whom any wavering (4b) must be unthinkable. Awareness of God and the enemy is virtually the hallmark of every psalm of David; the positive and negative charge which produced the driving-force of his best years.

13:5, 6. Certainty

The *I* of verse 5 is emphatic (as in NEB, *etc.*: 'But for my part I . . .'), and so, to a lesser degree, is *thy steadfast love.* However great the pressure, the choice is still his to make, not the enemy's; and God's covenant remains. So the psalmist entrusts himself to this pledged love, and turns his attention not to the quality of his faith but to its object and its outcome, which he has every intention of enjoying. The basic idea of the word translated *dealt bountifully* is completeness, which NEB interprets attractively as 'granted all my desire'. But RSV can hardly be bettered, since it leaves room for God's giving to exceed man's asking. As for the past tense in which it is put, this springs evidently from David's certainty that he will have such a song to offer, when he looks back at the whole way he has been led.

Psalm 14

Serpent's Brood

Here the spirit of godlessness reveals itself in two ways: in flouting God's law (1–3) and oppressing His people (4–6); that is, in both direct and indirect contempt of heaven. It is the reckless folly (1a, 2b, 4a) almost as much as the wickedness of it that emerges in the psalm, which 'looks down from heaven' on the scene as God views it. But the standpoint changes in the last verse to the earthly arena, where persecuted Israel waits longingly for the redress that will surely come.

The psalm is almost exactly duplicated at Psalm 53, where, however, the term 'God' replaces 'The Lord'. See further on verses 5b, 6, below.

14:1. God dismissed

The last word on atheism is said in Romans 1:22: 'Claiming to be wise, they became fools'; a judgment vindicated in the sequence 'What can be known about God is plain to them (19) . . . And . . . they did not see fit to acknowledge God' (28). The Hebrew for *fool* in this psalm is *nābāl*, a word which implies an aggressive perversity, epitomized in the Nabal of 1 Samuel 25:25. The assertion, *There is no God*, is in fact treated in Scripture not as a sincere if misguided conviction, but as an irresponsible gesture of defiance. In the context of Psalm 10:4 it is expounded as a gamble against moral sanctions; in Job 21:7–15 as impatience of authority; in Romans 1:10ff. as intellectual and moral suicide. There are elements of all these in the present passage; already verse 1b shows the outcome of this attitude in relation to the self (*corrupt*; *cf.* Gn. 6:12), to God (*abominable* refers primarily to Godward offensiveness) and to fellow man (*none . . . does good*), which are the areas explored in Romans 1, Job 21 and Psalm 10, referred to above.

14:2, 3. Man assessed

The point of these two verses is that the arrogant materialist of verse 1 is but an example, even though an extreme one, of man in general. The chief terms of that verse now reappear, directly or obliquely, with this wider reference. Not everyone is an aggressive fool of the Nabal type (see on 1a), but no-one is found to *act wisely*; a different word is now used for *corrupt*, but it is hardly a milder one (NEB, freely, 'rotten to the core'); and the *none* is now reinforced by *no, not one*. This is no exaggeration, since every sin implies the effrontery of supposedly knowing better than God, and the corruption of loving evil more than good. There is a reminder of the Flood in the vision of the Lord surveying the human race and finding it corrupt; but Romans 3:10–12 makes it clear that this condition is as perennial as it is universal.

14:4–6. The great miscalculation

The folly of evil, already emphasized in verses 1 and 2, is now seen as failure to discriminate (4) and failure to foresee (5f.). There is an animal complacency about the unconcerned exploiters and secularists of verse 4 which is only matched by that of the practised sinner of Proverbs 30:20. It is more impenetrable than the bluster of verse 1; this might well be twentieth-century man. On the *terror* to come (which 53:5 calls 'terror such as has not been') see further Isaiah 2:19ff.;

Revelation 6:15ff. *Cf.* C. S. Lewis: 'In the end that Face which is the delight or the terror of the universe must be turned upon each of us . . ., either conferring glory inexpressible or inflicting shame that can never be cured or disguised.'[1]

5b, 6. On *generation*, see on 12:7. At this point Psalm 53 diverges fairly sharply from Psalm 14, to the end of verse 6. The two texts can be set out as follows:

14:5b, 6	53:5b, c (Heb. 6b, c)
For God (is)	For God
with the generation of the righteous.	will scatter
The counsel of the poor	the bones of your besieger.
you would put to shame,	You have put (them) to shame,
but the Lord is his refuge.	for God has rejected them.

The degree of likeness and unlikeness between these suggests an intentional modification in Psalm 53 to meet a national crisis, *i.e.*, a threat of invasion or siege. The two versions, by their differences at this point, meet separate needs.

14:7. The great day to come
The older translations spoke here of bringing back Israel's captivity, which would have made this verse a late supplement to David's psalm. But there is general support now for the rendering *restores the fortunes* (or *well-being*), which is more comprehensive.[2] The Christian is taught by Romans 8:19–25 to pray such a prayer, in the context of the whole creation's 'eager longing' for liberty. A foretaste of that joy can be found in the opening of Psalm 126.

Psalm 15

A Man after God's Heart

The pattern of question and answer here may possibly be modelled on what took place at certain sanctuaries in the ancient world, with the worshipper asking the conditions of admittance, and the priest making his reply. But while the expected answer might have been a list of ritual requirements

---

[1] 'The Weight of Glory', in *Transposition* (Bles, 1949), p. 28.
[2] Anderson calls attention to the brief discussion of the Heb. expression in A. R. Johnson, *The Cultic Prophet in Ancient Israel* (University of Wales Press, 1962), p. 67, n.4.

(*cf.* Ex. 19:10–15; 1 Sa. 21:4f.), here, strikingly, the Lord's reply searches the conscience. It happens again in Psalm 24:3–6, and in Isaiah 33:14–17, whose fine climax anticipates closely, as this psalm does in general, the beatitude on the pure in heart.

15:1. God as man's host

The word *tent* conjures up two worlds: one of formal worship and sacrifice (Ex. 29:42), emphasized by the phrase, *thy holy hill*, and the other of simple hospitality, brought out by the words *sojourn* and *dwell*. The psalms often mingle the two ideas, seeing the worshipper as an eager guest, his pilgrimage a homecoming (*e.g.* 23:6; 27:4f., 84:11ff.). But this makes the question *who shall sojourn . . .?* all the more searching, since the encounter is personal, and 'evil can be no guest of thine' (5:4, NEB). See further on verse 5c, below.

15:2–5. Man as God's guest

The portrait is not an exhaustive catalogue; other features emerge in the answers of, *e.g.*, Psalm 24 and Isaiah 33, mentioned above, to say nothing of the Beatitudes or 1 Corinthians 13. This man is, above all, a man of integrity.

2. His character: true. The word *blamelessly* is a little negative for the Hebrew *tāmîm*, which implies what is whole, or whole-hearted, and sound. The second term, *right*, is fundamental to Old Testament morality; and this is no platitude, since there are ethical systems based not on this but on what promotes happiness or self-fulfilment.

In the final phrase, *truth* means what is sure and trustworthy, not merely correct. What this man says is one with what he is (contrast 12:2; Is. 29:13).

3. His words: restrained. The word for *slander* has a background of 'going around', to spy things out or spread them abroad (*e.g.* Heb. of Gn. 42:9ff.; *cf.*, in other terms, Lv. 19:16). It seems nearer scandal than slander. *Friend* is a Hebrew word whose meaning varies with the context; here it need signify no more than 'another person', and this impartiality is more suited to the portrait than a narrower loyalty would be. In the last clause, *takes up a reproach* can mean either 'casts a slur' (*cf.* Gelineau) or 'picks up something discreditable', in the sense of raking it up unnecessarily (*cf.*

Kirkpatrick). The whole verse enlarges on the theme of Proverbs 10:12: 'Hatred stirs up strife, but love covers all offences.'

4. His allegiance: clear-cut. What looks at first sight pharisaical in 4a is in fact no more than loyalty. This man is not comparing himself with others, but giving his vote: declaring what he admires and where he stands. Abram's attitudes to the two kings of Genesis 14:17–24 illustrate the point and the potential cost.

4c, 5. His dealings: honourable. The first two clauses (4c, 5a) need interpreting by other scriptures; the third (5b) is transparent. The final line (5c) rounds off the whole section and the psalm.

On the rash promise (4c), the point at issue here is one's *own hurt*, not another's (in contrast to Jephthah's or Herod's predicament): yet even so, Proverbs 6:1–5 teaches that on realizing one's mistake one can rightly beg release. The promise is not repudiated; the recipient can still insist; this middle course is therefore an honourable one to explore, between the extremes adopted by the quitter and the quixotic. Paul takes this further in 2 Corinthians 1:15–23 by distinguishing not only between vacillation and responsible second thoughts, but between keeping the letter of an undertaking, in some circumstances, and achieving its real purpose.

Money at interest (5a) is condemned in the Bible, not in general (*cf.* Dt. 23:20; Mt. 25:27[1]) but in the context of trading on a brother's misfortunes, as a comparison between Deuteronomy 23:19 and Leviticus 25:35–38 makes clear. The latter passage equally forbids selling him food at a profit. In the family, one carried the weak member; outside it the law allowed discretion, while forbidding extortion and encouraging generosity (*cf.* Ex. 23:9; Lv. 19:33f.). In this psalm, no distinction is hinted at between a brother and a stranger in need.

5c. His place: assured. The thought penetrates beyond the threshold and the welcome; indeed the question of verse 1 spoke of dwelling rather than gaining admission, for the qualities the psalm describes are those that God creates in a

---

[1] It would have been a weakness in the parable if the master's reply had put him clearly in the wrong.

man, not those He finds in him. The threat of insecurity expressed often in the Psalms by the word *moved* (*cf.*, *e.g.*, 10:6; 13:4, lit.) is met not by siding with the strong, but, as in, *e.g.*, 16:8; 46:5; 62:2, 6, by steadfast trust in God. Only so is the last Hebrew word of the psalm fully meaningful: 'he shall not be moved, ever.'

Psalm 16
'All my Delight'

The theme of having one's affections centred on God gives this psalm its unity and ardour. In so far as it can be divided, it sings of the chosen loyalty in verses 1–6, and the blessings that come to meet it in 7–11. Charles Wesley's hymn, 'Forth in Thy name', largely took its rise from verses 2, 8 and 11, and captured the spirit of the psalm in its final line: 'And closely walk with Thee to heaven.'

Title
See Introduction VI. *c.* 2, p. 38.

16:1–6. Faithful Servant
Almost every verse in this half of the psalm speaks of some aspect of single-mindedness: *i.e.*, of throwing in one's lot with God in the realms of one's security (1), welfare (2), associates (3), worship (4) and ambitions (5f.).

1. For the theme of *refuge*, see more fully Psalm 11, throughout.

2. The second line is very cryptic, as the variety of translations indicates.[1] But RSV and RV have the merit of simplicity and fidelity to the text, understood as (lit.) 'my good (or welfare) is not beyond (or additional to) thee',[2] a thought which is expressed more clearly in 73:25.

3. Here again the Hebrew text is difficult, but RV and RSV make sense of it by following certain MSS which omit an awkward 'and' (one Heb. letter) between *they* and *noble.*

---

[1] NEB emends the last two Heb. words and takes them with verse 3—an excessively drastic expedient.

[2] *Cf.* BDB, p. 755 (2, 4), with the explanatory note '*i.e.* does not lie outside thee'.

Other solutions involve bigger changes, most of which assume that *saints* and/or *noble* mean pagan deities, as they certainly could in a pagan poem, but hardly in this context without explanation. NEB offers an explanatory clause, but it is bound up with other textual conjectures. It is more likely that the pagan overtones of these words, if present at all, are to be detected only in their implied contrast to what is being asserted: *i.e.*, David is drawn to men of holiness and nobility, not in mere name (like the gods) but in character; *cf.* Isaiah 32:5, 8. *Saints* is lit. 'holy ones', as in the New Testament. This word is used in the Old Testament more often of heavenly beings than of earthly ones;[1] hence the clarifying phrase here, *in the land*, or 'on earth'. The term usually translated 'saints' in the Psalms in *ḥᵃsîdîm*, loyal or godly ones, as in verse 10.

4. There is a distinct echo of the story of the Fall in the phrase, *multiply their sorrows*, since very similar words were spoken to Eve in the Hebrew of Genesis 3:16. There could hardly be a more ominous allusion to what follows from apostasy. The nature of the choice is clear enough from the rest of the verse; but the word *god* is lacking, and the verb translated *choose* is debatable, suggesting to most translators 'hasten'[2]; to others, 'exchange'[3]; while some have tentatively considered 'acquire as a bride'[4], since 'bride-price' has the same consonants. The first translation, 'hasten', or its equivalent, remains the simplest.

5, 6. The thought of God Himself as David's *heritage*, voiced so eloquently here, and following on immediately from his repudiation of any *other god* (4), chimes in (as Perowne has pointed out) with his revealing reproach to Saul in 1 Samuel 26:19: 'they have driven me out . . . that I should have no share in the *heritage* of the Lord, saying, "Go, serve *other gods*".' Here he has triumphantly out-thought his enemy and his own doubts, stimulated by the very depth of the thrust.

---

[1] *Cf.*, *e.g.*, 89:5-7; but see 34:9; 106:16, which use the Heb. word 'holy', as here.

[2] *Cf.* AV, NEB, JB, LXX, Vulg.; but the Heb. lacks the word 'after', perhaps by haplography (copying a repeated group of letters only once), since the consonants of 'another' and of 'after' are the same.

[3] *Cf.* RV (RSV, Gelineau?) on the basis of 106:20; Je. 2:11; but this assumes here the transposition of two consonants and a construction as unnatural in Heb. as in English.

[4] *Cf.* Ex. 22:16 (Heb. 15); but it is always the worshipper who counts as the bride in such metaphors.

He remembers that disinheritance can even be an honour and a pointer to the only real security, since God had likewise given His priests no block of territory to call their own, only the assurance, 'I am your portion and your inheritance' (Nu. 18:20). So David, and every singer of his psalm, can now see that this is no peculiarity of priesthood but a pointer to the true riches of each member of God's Israel, that 'kingdom of priests' (*cf.* Ex. 19:6). *My chosen portion*, moreover, should be rendered 'my allotted portion', as in NEB; this God-centredness is not extravagant piety but simple obedience. Nor is this wealth insecure because unseen (5b), nor again unreal because it is intangible (6): the most favoured tribe at the allotment of boundaries (*lines*, 6; *cf.* Jos. 19:51) could boast nothing as *goodly* as this.[1] Here is the scale of values that we recognize again in, *e.g.*, Philippians 1:21; 3:8.

16:7–11. Faithful Lord
Some of the particular blessings of the 'goodly heritage', which is God Himself, now come into focus. To have Him is to enjoy not only guidance (7) and stability (8), but resurrection (9f.) and endless bliss (11).

7. There is nothing facile in the divine guidance depicted here: on God's side it is *counsel* rather than coercion, and on man's side the kind of heart[2]-searching that may drive away sleep. Psalm 127:2 deplores this restlessness when it is mere worry, but the word *instructs* here has a purposeful firmness (*cf.* 'chasten', 6:1; 94: 12; *etc.*), as of schooling one to face hard facts. See also on 17:3.

8. The bold words, *I shall not be moved*, which can be pure bravado (*cf.* 30:6), are only worth singing as the climax of such a sober, realistic verse as this. See also on 15:5c. *At my right hand* suggests, as it does to us, a person who will stand by one; more specifically this help might be in court or in battle (*cf.* 109:31; 110:5). Other senses of the right hand come in verse 11 and in 110:1.

---

[1] Verse 6 could be taken to refer to additional, *i.e.*, material blessings, but the main thrust of the psalm, and the continuation of the inheritance metaphor from verse 5, tell against this.

[2] For *heart*, the Heb. here is lit. kidneys (AV, RV 'reins'), pictured as the seat of deliberation and choice (probably no more literally than in our use of 'heart', 'spleen', 'guts', *etc.*). It might almost be translated 'conscience'. On the possibility that 'glory' (9; RSV 'soul') was originally 'liver', see footnote to 30:12.

At Pentecost Peter quoted this closing paragraph of the psalm, from the LXX, as a prophecy of the Messiah, for whom alone such words would be perfectly and literally true (*cf.*, *e.g.*, the *always* of this verse).

9, 10. Several times in the Psalms the sense of being already face to face with God grows into the certainty of enjoying this intimacy for ever (see on 11:7), for God is not one to *give . . . up* His friends. Admittedly some commentators see here no more than recovery from an illness (*cf.* Is. 38:9-22); but the contrast in Psalms 49 and 73 between the end of the wicked and that of the righteous supports a bolder view. And at its full value, as both Peter and Paul insisted (Acts 2:29ff.; 13:34-37), this language is too strong even for David's hope of his own resurrection. Only 'he whom God raised up saw no corruption'.[1]

11. This verse is unsurpassed for the beauty of the prospect it opens up, in words of the utmost simplicity. The *path of life* is so called, not only because of its goal but because to walk that way is to live, in the true sense of the word, already (*cf.* 25:10; Pr. 4:18). It leads without a break into God's presence and into eternity (*evermore*). The *joy* (lit. joys) and *pleasures* are presented as wholly satisfying (this is the force of *fullness*, from the same root as 'satisfied' in 17:15) and endlessly varied, for they are found in both what He is and what He gives—joys of His face (the meaning of *presence*) and of His *right hand*.[2] The refugee of verse 1 finds himself an heir, and his inheritance beyond all imagining and all exploring.

Psalm 17

A Plea for Justice

David's first concern is to plead his innocence, opening himself to God's scrutiny. This is the prelude to a call for protection, which dominates the second half of the psalm. The first mention of his danger is in verse 7, which leads into a vivid

[1] Acts 13:37. The LXX, quoted in Acts, has 'corruption' where the Heb. has *the Pit; i.e.*, it reinterprets this symbolism in non-spatial terms, by a play on the word for Pit, whose consonants are those of the verb 'to corrupt'. On *glory* (9) see footnote to 30:12.
[2] The expression is '*in*' (not 'at', as verse 8) 'thy right hand'; *i.e.*, God's right hand is dispensing blessings and gifts: *cf.* Gn. 48:14ff.; Pr. 3:16.

account of the encircling enemies and a strong plea for their overthrow. The final verse leaves these earthly preoccupations behind. Night will give way to a cloudless morning.

Title
See Introduction VI. *c.* 2, p. 38.

17.1 5. The appeal to truth
If these claims sound extravagant, God Himself could use such language of Job (Jb. 1:8; 42.0) without for a moment implying his sinlessness. See also on Psalm 5:4-6. David is not complacent, but concerned for integrity: man's truth and God's. He searches his heart and finds assurance that his piety is no pretence (*cf.* 1 Jn. 3:18-21); he therefore appeals to God to adjudicate accordingly, for his name needs to be cleared (2). God as judge can surely do no less, and David has nothing to hide.

3. Note the allusion, as in 16:7, to the searching thoughts that come with sleeplessness: they can be God's visitation as well as the mind's introspection: *cf.* 77:2-6; also, more cheerfully, 63:5f.; 119:62.

4. The word translated *avoided* usually means 'kept' or 'watched'. But the latter can have a hostile sense, as in 56:6 (Heb. 7), and another voice of the verb means to beware; so the RSV (*cf.* AV, RV) finds no need to alter the text or the verse-division, as do NEB, JB. David could have had in mind the incident of 1 Samuel 25:32ff., where he recognized the voice of God to him through Abigail, restraining him from violence.

5. On *slipped*, lit. 'been moved', see on 15:5c.

17:6-9. The appeal to love
Now it is a straight plea to a friend and protector, not a case presented to the judge.

7. The first two lines, in English, translate just four highly-charged Hebrew words. *Wondrously show* calls to mind the word for God's miraculous interventions (see on 9:1) and for His rebuke to Sarah in Genesis 18:14: 'Is anything too hard (lit. wonderful) for the Lord?' *Steadfast love*, or 'true love' (NEB), is that faithfulness to a covenant, to which marital

87

devotion gives some analogy. It is the word which older versions translated 'lovingkindness', before its connection with covenanting and its strong element of fidelity were fully appreciated. *Cf.* 62:12. *Saviour* and salvation in the Old Testament are primarily concerned with material evils, as here, but can pass readily into the spiritual realm, as in 51:12, 14. To seek *refuge* is a frequent concern of the Psalms, particularly those of David, where it is almost as much a hallmark as is the mention of enemies (a fact which chimes in with David's early perils; see the quotation from Kirkpatrick at 18:2). Probably the final phrase should be taken with 'saviour' and translated 'with (not *at*) *thy right hand*'; *cf.* NEB.

8. *The apple of the eye* is the pupil. This figure of speech is followed by that of the protective *wings* in the song of Moses (Dt. 32:10, 11), just as it is here, and the second metaphor is eloquently enlarged upon in that passage. Elsewhere it is a standard figure of speech (*cf.* Ru. 2:12; Pss. 36:7; 57:1; 63:7; 91:4).

17:10–12. The lust to kill

This is a study of heartlessness, described both directly and in terms of the predator, human or animal. The ugly scene of encirclement reappears in 22:12–18 in a form which shows where it logically ends: at Calvary.

10. The Hebrew is cryptic in the first line, which consists of two words, 'they-closed their-fat'. 'Their fat' (or, adverbially, 'in their fatness') probably refers to their literal appearance, which told its own tale of self-love (*cf.* 73:7), faithfully reflecting their inward state (*cf.* 119:70, 'their heart is gross like fat'). 'They closed' may be intransitive, as when we say that an unresponsive person 'closed up'; hence JB, 'entrenched in their fat'; *cf.* AV, RV. But RSV and NEB take it as transitive, rather as in 1 John 3:17, and 'their fat' as meaning 'their (gross) heart'. The former translation, which seems slightly less forced, makes the callousness a gradual growth; the latter makes it a conscious choice. Either process is, of course, all too possible.

11. *They track me down* is an emendation of '(in) our steps' (AV, RV), partly to avoid the change from 'me' and 'my' in the rest of the psalm to 'our' at this point (the remainder of the verse leaves the pronouns unspecified). But the Hebrew

is not implausible: David's companions are never far from his
thoughts, and the enemy likewise is now plural, now singular.[1]

17:13, 14. The rewards of lust

Two insights into what is stored up for the wicked are put
side by side here, with startling effect. The first, *i.e.*, encounter
with God (13), is a familiar pattern of judgment, vigorously
pictured as halting these men in their tracks (*confront them*;
or, RV mg., 'forestall them'). The second (14) is its apparent
opposite: heaping on them the very things they love. They
are *men . . . of the world*: give them their fill of it![2] To have
everything but God is judgment enough—a theme made
explicit by the utter contrast of the final verse.

The phrases, *by thy sword* (13) . . . *by thy hand* (14), lack the
preposition 'by', but it is rightly supplied in translation if
these nouns are being used instrumentally with *Deliver*.[3]
Alternatively the nouns could be in apposition to 'wicked'
and 'men', as in AV, RV mg.: 'from the wicked, which is thy
sword: from men which are thy hand'—a way of asserting
God's use of evil men as means of judgment; *cf.* Isaiah 10:5ff.
But this seems too big a subject merely to glance at in an
aside; therefore the rendering of RSV, *etc.* is preferable.

17:15. The reward of love

This superb verse soars straight up from the prosperous low-
lands of verse 14, where all was earthbound. The contrast is
pointed by the emphatic opening, *As for me* (*cf.*, *e.g.*, Jos.
24:15b, or the 'But I . . .' of Ps. 13:5), and by the word *satisfied*
which is the same Hebrew verb as 'have more than enough'
in the verse before. See also on 16:11. So the two goals of
men are set side by side, somewhat as they are in Philippians
3:19f.

The significance of *righteousness* for seeing God face to face
is not purely judicial. Only like can communicate with like:
cf. Titus 1:15 with Matthew 5:8. The promise that 'we shall

---

[1] The singular in verse 12 (Heb.) may be viewing the enemy either
collectively or distributively (*i.e.*, 'each of them is like a lion'). Kirkpatrick
suggests a possible reference to a conspicuously ferocious member of the
group (*e.g.* Saul?).
[2] This interpretation of verse 14 is that of, *e.g.*, RSV, also expressed
powerfully in JB. But the Heb. tenses allow equally the rendering of AV,
RV and, emendations apart, NEB.
[3] G-K, 144 m.

see him as he is' not only ensures that 'we shall be like him' (1 Jn. 3:2; *cf.* 2 Cor. 3:18) but already, in measure, presupposes it. To know God face to face and see His *form* was the supreme privilege of Moses (Dt. 34:10; Nu. 12:8), and since he saw Him not in dreams but waking (Nu. 12:6f.) some expositors[1] suggest that the words *when I awake* meant to the psalmist no more than this. But a variety of strong expressions in the psalms (see on 16:9ff., and the references listed at 11:7) support the view that *awake* is used here of resurrection, as it undoubtedly is in Isaiah 26:19; Daniel 12:2. It is a climax which abundantly answers the prayer of verse 7, 'Wondrously show thy steadfast love.'

Psalm 18
A Warrior King Looks Back

This exuberant thanksgiving is found also, with a few minor variants, in 2 Samuel 22, introduced by a similar historical note. For all its length, its structure is coherent and clear, and its energy unflagging. Although some have assumed from the final verse that the king in question was not David but one of his descendants,[2] the verse does not require this, and the zest and vividness of the writing point to first-hand experiences such as David pre-eminently had. An incidental pointer to him is the allusion to fighting on foot (29, 33),[3] since later kings soon took to chariots (*cf.* 1 Ki. 22:34; 2 Ki. 9:21), which were introduced on a large scale by Solomon. But much in this psalm 'agrees better with Christ', as Calvin said, than with David; and in Romans 15:9 Paul needed no argument to support his treating verse 49 as part of a prophecy of the Messiah.

Title
On *the choirmaster*, see Introduction VI. *c.* 3, p. 40. The historical note is substantially that of 2 Samuel 22:1, with the addition here of words *the servant of the Lord*, as in the title of Psalm 36.

---

[1] *E.g.*, Kirkpatrick, Weiser. For the contrary view see, *e.g.*, Briggs, Dahood.
[2] *E.g.* Mowinckel, I, pp. 75, 77. On this, see above, p. 45.
[3] *Cf.*, *e.g.*, Weiser, p. 186.

As if to match this, the final verse speaks of 'his anointed', another term which was to enlarge its meaning as the Old Testament approached fulfilment in the New. The psalm marks the point, early in David's reign, at which his power was at its height (*cf.* 2 Sa. 8:14b), evidently before his great sin had left its mark on him (*cf.* Kirkpatrick on verses 20–23) and its shadow on his kingdom (*cf.* 2 Sa. 12:10ff.).

18:1–3. The refuge

1.[1] This word for *love* is an uncommon one, impulsive and emotional. Found elsewhere only in its intensive forms, it usually expresses the compassionate love of the stronger for the weaker.

2. In this rush of metaphors David re-lives his escapes and victories (*cf.* the psalm's title), and probes into their meaning. 'The *rock*, or cliff (*sela‘*) where he had been so unexpectedly delivered from Saul (1 Sa. 23:25–28); the *stronghold*[2] ...; "the rocks[3] of the wild goats" ... were all emblems of Him who had been throughout his true Refuge ...' (Kirkpatrick).

18:4–19. The rescue

The titanic scale of this scene is in strange contrast to the small human figure of the singer, to rescue whom God does battle in person against *death* and *perdition*[4] (4, 5), armed with His most fearsome weapons. Such is the worth, the psalm implies, of an individual, and such is that individual's debt to God. King though David is, the whole psalm is in the singular and has the freshness of personal experience. David is blessed because God has 'delighted' (19) in him, not simply because he represents his people. They will be blessed for his sake (as the church is for Christ's sake) rather than he for theirs. *Cf.* 2 Kings 8:19; Isaiah 55:3.

6. From the Hebrew tenses, the second half of this verse appears to be David's prayer: '... let him hear ..., and let my cry reach his ears.' The answer follows dramatically in the next verse.

---

[1] This verse is absent from 2 Sa. 22.

[2] Or *fortress*, RSV (*meṣûdâ*): the cave of Adullam, where David first formed his band of outlaws; a refuge in many crises, and a place of many memories (1 Sa. 22:4; 24:22; 2 Sa. 5:17; 23:13f.).

[3] See 1 Sa. 24:2, where the Heb. noun is *ṣûr*, as in the second occurrence of *rock* in our verse.

[4] The Heb. is Belial. See footnote on 41:8.

7ff. The theophany (*i.e.* God made manifest) recalls the deliverance at the Red Sea by fire, cloud and the parting of the waters (*cf.* verse 15); also the phenomena at the mount Sinai, which 'quaked greatly', 'wrapped in smoke', when God 'descended upon it in fire' (Ex. 19:18). There is no description of God's form; we glimpse only what Job calls 'the outskirts of his ways' (Jb 26.14). Some expositors see this passage as reflecting a cultic re-living of the exodus and the Sinai covenant, actualized for the worshippers in a ritual in which the reigning king played a leading part.[1] Since the existence of such a ritual, however, is no more than an inference from passages such as this, it is unnecessary to interpose it between the primal events and David's consciousness. Enough that he sees his perils and deliverance as no less crucial and miraculous than those of Moses' day, to be described in the same tremendous terms, since God Himself 'reached from on high' (16) to save him. There are similar echoes of the exodus in Judges 5:4f. and in Habakkuk 3.

8. Everything in the description speaks of judgment, but as this is directed against the powers of evil it means salvation to their victim. *Smoke*, as in Isaiah 6:4, dramatizes the reaction of holiness to sin, and *nostrils* are in Hebrew the organ of anger. *Devouring fire* is synonymous in Deuteronomy 4:24 with divine 'jealousy' or intolerance; *coals* are rained down from God's chariot-throne on the doomed city in Ezekiel 10:2. So the list continues, as the storm approaches, darkens, and finally unleashes itself.

9. The NEB's imperious phrase, 'He swept the skies aside', requires a small vowel change,[2] which is attractive but hardly justified. *He bowed the heavens* is a comparably expressive prelude to the great downward sweep of the chariot.

10ff. *Cherub ... darkness ... clouds ... brightness ...* Thunderstorm and supernatural beings are again mingled in this fashion in Ezekiel 1:4ff., where the cloud discloses 'living creatures', *i.e.* cherubim,[3] in attendance on God. These beings are found in contexts that emphasize God's inviolable holiness: as guardians of the tree of life (Gn. 3:24), of the Holy of Holies (Ex. 26:31, 33) and of the mercy seat (Ex.

---

[1] See Introduction, III, pp. 9ff., 13ff.
[2] *I.e.*, *wayyaṭ* for *wayyēṭ*.
[3] *Cf.* Ezk. 9:3.

25:18–22), and as bearers of the chariot-throne on which God rides to judgment (Ezk. 1:22ff.; 10:1ff.).

16–19. After the enormous scale of the theophany, the close personal concern of this climax is striking. The display of power terminates not in a sweeping gesture but in action at the point of need. *He reached* (16), rather than 'sent' (AV, RV), since the ambiguity of the phrase is resolved by 144:7, where it is God's hand, not His messenger, that is put forth (lit 'sent') in a similar context. And if verse 16 matches the metaphor of the 'torrents' (4), the *broad place* of verse 19 answers that of the 'distress', *i.e.* straits, of verse 6. In God's hands, absolute power (*cf.* the theophany) serves the ends of perfect freedom.

18:20–30. 'His way is perfect'
On the apparent self-righteousness of verses 20–24, see on 17:1–5 and on 5:4–6. But while, as those passages show, David could quite properly use this language within a limited frame of reference, the Messiah could use it absolutely; and the psalm is ultimately Messianic (see the end of the prefatory comment, above). Every theme in it was to gain new depth with Christ.

The main concern of the passage is, in fact, to praise God as the protector of those who 'commit their souls in well-doing unto a faithful Creator' (1 Pet. 4:19, RV). With 'David the servant of the Lord' (see the title) compare the Servant speaking to this effect in Isaiah 50:7ff., or Paul in 2 Timothy 4:6–8.

22. The two expressions, *ordinances* (or 'judgments') and *statutes*, often found together in Deuteronomy, are a favourite summary of God's law, mainly as it concerned matters between man and man on the one hand, and man and God on the other. See, *e.g.*, Exodus 21:1ff.; Leviticus 3:17. This rather technical language suggests that David was familiar with the written law (see also on verse 31), an impression strengthened by 19:7ff. Weiser points out that behind the law was the covenant; therefore this protestation was an appeal to God's 'covenantal faithfulness', rather than a legalistic exercise.

25. The word *loyal* (*ḥāsîḏ*) is a further mark of this outlook. It is connected with 'steadfast love' (*ḥeseḏ*), the pledged love between covenant partners (see on 17:7), and is a standard term in the Psalms for God's servants. Other translations of it in RSV are 'godly' (*e.g.* 16:10), 'saints' (*e.g.* 30:4; but see on 16:3) and 'faithful' (*e.g.* 50:5, further defined in the phrase 'who made a covenant with me by sacrifice'). It is used of God Himself in 145:17 and Jeremiah 3:12, in both of which places it could well be translated 'faithful' or 'loyal', as here.[1]

26. In the first line, man 'With the savage . . . ,' rests on a double conjecture,[2] gratuitously emending a straight-forward and well-attested text. *Show thyself perverse* (NEB 'tortuous') is a verb that takes up the idea of *crooked*; it is the twisting or wrestling which Naphtali's name commemorated (Gn. 30:8). The principle is illustrated by God's use of Laban to educate Jacob, and perhaps supremely by His unsettling treatment of the devious Balaam.

27-30. All these verses, and some of the second lines, open with an emphasis on God, which could be rendered 'As for thee, thou dost . . . ', or 'For it is thou that dost . . . ' (*etc.*)—for the whole psalm is praise, not concealed boasting.

27. Thus 'humble folk' (NEB) catches the meaning of the Hebrew '*ānî* better than *a humble people*, for David is speaking primarily of circumstances rather than virtue. These are the under-dogs, who meet us frequently in the Psalms, not only as the 'humble' (here), but translated better as 'the poor' (*e.g.* 10:2), 'the afflicted' (*e.g.* 22:24), 'the weak' (35:10) and 'the needy' (68:10). They correspond to the 'poor' in the first Beatitude, as being those who are in need and know it. A companion word, '*ānāw*, is also translated in most of these ways; but as far as it has a separate meaning it is that of the third Beatitude, which names the 'meek' (see on 25:9; *cf.* 37:11), who refuse the way of self-assertion. It is used of Moses in this sense in Numbers 12:3.

29. With these exploits (*cf.* verse 34) compare those of the 'mighty men', in 2 Samuel 23:8ff. But *crush* and *troop* could be translated 'run' and 'bank' (*cf.* Heb. of 65:11, EV 10), as in NEB. For the bearing of this verse on David's authorship, see the prefatory comment to the psalm.

30. The striking opening, *This God*, is echoed in verse 32 (*cf.* JB), where the phrase in our verse, *his way is perfect*, is capped by the answering phrase (lit.) 'he has made my way

---

[1] Here 'show thyself loyal' is a verb, from the same root as the adjective.
[2] It assumes that 'man' ($\sqrt{g\text{-}b\text{-}r}$) has crept into 25b from 26a (Heb. 26b, 27a), where it should hypothetically replace 'pure' ($\sqrt{b\text{-}r\text{-}r}$) and be understood in a hostile sense.

perfect'. Obviously *perfect* (*tāmîm*) has a far richer content as a description of God's activity than of man's, but His flawless wisdom, love and power are mirrored in the relative soundness of thought, motive and achievement (here it is especially achievement) which He produces in His servants.[1] Yet after the early climax of his career, did David lose the impetus towards this (*cf.* Phil. 3:12ff.), as if settling for the tamer sense of *tāmîm, i.e.* 'safe' (*cf.* 32, RSV)?

18:31-45. Victory and rout

The speed and buoyancy of the poetry capture the excitement of attack and pursuit. All is as light and swift here as it was cataclysmic in the rescue scene of verses 4-19; but all is equally from God. 2 Samuel 8 gives the prose summary of campaigns such as these, insofar as the psalm is retrospective (see on verses 37ff., below).

31. The confident monotheism and the recurrent use of the word *rock* (*ṣûr; cf.* verses 2, 46) point to the Song of Moses as part of David's inspiration for this psalm. With verse 30 compare Moses' words 'The Rock, his work is perfect', and with verse 31, 'Their rock is not as our Rock' (Dt. 32:4, 31). See also on verse 47, below.

32. This verse pairs with verse 30, where see comment.

33, 34. *Cf.* the physical prowess in verse 29. The *bow of bronze* was apparently a wooden bow strengthened with the metal.

35. For the remarkable expression in the Hebrew text, 'thy gentleness made (or will make) me great' (*cf.* AV, RV, RSV mg.), various commonplace substitutes have been suggested since ancient times. But the truth it expresses is profound, and the only question is whether David had the perception to see it. On so subjective a matter the text should have the benefit of the doubt. The Hebrew noun is akin to the adjective '*ānāw*, humble, meek, the second word discussed at verse 27 above; and while it was the gentleness God exercised that allowed David his success, it was the gentleness God taught him that was his true greatness.

37-45. Most of the tenses here are imperfects, which in Hebrew signify either future or continuous actions. While RSV could be right in placing these in the past, it is more likely

---

[1] *E.g.* it is translated 'blameless' in verses 23, 25 (Heb. 24, 26).

that they are looking ahead, reckoning that the victories already won are a promise of greater things. The Accession Decree of Psalm 2:7–9 offers 'the ends of the earth' to the Lord's anointed, and while these verses take up the stern aspect of this,[1] others will dwell on the prospect of Gentile conversions (*cf.* 22:27; also Is. 55:5 with our verse 49). The New Testament endorses both these emphases (*e.g.* Rev. 2:26f.; 7:9ff.).

18:46–50. Doxology

46. The attractive naivety of Gelineau and JB, '(Long) life to the Lord!', is wrong. *The Lord lives* is an affirmation, unlike the homage cry of, *e.g.*, 1 Kings 1:25, 39 (see Heb.). This truth was seen as the great contrast between Yahweh, who 'does whatever he pleases', and the idols who 'have mouths but do not speak' (115:3, 5); also perhaps between His unfailing life and the cyclic vicissitudes of Baal. The cry 'Baal lives' had to alternate with 'Baal is dead'. And the complement of the tireless energy of the Lord who 'lives' is the endless stability of *my rock*. See also the comments on verses 2 and 31.

47. The opening words, *The God*, correspond to the emphatic 'This God—' of verse 30 (*cf.* verse 32). If the Song of Moses was in mind (see on verse 31, above), the *vengeance*, or retribution, would be seen clearly as what God *gave* His servant to carry out, since He affirms there that 'vengeance is mine' (Dt. 32:35). Only in God's hands, or in trust from them, is retribution right (Rom. 12:19; 13:4).

49, 50. Paul quotes verse 49 as the first in a series of four prophecies to show that Christ came for the Gentiles as well as the Jews (Rom. 15:8–12). While David may have thought only of Yahweh's fame spread abroad, his words at their full value portray the Lord's anointed (50), ultimately the Messiah, praising Him *among*—in fellowship with—a host of Gentile worshippers. Although every Davidic king might make this psalm his own, it belonged especially to David whose testimony it was, and to Christ who was his

---

[1] *Cringing* (44) is a translation probably derived from the idea of insincerity, which is one element of the Heb. verb. But J. H. Eaton, *JTS* 19 (1968), pp. 603f., draws attention to this verb's other sense, 'grow lean' (*cf.* Ps. 109:24), and sees the vanquished as cut down to size, their arrogance gone. 'They become small in view of me.'

'offspring' (*descendants* is this singular/collective noun) *par excellence*, just as He was the supreme offspring (Gal. 3:16) of Abraham.

Psalm 19
The Skies, the Scriptures

The very sound of the two movements of the psalm tells something of their two concerns: the broad sweep of God's wordless revelation in the universe, expressed in the exuberant lines of verses 1–6, and the clarity of His written word, reflected in the quiet conciseness of verses 7–10, to which the heart-searching of 11–14 is the worshipper's response.

It is unimportant to decide whether two psalms have been brought together, or whether the two themes complemented one another from the first within a single poem (although the abrupt end of verses 1–7 tells against the former view). What is bequeathed to us is one psalm, whose two parts greatly illuminate one another. Again, whether or not David drew on existing poetry for his description of the sun, his praise was wholly for its Creator; and all the more pointedly so if he was capturing this language for the first time for its proper use.

The psalm is quoted in Romans 10:18, and its thought may also underlie the argument of Romans 1:18ff., that God's eternal power and deity are 'clearly perceived in the things that have been made'. Its theology is as powerful as its poetry.

19:1–6. The eloquence of nature
Different ages need this reminder—for such it is (Rom. 1:19)—in different ways. The ancients were tempted to 'kiss their hand' to sun and moon and the host of heaven (*cf.* Jb. 31:26f.; 2 Ki. 23:5); the moderns to explain them away as fortuitous, in one mood, or to revert to astrology in another. Only the Christian is moved to filial wonder and joy at the thought of their Maker.

2. The expression, *pours forth*, suggests the irrepressible bubbling up of a spring, and therefore perhaps the unfailing variety with which the days reflect the Creator's mind. The book of Job enlarges on this, especially in the sky-scapes of chapters 37 and 38. *Knowledge* is well matched with *night*, since without the night skies man would have known, until recently, nothing but an empty universe.

3, 4. The paradox of wordless speech is brought out by the modern versions, rightly, as against AV; but RSV's speculative repetition of *voice* is clumsy and not in fact supported by the LXX (quoted in Rom. 10:18), which uses, instead, a synonym for voice ('cry, sound') in verse 4. Translate it, therefore, 'yet their cry goes out . . .'. Such a synonym is a defensible rendering of the existing Hebrew word, whose commoner meaning is 'line' (AV, RV, RSV mg.).[1] The parallel noun, *words*, in 4b, supports 'cry, sound', *etc.*, as against 'line'; although the latter makes resonable sense if it indicates that no boundaries restrict these witnesses (*cf.* 2 Cor. 10:13). But a suggestion by Weiser that it means 'their plumbline', and thus 'their law', would give these natural phenomena too specialized a role.

4. 7. Addison's hymn sums up these verses very finely:

(LAST VERSE) · 'What though nor real voice nor sound
　　　　Amid their radiant orbs be found;
　　　　In reason's ear they all rejoice,
　　　　And utter forth a glorious voice,
　　　　For ever singing as they shine,
　　　　"The hand that made us is divine."'[2]

4c–6. *The sun*, suddenly and emphatically introduced in 4c, now dominates the scene, exultant and magnificent, yet obedient. God has assigned it its place to occupy (4c) and its *course* to run; the whole sky its mere *tent* and track. Such are God's servants and visible establishment ('the outskirts of his ways', Jb. 26:14).

5, 6. Some commentators (*e.g.* Weiser) see a poetic allusion

---

[1] In verse 4a RSV has emended the Heb. consonants *q-w-m* to *q-w-l-m*, as in 3b (Heb. 5a, 4b). But the Heb. as it stands can be argued to mean 'their cry', either by analogy with Ecclus. 44:5 mg. (*i.e.*, cord, chord, musical note; *cf.* NEB here, 'their music'; see G. R. Driver in P. R. Ackroyd and B. Lindars (ed.), *Words and Meanings* (CUP, 1968), p. 54), or, with Dahood, by taking the root *q-w-h* in, *e.g.*, Ps. 40:2; Jb. 17:13 to mean 'call'. Dahood is here following J. Barth, *Etymologische Studien* (Leipzig, 1893), pp. 29ff.

[2] J. Addison, 'The spacious firmament on high'.

to tales of a sun-god who returns each night to the ocean and to his bride, and sets out again in the morning. A more likely allusion is to a human wedding, when the bridegroom, spendidly arrayed, sets forth to the house of the bride to claim her. Such is the radiance and festive mood of the journey. All would agree that the psalm, if it glances at mythology, repudiates it. The sun may be 'like' a bridegroom or a runner; it is in fact no more than a glorious part of God's 'handiwork' (1). But as such, it proclaims the extent (6a) and penetration (6b) of His rule.

19:7-14. The clarity of Scripture

'Two things', according to Kant, 'fill the mind with ever new and increasing admiration and awe ... the starry heavens above and the moral law within.'[1] The psalm transcends the second of these themes by looking to the divine law revealed; evoking not only 'admiration and awe' but the person-to-Person response of verses 11-14. In this section the revealed name of God, Yahweh (the Lord), is heard seven times; earlier, true to the theme of general revelation, only the least specific term for God (El, verse 1) was used, and only once.

7-10. As in Psalm 119, where still more synonyms are used, these six facets of revelation are not sharply distinguished, yet each has a certain character of its own. Here we shall study them by means of the nouns, adjectives and verbs in turn.

a. The nouns. *Law* (*tôrâ*) is the comprehensive term for God's revealed will. *Testimony* (*'ēdûṯ*) is its aspect as truth attested by God Himself (*cf.* 1 Jn. 5:9); it is also a term for His covenant-declaration (*cf.* Ex. 25:16 with, *e.g.*, Dt. 9:9). *Precepts* and *commandment* indicate the precision and authority with which God addresses us, while *fear*, or reverence, emphasizes the human response fostered by His word. *Ordinances*, or judgments (*mišpāṭîm*), are the judicial decisions He has recorded about various human situations (*cf.* on 18:22).

Together, these terms show the practical purpose of revelation, to bring God's will to bear on the hearer and evoke intelligent reverence, well-founded trust, detailed obedience.

---

[1] *Dialectic of Pure and Practical Reason*, conclusion.

99

b. The adjectives. For *perfect*, see on 18:30, and *cf.* the description of God's will in Romans 12:2. *Sure*, by its passive form, can mean not only what is firm but what is confirmed: *cf.* 'verified' in Genesis 42:20. *Right* means morally right, or straight. On *pure* and *clean*, David's own comment is in Psalm 12:6, seen in contrast to 1911 4. *True* is lit. 'truth', in the sense of dependability. In all, these epithets move in a different world from the compromise, insincerity and half-truths of human intercourse.

c. The verbs. The first four, *reviving, making wise, etc.*, (7, 8) enlarge on what Scripture does for men; the remaining two (since *righteous* (9) translates a verb here) on what it is in itself. On *reviving*, see on 23:3. In the phrase (they are) *righteous altogether*, the adverb means, rather, 'together', *i.e.* all alike: *cf.* NEB, JB, 'righteous every one'. Matthew Henry comments, 'they are all of a piece'.

11–14. Here is the spiritual counterpart of verse 6c: 'there is nothing hid . . .' The fact is not only stated but demonstrated by David's quickened concern aroused by the blessings (10, 11b) as well as the warnings (11a) of Scripture. The two-edged sword has penetrated.

12, 13. It was the Mosaic law which made these inner distinctions between sins, yet succeeded (as these verses show) in leaving no sin condoned. Verse 12a recognizes that a fault may be *hidden* not because it is too small to see, but because it is too characteristic to register. On both verses see Numbers 15:27–36, where the outward triviality of the incident underlines the gravity with which God viewed its motivation. A Jewish admonition is to the point: 'Do not say, "I sinned, and what happened to me?" . . . Do not be so confident of atonement that you add sin to sin' (Ecclus. 5:4f.).

14. The psalm ends, not on the note of avoiding sin, but on that of offering back to God the mind's fitting response to His own words, as a pure sacrifice (*cf.* Ho. 14:2). This is the probable implication of *acceptable*, a term often found in sacrificial contexts. And God is addressed not as the sinner's accuser or judge but as his refuge (*my rock*; see on 18:2) and champion (*my redeemer*, as in, *e.g.*, Lv. 25:25; Jb. 19:25). This sinner can call himself 'thy servant' (11, 13): he belongs to Him by the covenant which the law itself presupposes.

Psalm 20
'The Day of Trouble'

This 'day of trouble' is one of impending battle, as the chariots of verse 7 make clear. The shape of the psalm brings the scene before us as the king prepares to march; his prayers and sacrifices offered, his plans prepared and his men grouped with their standards. First there is the congregation's Godspeed to him (1–5), a corporate invocation of blessing. In reply, a single voice, perhaps of the king himself, tells of the certainty of God's answer ('Now I know . . .', 6–8). Then the people respond with a final prayer for him (9), brief and urgent.

It is one of the most stirring of the Psalms, by its tense awareness of life-and-death issues soon to be resolved. Its companion piece is the next psalm, all exuberance and delight.

20:1–5. The Lord answer you!

1. *You* is singular throughout, identified in verse 6 as the Lord's anointed. In this one man the whole people see themselves embodied and their national life sustained: he is 'the breath of our nostrils', the protective 'shadow' (La. 4:20), 'the lamp of Israel' (2 Sa. 21:17). In reality such a role must prove too big for any but the Messiah, whom it thus foreshadowed.

The divine *name* was not regarded in Israel as magically potent (as in some heathen systems) but as a token of God's self-revelation and His readiness to be invoked (7)—with the added reminder here of His commitment to *Jacob* and his posterity. With the priestly blessing of Numbers 6:24ff. God let His name be 'put . . . upon the people of Israel', as if marking them as His possession. And to this idea was added that of their acting on His behalf, which is the thought of verse 5 and of Asa's avowal 'We rest on thee, and in thy name we go' (2 Ch. 14:11, AV). All these aspects are carried over into the New Testament: *e.g.* John 14:14; 17:6; Acts 3:6; Revelation 3:12.

2, 3. This word for *sanctuary* is simply 'holiness', a synonym here for *Zion*, where already God's ark, but not yet His Temple, signified His presence (2 Sa. 6:17). The spirit of this prayer is very different from that of reliance on the ark itself in the days of Eli, or on *sacrifices* in the days of the prophets, as means of forcing God's hand. It is God who confers their entire value on them (*regard with favour* is lit. 'make, or reckon, rich').

4. Although, in the Hebrew, *grant you your heart's desire* differs slightly from the expression in 21:2, it beautifully links the two psalms as prayer and thanksgiving on either side of a crisis. *Plans* is the word sometimes translated as counsel or strategy: *cf.* Isaiah 11:2; 36:5, where the limitations of human planning, recognized in the psalm, are exposed from above and below.

5. *Victory*, here and in verses 6 and 9, translates related words from the root 'save' (*cf.* the name Jesus). Such a meaning, in contexts of battle, adds a positive content to 'salvation', beyond that of bare deliverance. On *the name*, see on verse 1. *Set up our banners* (a single word in Heb.) recalls the orderly array of the tribes in Numbers 2:2, *etc.* ('each by his own standard') and the visual impact of 'an army with banners' in the Song of Solomon 6:4, 10. A different word is used in Psalm 60:4. Note finally, on this verse, the far-reaching implications of *fulfil*, in relation to plans (4) and petitions: *cf.* Ephesians 3:20; 2 Thessalonians 1:11.

20:6-8. He will answer

On the sudden change to assurance, see the concluding comment on Psalm 6. Even the dimensions of the scene are enlarged: the help sought from Zion (2) is now seen as sent from heaven itself.

7. The word *boast* (or 'trust', AV, RV) is a translator's inference, though a reasonable one; the only verb in the sentence is 'we will make mention' (RV). This verb is thought to have had the special meaning of proclaiming the name of God in worship, bringing His power into the midst (see on verse 1), rather as Christians invoke the name of Christ for protection or victory. But the preposition in this phrase brings it more into line with Old Testament expressions of allegiance or regard (*e.g.* Is. 48:1, 'confess').[1] In Joshua 23:7 it is coupled with 'swear by', and in our colloquial use this comes very near the sense of the opening of our verse, as when we say that a person 'swears by' some favourite remedy or

[1] See Childs, p. 14.

device. *Chariots* and *horses* were the most formidable force of ancient times, but they brought memories to Israel of miraculous victories, *e.g.* at the Red Sea and the river Kishon (Ex. 14; Jdg. 4).

20:9. Answer us
Literally the Hebrew reads (with the traditional punctuation) 'Lord, give victory; let the King answer us (or, the King will answer us) in the day of our calling'. But RSV's first line, *Give victory to the king, O Lord* is consistent with the Hebrew, and makes this line of equal length with the second.[1] This seems marginally preferable, although the sense is broadly similar either way.

The final phrase, lit. 'in the day of our calling', has a telling echo of the opening verse. The fact that the time of trouble has been made the time of prayer makes the buoyant spirit of verses 6–8 a matter not of wishful optimism but of realistic faith.

Psalm 21
The Day of Rejoicing

This jubilant psalm has the sound of a coronation ode, or a hymn for a royal anniversary. But it could well celebrate a victory, since a comparison of verse 2 with Psalm 20:4 suggests that Psalms 20 and 21 are paired as petition and answer (although the Heb. of these two verses is not as closely matched as the English). The structure, again, is similar in consisting of two main blocks of material; but here the king's faith is heard first (1–7), and the congregation's address to him second (8–12). In both psalms a final verse, calling directly on God, clinches the prayer and praise.

21:1–7. The king and the Lord
The king himself may be speaking in the third person, or else another on his behalf: in either case only God and he are in

---

[1] But the second line of the MT has the third person: 'let him answer', or 'he will answer'. LXX, Syr. and Jerome read an imperative, 'answer us', involving a difference of one consonant from MT, *i.e.*, (*wa*) *ᵃnēnû* for *yaᶜᵃnēnû*.

the picture in these verses. At verse 8 the perspective will
change and the king be addressed with promises of dominion.

1, 2. *Thy help* is the same word as 'thy victory' in 20:5,
where see comment. On verse 2, see on 20:4

3. The friendly confrontation of *thou dost meet him* stands
out in welcome contrast to the encounter with death in 18:5
(Heb. 6), and to God's encounter with the wicked in 17:13,
expressed by the same word. *Cf.*, in a context of compassion,
79:8; Isaiah 21:14. As to the *crown*, its worth derives from the
Giver rather than the gold: a fact which David forgot in
accepting the trophy of 2 Samuel 12:30; but it is underlined
again in Ezekiel 21:25–27.

4ff. While the gift of *life . . . for ever and ever* might have
implied to an Old Testament reader either a hyperbole like
that of Daniel 2:4, *etc.*, or an allusion to the endless dynasty
promised to David in 2 Samuel 7:16, the New Testament
has filled in the picture firmly with the figure of the ultimate
king, the Messiah, for whom the whole stanza is true without
exaggeration. In Him the *glory . . . splendour and majesty* of
verse 5 reveal their full range of depth (Jn. 13:31f.) and height
(Rev. 5:12), as does *the joy of thy presence* (6; *cf.* Heb. 12:2).
See also on verse 9, below.

21:8–12. The king and his enemies
If the psalm originally celebrated a specific deliverance (see
introductory comment), it saw in this the promise of final
triumph. It has the crusading spirit dedicated to hunting out
every enemy, not allowing him the initiative (*find out . . .
find out*, 8), and to ridding the world of his kind (10). This
again outruns the power of any king, as 9b acknowledges, and
the scale of events calls once more for the Messiah. 2 Thessalonians 1:7b–9 may owe something to this passage, with its
theme of Christ's appearing and of attendant fire and judgment. *When you appear* (9) is lit. 'at the time of your face', *i.e.*,
of your presence (*cf.* Rev. 6:16). 'In the time of thine anger'
(AV, RV) is a less literal translation.

21:13. The Lord alone
This single verse to round off the psalm corresponds to the
close of Psalm 20. But here man is out of sight, though not
unheard; his part is to stand aside, admire and give thanks.

Psalm 22
The Psalm of the Cross

No Christian can read this without being vividly confronted with the crucifixion. It is not only a matter of prophecy minutely fulfilled, but of the sufferer's humility—there is no plea for vengeance—and his vision of a world-wide ingathering of the Gentiles. The Gelineau translation entitles it 'The suffering servant wins the deliverance of the nations'.

No incident recorded of David can begin to account for this. As A. Bentzen points out, it is 'not a description of illness, but of an *execution*';[1] and while David was once threatened with stoning (1 Sa. 30:6), this is a very different scene. The theory that the king underwent a ritual humiliation at an annual festival in Israel as in Babylon, would provide a plausible setting for such a psalm;[2] but the existence of such an Israelite ritual is only an inference from passages like this, unsupported by direct evidence. Whatever the initial stimulus, the language of the psalm defies a naturalistic explanation; the best account is in the terms used by Peter concerning another psalm of David: 'Being therefore a prophet, . . . he foresaw and spoke of . . . the Christ' (Acts 2:30f.).

The turning-point is at the end of verse 21, where the alternate cries and prayers give way to praise and to a broadening vision of God's perfect rule. Hebrews 2:12 quotes verse 22, from this section, as an acknowledged Messianic prophecy.

Title
See Introduction VI. *c.* 3, pp. 41f.

22:1–21. The power of darkness
This part of the psalm is marked by a throbbing alternation of 'I/me'-sections, of increasing length (verses 1–2, 6–8, 12–18), with 'Thou'-sections of increasing urgency and immediacy (verses 3–5, 9–11, 19–21). The pattern will change at verse 22 from this alternation to a rapidly expanding circle of praise and vision.

[1] A. Bentzen, *King and Messiah* (Lutterworth, 1955), p. 94, n.40. The italics are his.
[2] See Introduction, III, pp. 10f.

1. Why . . .? Our Lord's cry of dereliction (quoting this verse in His native Aramaic) told, it would seem, of an objective reality, namely the punitive separation He accepted in our place, 'having become a curse for us' (Gal. 3:13). For David, on the other hand, the meaning would be close to that of the second line, *Why art thou so far from helping me?*—for the Psalms use such terms practically, not theoretically: *cf.* 'remember', 'hear', 'awake'. It is not a lapse of faith, nor a broken relationship, but a cry of disorientation as God's familiar, protective presence is withdrawn (as it was from, *e.g.*, the blameless Job) and the enemy closes in.

3–5. Yet thou . . . David stops floundering in his own grief, which would suck him further down, to reach for 'the rock that is higher than I'. (*Thou* is emphatic, and so by their position are the expressions *In thee . . . to thee . . . in thee* (4f.), just as in RSV and NEB.) What is more, he makes for the highest ground of all: the theme of God as *holy*, and of the church as praising[1] Him—not, initially, of God as compassionate or himself as pitiable, though this will follow. He also looks back resolutely to other times (4, 5) and other men's experiences of help.

6–8. But I . . . The scorn hurts because he belongs, and cares. Warm, quick affection, not olympian detachment, was the mark of both David and his greater Son; yet Jesus diverted pity from Himself to others. 'Weep for yourselves and for your children.' Notice the false premise from which the unbelievers argue in verse 8, as always: that God is there for our convenience, if He is there at all (*cf.* 'command these stones'; 'throw yourself down'; 'come down from the cross').[2] The very gestures and words of verses 7 and 8 were reproduced at Calvary (Mt. 27:39, 43).

9–11. Yet thou . . . Having fixed his mind on God's glory and fame in verses 3–5, David dwells now on His personal,

[1] With the expression, *enthroned on the praises of Israel* (or 'inhabiting' them, *cf.* AV, RV), the Old Testament characteristically draws out the inner meaning of its visible institutions. See also on Ps. 51:17. God's earthly throne or palace is not in the Temple but in the hearts of His people (Is. 66:1f.) and on their lips. But the metaphor also puts the question to the church, whether its hymnody is a throne for God or a platform for man.

[2] *He committed* (*gal*) is the rendering of the Heb. consonants adopted by the most ancient versions and quoted in Mt. 27:43. But MT has the imperative (*gōl*), 'Commit . . .'. The former is grammatically the less disjointed.

lifelong care of him. God is no casual acquaintance, to offer perfunctory help. *Cf.* 139:13-16; Job 10:8-12. The link between the translations, *didst keep me safe* (RSV) and 'didst make me trust' (RV) is the fact that well-founded trust and safety go hand in hand. Further, Jeremiah 12:5b ('fall down') suggests that the basic meaning of this Hebrew verb may be to lie prone[1] (*cf.* our verse 10, 'upon thee was I cast'); hence NEB's translation 'laid me'. Perhaps the best is JB: 'you entrusted me to my mother's breasts.'

12-18, Ravening and roaring. This is a scene often enacted: the strong closing in on the weak; the many on the one. The crowd is pictured as bestial (bulls, lions, dogs, wild oxen), but it is all too human, whether the deed is done with subtlety or with the brutality of Calvary. The context suggests some of the motives for which men do these things to one another: resentment at those who make high claims (8); the compulsion of crowd-mentality (12, 16a; *cf.* Ex. 23:2); greed, even for trivial gains (18); and perverted tastes— enjoying a harrowing spectacle (17) simply because sin is murderous, and sinners have hatred in them (*cf.* Jn. 8:44).

While verses 14, 15, taken alone, could describe merely a desperate illness, the context is of collective animosity and the symptoms could be those of Christ's scourging and crucifixion; in fact verses 16-18 had to wait for that event to unfold their meaning with any clarity.

They have pierced (16) or, simply, 'piercing', is the most likely translation of a problematic Hebrew word. A strong argument in its favour is that the LXX, compiled two centuries before the crucifixion, and therefore an unbiased witness, understood it so. All the major translations reject the Massoretic vowels (added to the written text in the Christian era) as yielding little sense here (see margin of RV, RSV, NEB), and the majority in fact agree with LXX. The chief alternatives (*e.g.* 'bound' or 'hacked off') solve no linguistic difficulties which 'pierced' does not solve[2], but avoid the apprent prediction of the cross by exchanging a common Hebrew verb

---

[1] G. R. Driver, 'Difficult Words in the Hebrew Prophets', in H. H. Rowley, ed., *Studies in Old Testament Prophecy* (T. & T. Clark, 1950), p. 59.
[2] The same form, *kārû*, has been proposed for all three. But the existing Heb. consonants, *k'ry*, are consistent with the plural construct of the Qal participle of *kûr*, 'piercing', spelt with aleph as a vowel-indicator (*cf.* the longer spelling of Ramoth in Jos. 20:8 as against Jos. 21:36, Heb.).

(dig, bore, pierce) for hypothetical ones, attested only in Akkadian, Syriac and Arabic,[1] not in biblical Hebrew.

19-21. But thou . . . This is the climax of the 'Thou' sections, and the turning-point of the psalm. The first 'Yet thou' was deliberately objective (3-5); the second less so (9-11); the third is a series of urgent cries, as the enemies seem to move in; murderous, unclean, ravenous, irresistible. On the rare word for *my help* (19), and its possible connection with the title, see Introduction, pp. 41f. *My life* (20b) is lit. 'my only one'—all I have left, and my dearest possession; *cf.* NEB 'my precious life'. Seen against this, *the power of the dog* is a grimly eloquent phrase.

In verse 21 only the RV captures anything of the sudden, dramatic change, kept back in the Hebrew to the last word. Instead of *my afflicted soul*, which is an emendation (*cf.* RSV mg.), the Hebrew text has merely a verb in the perfect tense. If this is the true text, this single word is a cry that greets a last-minute deliverance. '. . . And from the horns of the wild oxen. *Thou-hast-answered-me!*'

22:22-31. The spread of joy
22-26. The votive feast. Verse 25 gives the setting of these verses, for the law encouraged those who vowed some service to God, should their prayer be granted, to fulfil the vow with a sacrifice, followed by a feast (26) which might last as long as two days (Lv. 7:16). They were not to keep their happiness to themselves and their children, but invite their servants and other needy folk (*cf.* verse 26), especially the Levites, to eat with them before the Lord (Dt. 12:17–19). And they must tell the congregation what God had done for them (22; *cf.* 40:9f.; 116:14), calling on them to join in such a psalm as this (*cf.* 34:3 and the accompanying testimony).

But Hebrews 2:11, 12 relates verse 22 to the Messiah, as one who is 'not ashamed to call (us) brethren'; who therefore stands *in the midst* (22), not only on high, and at whose thanksgiving feast the humble[2] are welcome to *eat and be satisfied* (26) and (in no mere form of words but in reality) to *live for ever* (26).

---

[1] *Cf.* G. R. Driver, *ET* 57 (1945/6), p. 193.
[2] While 'afflicted', in the singular, is clearly right in verse 24, the nuance in 26 is towards 'meek' (AV, RV) or 'humble' (NEB). The two words are discussed at 18:27.

27–31. The boundless kingdom. Now David's language overflows all its natural banks as the thanksgiving proper to even a king (whose own fortunes affect those of many others). The fruits of his deliverance are transcendent, glimpsed already in the blessing, 'live for ever' (26), called down on his guests. Now they spread out in space and time until the Lord receives the homage of the Gentiles (27f.) and the worship of the proud (29). Verse 29 glances significantly at verse 26, if the Hebrew text is allowed to speak for itself as in RV: 'All the fat ones of the earth shall eat and worship.' *I.e.*, those who are at present self-sufficient will put aside their arrogance to join the humble at the feast (*cf.* 26), if they would gain the life which is not theirs to command (26c, 29c).[1]

Finally the vision extends to unborn generations (30f.), in terms which anticipate the preaching of the cross, recounting God's righteousness (or *deliverance*, a secondary meaning of the word) revealed in the action He has taken. The psalm which began with the cry of dereliction ends with the word *he has wrought it*, an announcement not far removed from our Lord's great cry, 'It is finished.'

Psalm 23
Shepherd and Friend

Depth and strength underlie the simplicity of this psalm. Its peace is not escape; its contentment is not complacency: there is readiness to face deep darkness and imminent attack, and the climax reveals a love which homes towards no material goal but to the Lord Himself.

23:1–4. The Shepherd
1. The Lord, as often in the Psalms, occupies here the first and emphatic place, and the *my* reveals a pledged relationship which dares to link *The Lord* (*is*) . . . with the incongruous *I shall.* . . . Everything in the psalm flows from that. In the word *shepherd*, David uses the most comprehensive and

---

[1] Alternatively the two halves of verse 29 may refer to the living and the dead respectively; *cf.* Phil. 2:10.

intimate metaphor yet encountered in the Psalms, preferring usually the more distant 'king' or 'deliverer', or the impersonal 'rock', 'shield', *etc.*; whereas the shepherd lives with his flock and is everything to it: guide, physician and protector.

2. The *green pastures*, or grassy meadows, and the 'waters to rest by' (*cf.* the 'resting place' which the ark sought out for Israel in Nu. 10:33) are mentioned first because they show how the shepherd, unlike the hireling, thinks and observes in terms of his flock. He would be poor at the job if he did not; as inadequate as the father who has not learnt to think and feel as a family man. God would not have taken on a flock, a family, if He had not intended that He and they should be bound up with one another.

3. After the tenderness of verse 2, God's firm, faithful dealings in this verse and the next can be seen in their true light. *He restores my soul* is an expression open to more than one interpretation. It may picture the straying sheep brought back, as in Isaiah 49:5, or perhaps Psalm 60:1 (Heb. 3), which use the same verb, whose intransitive sense is often 'repent' or 'be converted' (*e.g.* Ho. 14:1f.; Joel 2:12). Psalm 19:7, by its subject (the law) and by the parallel verb ('making wise'), points to a spiritual renewal of this kind, rather than mere refreshment. On the other hand, *my soul* usually means 'my life' or 'myself'; and 'restore' often has a physical or psychological sense, as in Isaiah 58:12, or using another part of the verb, Proverbs 25:13, Lamentations 1:11, 16, 19. In our context the two senses evidently interact, so that the retrieving or reviving of the sheep pictures the deeper renewal of the man of God, spiritually perverse or ailing as he may be.

It is the same with the *paths of righteousness*, which, in terms of sheep, mean no more than 'the right paths', but have, further, a demanding moral content for the human flock (*cf.* Pr. 11:5), whose ways will either shame or vindicate their Shepherd's good name. Ezekiel 36:22-32 draws out this searching implication of the phrase *for his name's sake*, but adds the corollary that, to uphold that name, God will make new men of us, whose ways will be His own.

4. The dark *valley*, or ravine, is as truly one of His 'right paths' as are the green pastures—a fact that takes much of the sting out of any ordeal. And His presence overcomes the worst thing that remains: the *fear*. *Shadow of death* is the literal meaning of the single Hebrew word *ṣalmāweṯ*,[1] which occurs nearly twenty times in the Old Testament, and RSV is right to retain it here. In many of this word's occurrences 'death' could be a kind of superlative, as in NEB's rendering here, 'dark as death', and in the term 'deep darkness', used by RSV elsewhere. Such a translation here (*cf.* RP's footnote, 'the darkest valley') would widen the reference of the verse to include other crises besides the final one. But although darkness is the leading thought in most of the Old Testament contexts, death is dominant in a few, including (in my view) the present verse. In Job 38:17 the gates of *ṣalmāweṯ* are equivalent to 'the gates of death' in the same verse, in Jeremiah 2:6 this term describes the peril of the desert, which is a place of death rather than of special darkness; and elsewhere the LXX makes 'shadow of death' its most frequent translation of the word. In Matthew 4:16 the insertion of 'and' ('the land and shadow of death') treats 'death' as more than a mere reinforcement of 'shadow', and in the Benedictus it marks a climax after 'darkness' (Lk. 1:79).

Thou, at this point of danger, replaces the more distant 'He', in a person-to-person address; for the Shepherd is no longer ahead, to lead, but alongside to escort. In times of need, companionship is good; and He is armed. The *rod* (a cudgel worn at the belt) and *staff* (to walk with, and to round up the flock) were the shepherd's weapon and implement: the former for defence (*cf.* 1 Sa. 17:35), the latter for control—since discipline is security. Setting aside this metaphor, only the Lord can lead a man through death; all other guides turn back, and the traveller must go on alone.

23:5, 6. The Friend

5. The shepherd imagery has served its purpose, to be replaced by one of greater intimacy. (The attempt to sustain the first metaphor, which is sometimes made, would turn it through a full circle, picturing men as sheep which are pictured as men—with their table, cup and house—which is hardly a profitable exercise.)

It is one thing to survive a threat, as in verse 4; quite

[1] Many moderns revocalize the consonants, to read a hypothetical form *ṣalmût*, which would contain no reference to death. But the ancient versions do not support this conjecture.

another to turn it into triumph. Every detail here is in that key, from the well-set *table*[1] (for *preparest*, see on 5:3) to the festive *oil* (*cf.* 104:15; Lk. 7:46) and brimming *cup*. The picture may be one of cool assurance under pressure, an Old Testament equivalent of Romans 8:31-39 or 2 Corinthians 12:9f.; a witness to infinite resources in the worst of situations. But since the enemy is never taken lightly in Scripture, except by a Ben-hadad or a Belshazzar, it more probably anticipates a victory celebration, where the enemies are present as captives; or an accession feast with defeated rivals as reluctant guests.

6. But the prospect is better than a feast. In the Old Testament world, to eat and drink at someone's table created a bond of mutual loyalty, and could be the culminating token of a covenant. It was so in Exodus 24:8-12, when the elders of Israel 'beheld God, and ate and drank'; it was so again at the Last Supper, when Jesus announced 'This cup is the new covenant in my blood' (1 Cor. 11:25).

So to be God's guest is to be more than an acquaintance, invited for a day. It is to live with Him. There is a suggestion of pilgrimage in the picture of a progress that ends at *the house of the Lord*; but it is also a journey home, for it was not only the Levites who considered the courts of the Lord their true home (as in Pss. 42 and 84) but also, in heart and mind, David the man of affairs: *cf.* 27:4; 65:4.

Mercy is the covenant-word rendered 'steadfast love' elsewhere (see on 17:7). Together with *goodness*[2] it suggests the steady kindness and support that one can count on in the family or between firm friends. With God these qualities are not merely solid and dependable, but vigorous—for to *follow* does not mean here to bring up the rear but to pursue, as surely as His judgments pursue the wicked (83:15).

For ever is lit. (in this verse) 'to length of days', which is not in itself an expression for eternity. But since the logic of God's covenant allows no ending to His commitment to

---

[1] It is misplaced ingenuity to emend this to 'spear', on the supposition that one consonant has been duplicated. (E. Power, *Bib.* 9 (1928), pp. 434-442; supported by J. Morgenstern, *JBL* (1946), pp. 15-17, and by W. F. Albright, *ibid.*, p. 420.) Morgenstern (but not Albright) also interprets the *cup* as a drinking trough, thereby maintaining the shepherd/sheep metaphor. (I owe this reference to A. R. Millard.)

[2] *Cf.* A. R. Millard, 'For He is Good', *TB* 17 (1966), pp. 115-117.

a man, as our Lord pointed out (Mt. 22:32), the Christian understanding of these words does no violence to them. 'Neither death, nor life, . . . will be able to separate us from the love of God in Christ Jesus our Lord.'

Psalm 24
King of Glory

In this majestic psalm we move as if in procession with the King of Glory from the provinces of His realm to 'the central height' and the city at the summit. If a ceremonial occasion gave rise to the psalm, some would locate it in the supposed enthronement festival (see Introduction III, pp. 9ff.). Yet we need hardly look further than the escorting of the ark by David 'with song and lyres and harps . . .' from Kirjath-jearim to mount Zion (1 Ch. 13:8), which is certainly commemorated in Psalm 132, and for which Psalm 68 may also have been written.

Traditionally this is sung on Ascension Day, and has inspired some of the great hymns for that occasion. Delitzsch however has pointed out that the theme is better seen as that of Advent, the Victor's arrival to possess the citadel He has conquered, just as David and the ark transformed the Jebusite stronghold into the hill and city of the Lord. The psalms cited in 1 Chronicles 16 as sung on that occasion (96 and parts of 105 and 106) have God's final coming as their climax.

24:1, 2. The All-Creating
Characteristically, the first and emphatic Hebrew word is *the Lord's*, in verse 1, and *he* in verse 2. To Him as Creator and Sustainer (2), pictured as a city's founder and establisher, belongs the earth in all its aspects: fruitful earth (1a), peopled earth (1b), solid earth (2). *Fullness* (translated in 98:7 as 'all that fills it') conjures up its wealth and fertility, seen here not as man's, for exploitation, but, prior to that, as God's, for His satisfaction and glory (*cf.* the same Heb. expression in Is. 6:3). This view of it is not impoverishing but an enrichment: *cf.* 1 Corinthians 3:21b, 23, and (quoting our verse) 10:25f., 31.

The Psalms claim the peopled earth (1b) for God as Creator

(2), King and Judge (*e.g.* Ps. 9:7f.). The New Testament goes further still (Jn. 3:16f.).

2. *Upon* could be translated 'above', as in 8:1 (Heb. 2), but the poetic image is of the solid earth rising out of the waters, and the allusion is to Genesis 1:9f.; *cf.* 2 Peter 3:5. RSV rightly has *rivers* rather than the older versions' 'floods' or the 'waters beneath'. To the Old Testament, 'the foam of perilous seas' tends to dominate such a scene, making the deep a reminder of formlessness (Gn. 1:2), menace (Ps. 46:5) and restlessness (Is. 57:20). But (against heathen belief) 'the sea is his', as surely as 'the dry land'. See also on 46:2–4; 74:13; 96:11.

3–6. The All-Holy

With this stanza compare Psalm 15, and the comments there. To *ascend* and *stand* presents a fine picture of worship, balancing the other main expression, to 'bow down'. It is to make a deliberate quest (*cf.* Mk. 9:2), to mount to a vantage-point (*cf.* Gn. 13:14ff.; 19:27f.), to converge on it with other seekers (Is. 2:2f.), and finally to stand before the throne (Rev. 7:9).

4. On *clean hands* see Isaiah 1:15; 33:15; 1 Timothy 2:8. On *a pure heart* see on 17:15. The meaning of *lift up his soul* is illuminated by 25:1, where it is a parallel to 'trust'. This false (*i.e.* empty) object of trust may be an inadequate helper (*e.g.* an idol, or 'the help of man', 60:11) or an unworthy stratagem such as the lies of 12:2 (Heb. 3), for which this word is also used. On *swear deceitfully*, see on 15:4c.

5. *Vindication* is lit. 'righteousness', and is here akin to justification, the judge's pronouncement in favour of one's claim or plea. Whatever is functioning as it should is 'righteous': in court, the man in the right; in character. the honest man; in the run of affairs, success. Probably all three are present in this context. This man has the smile of God upon him: he is accepted, he is helped to live an upright life, his affairs under God's *blessing* will run as they should. See also on 23:3b; 65:5.

6. For the meaning of *generation* see on 12:7; and on seeking God's face see on 11:7 and 17:15. *Jacob*, in the Hebrew text, stands alone (*cf.* AV), and makes little sense without the LXX's prefix, *God of*. Either this Hebrew word has dropped out in the copying, or possibly we should read 'seek thy face like Jacob' (assuming haplography of the consonant *k*), alluding to the blessing and the face-to-face encounter at Peniel (Gn. 32:29f.).

24:7–10. The All-Victorious
This stirring challenge and response (which may have been ritually enacted at the arrival of David's procession at the gates) brings before us in the fewest of words the towering stature of the unseen King, the age-old fortress He is entering to make His own (see the opening comments on the psalm), and the link between this climax and the earlier history of redemption—for the expression *mighty in battle* is but a stronger form of God's title of 'warrior' first heard in the song of victory at the Red Sea (Ex. 15:3). The ascent completes a march begun in Egypt; indeed the psalms that are quoted in 1 Chronicles 16 as sung on this occasion look back as far as Abraham and on to the coming of the Lord as Judge. If the earth is His (1, 2) and He is holy (3–6), the challenge to the 'ancient doors' is not an exercise in pageantry, but (as in 2 Cor. 10:3–5) a battle-cry for the church.

Psalm 25
An Alphabet of Entreaty

The Hebrew alphabet, with an occasional irregularity, supplies the framework of the psalm, in which the pressure of enemies, the need of guidance and the burden of guilt take turns to be the dominant concern. The tone is subdued, and the singer's trust is shown in patient waiting rather than the outburst of joy which sometimes marks the climax of such a psalm. Right outside the alphabetic scheme, the final verse claims for Israel what David has petitioned for himself, so making of a personal plea a hymn for the whole congregation.

Enemies
Enemies, seldom absent from a Davidic psalm, are implied to be ideologically as well as personally opposed to David. Their victory would discredit not only him (2) but what he

stood for: that is, the conviction that a man must live by the help of God, not by his wits (3). Verses 20, 21 return to this and clarify it by looking to *integrity and uprightness* as his defence (which his enemies would despise as naïve), confessing that but for God these would be no match for the worldly weapons of treachery (3; *cf. the net*, 15) and hatred (19). So the enemy has failed to dictate to David the terms of battle. Those who sing the psalm profess the same attitude as his.

Guidance

This is a major theme. The first plea is for instruction in the general will of God: note the plurals, *to know thy ways . . . thy paths* (4). This is free of the self-interest that may motivate requests for special guidance, and it lays the foundation for right decisions, a foundation of 'faculties trained . . . to distinguish good from evil' (Heb. 5:14). The other marks of this prayer are, first, persistence—a patient alertness for 'the first signal of his hand,' seen in verses 5c, 15 (*cf.* 123:2); second, penitence—recognizing that one is no apt or deserving pupil but a *sinner* (8), with a sinner's bias and guilt; third, obedience—the biddable attitude implied in the word *humble* or meek (pl. of '*ānāw*, 9, the second word discussed at 18:27); and fourth, reverence (*fear*; 12, 14)—the simple piety which God honours with His *friendship* (14).'Friendship' is the Hebrew word *sôd*, meaning both 'council' and 'counsel': both the circle of one's close associates and the matters that are discussed with them (*cf.* 'council', Je. 23:18, 22; 'secret', Am. 3:7).This whole approach to divine guidance is personal and mature, unlike the basically pagan search for irrational pointers and omens (*cf.* Is. 47:13).

Guilt

The references to this are brief but earnest and recurrent. Its solvent is not time but divine grace (7), pledged by the covenant (see on 'goodness and mercy', 23:6). God's 'remembering' is active and certain (see on 8:4); the alternative forms which it can take are well put as *remember . . . sins* or *remember me* (7). But there is no glibness in the appeal to covenant love, as if it merely averted punishment. God *instructs sinners* not only out of goodness and mercy (*cf.* 7) but as being Himself *good and upright* (8), and therefore concerned to reproduce these qualities in others. David, for his part, mourns his guilt (11), sensitive to the estrangement (*cf. Turn . . . to me*, 16; *forgive*, 18) which is the deepest trouble of verses 16–18.

Trust
The word itself is used at the outset (2), but the attitude also comes through in the statements about God (*e.g.* 5b, 8–10, 14f.) and in the emphasis on waiting for Him (3, 5, 21; indirectly, 15). To *wait* is to accept His time and therefore His wisdom; it marked the difference between David's and Saul's attitudes to God (1 Sa. 26.10f.; 13:8-14), and between Isaiah's and Israel's (Is. 30:15-18). The word for it in the psalm suggests a certain tenseness: the trust is eager, waiting in hope rather than resignation. This hope is unfulfilled at the close, but the waiting continues. Perhaps the psalm is thereby all the more relevant to those who are not granted the radiant assurance that breaks out in, *e.g.*, 6:8ff.; 20:6ff.; *etc. Cf.* the quiet encouragement of Isaiah 30:18; 64:4.

Psalm 26

Pure Devotion

An absorbed delight in the presence and house of God makes the core of this psalm (verses 6–8) a personal confession that shames our 'faint desires'. The surrounding verses point to the source of this joy, in the realm of choice rather than temperament: the costly choice of allegiance which has thrown David back on God's protection and made clear to him where his heart and treasure lie, and in what company he is supremely at home.

In each of Psalms 26–28 the Lord's house comes into view. In Psalm 26 the worshipper, as he approaches, is searched by God's demand for sincerity (*cf.* Pss. 15 and 24) and, in the last verse, rejoices to have found access. In Psalm 27 he sees this house as sanctuary from his enemies, and as the place of vision, face to face with God. In Psalm 28 he brings forward his petition, spreading his hands as a suppliant towards the holy of holies, and receives his answer.

26:1–3. Nothing to hide
In this opening, David's fellow men are not yet in the picture, though his defensiveness tells its own tale of them. With the cry 'Yahweh, be my judge!' (JB), he wisely appeals over the heads of friends and enemies alike. It is the secret of true independence, as Paul was to find in the slow current of opposition and intrigue: *cf.* 1 Corinthians 4:3–5. On the claim to be in the right, and on readiness to be judged, see on Psalm 5:4–6; note too that God Himself used the word *integrity* of David in 1 Kings 9:4. Its basic meaning is wholeness, usually in the sense of whole-heartedness or sincerity, rather than faultlessness. When David thought of his ways in detail, not merely of his over-all loyalty, his pleas to be searched and known became no longer a demand, as here (2), but a surrender (139:23f.).

The phrase, *without wavering* (1) is lit. 'I shall not (or, do not) slip', referring either to the outcome of his trust, as in AV, or more probably to its quality. Another expression with two possible meanings is *in faithfulness to thee* (3), lit. 'in thy truth' (AV, RV, NEB), since 'truth' in the Old Testament is largely faithfulness. But grammatically this is more easily taken to be God's than David's, and it would then match *thy stead-fast love*. Perhaps we can trace a meaningful shift of emphasis from '*my* integrity' in verse 1 to '*thy* faithfulness' here.

26:4, 5. Nothing in common
If these verses sound arrogant, we mistake them. These men are potential allies, potential enemies; and David has made his choice. Hating their *company* is not a matter of social preference but of spiritual alignment; 'company' here means congregation or party, a rival group to God's own. David's character and his kingdom were both at stake in this choice of associates, as is the character of any enterprise. In each of these two verses there is a decisive tense followed by an open one; a clear-cut attitude and a resolve to maintain it. *Cf.* NEB: 'I have not . . . nor do I . . .; I hate . . . and will not . . .'. See also on verse 11.

26:6–8. Into His courts
The dry precision of the law books blossoms into life with this glimpse of a singing procession round the altar in the open court. The scene is even more animated in, *e.g.*, 27:6; 42:4;

68:24ff. Between the altar and the tent stood the laver, where the priests washed their hands and feet before approaching either of them (Ex. 40:30–32); and David takes this to heart in the spirit of Psalm 24:4 (where see references).

7. For examples of a personal *song of thanksgiving*, which would accompany the sacrifice of Leviticus 7:12ff., see *e.g.* Psalm 40 or 116; and for corporate remembrance of God's miracles of salvation (*wondrous deeds*) see such psalms as 78, 105, *etc.* In both these ways the past lives on to enrich the present and give precision to one's praise.

8. *Love*, like the *hate* in verse 5, is fundamentally an expression of choice: this is where his heart is, not with the worldly. But the heart has warmed to the choice and to the company. The word *habitation* need not be changed to 'beauty' (NEB), which is the LXX reading of the Hebrew consonants in the reverse order. *Habitation* adds its emphasis to the phrase *where thy glory dwells*, in case we should miss the marvel of God's taking up residence among us. In the wilderness His *glory* had dwelt visibly on the tabernacle (Ex. 40:34ff.), and in Judaism the word for 'dwelling', *shekinah*, which is akin to *dwells* here, became a standard term for this. But John 1:14 announces the reality foreshadowed in the cloud and fire: 'the Word became flesh and dwelt'—note the term[1]—'among us . . . . ; we have beheld his glory, glory as of the only Son from the Father.'

26:9, 10. Men with no future

The picture behind the term for *sweep . . . away* is of gathering up what is to be thrown out, much as in the parable of the tares in Matthew 13:30. David is conscious that however strongly he has meant to reject the way of the wicked (4, 5), it is God's verdict on him that counts, and he must come to Him as a suppliant. It is left to the final stanza to sum the matter up.

26:11, 12. Love without fear

These two verses give a rounded view of a godly man's profession. Its first element is *integrity*, *i.e.*, whole-heartedness

---

[1] 'Dwelt', or 'tabernacled', probably contains an intentional allusion to the Tent of God in the wilderness; moreover the similarity between the Greek word *skēnē* (tent) and Heb. term Shekinah may well have influenced John's choice of verb.

(see on verse 1); and here David shows his will to persist on this path, by his change of tense from 'I have walked' (1) to 'I (will) walk' (*cf.* the last comment on verses 4, 5, above). This is loyalty, not self-righteousness, since the second element is deep humility (11b): a confession of inability to do without help (*redeem me*) and unfitness to claim it as of right (*be gracious*). The third element is assurance (12), for no-one pleads (11b), or trusts (1b), in vain. So the psalm which began defensively, much aware of the anti-church (see on verse 5), ends with praise and the joy of adding one's voice to those of multitudes of fellow believers (for *congregation* is in the plural here).

Psalm 27

My Light and my Salvation

This ardent, eloquent psalm enlarges on the themes it shares with its more subdued neighbours, Psalms 26 and 28: the Lord's protection, the joy of His house, and the singer's unquestioning loyalty and trust. See the second introductory paragraph to Psalm 26.

27:1-3. Whom shall I fear?

Light is a natural figure for almost everything that is positive, from truth and goodness to joy and vitality (*e.g.*, respectively, Ps. 43:3; Is. 5:20; Ps. 97:11; 36:9), to name but a few. Here it is the answer to *fear* (1, 3) and to the forces of evil. These are not underrated: the *stronghold*, or refuge, is a reminder that they may threaten one's very *life*. In verse 2 RSV has needlessly relegated to the margin the picture of the enemy as a pack of hunting animals; it also misses the emphatic *they* in the dénouement: 'it is they who stumble and fall' (NEB). In verse 3 we can get the feel of these threats by remembering David's desperate situation in 1 Samuel 23:26f., or Elisha's in 2 Kings 6:15. *Cf.* also Exodus 14:19f. (mg.), 24, where the Lord was both a light to walk by and an intangible barrier against the pursuer.

27:4-6. Sanctuary

As in the well-known 23:6, this is not an ambition to be a priest or Levite but to enjoy the constant presence of God which is typified by their calling. Note the singleness of purpose (*one thing*)—the best answer to distracting fears (*cf.* 1–3)—and the priorities within that purpose: *to behold* and *to inquire*; a preoccupation with God's Person and His will. It is the essence of worship; indeed of discipleship. It will be elaborated in verses 7–12.

The present verses ring the changes on the theme of the Lord's house, taking up various terms that one can use for a dwelling place. *Temple* (4) is the standard word for a divine or royal residence (*cf.* 45:15 (Heb. 16), 'palace') and need not imply that Solomon's Temple was already built. Either this word or *tent*, as the place of worship (6), is being used for its associations rather than its materials (see also on Ps. 5:7), for they cannot both be literal; note too the vivid terms of verse 5, where *shelter* should perhaps be 'lair' (the same word as the lion's 'covert' in 10:9; *cf.* also 76:2a (Heb. 3) with Am. 1:2; 3:8). The *tent* in this verse (5) speaks of the devoted protection that a guest would receive from his host, and the *rock* brings back memories of David's mountain fastnesses: see on 18:1–3. With the *tent* of worship in verse 6, and the exuberant thanksgiving, *cf.* 2 Samuel 6:14–17; Psalm 26:6–8.

27:7-12. Thy face . . . , Thy way
The triumphant scene just pictured is still to come; meanwhile there is little sign of God's favour or that of anyone else. David gets back to the 'one thing' he has set his heart on (*cf.* 4), and holds on to the fact that the first move, after all, has come from God. He will not ask for our love (8a) and then withhold His own (9a). The point of verse 10 is probably hypothetical (*cf.* AV, NEB, JB): not that both of David's parents have in fact disowned him, but that beyond their breaking-point the love of God would still persist; indeed that it begins where man's leaves off. *Cf.* 'Can a woman forget . . . ?' (Is. 49:15).

But David is not only a worshipper seeking God's *face* (8ff.); he is a pilgrim committed to His *way* (11), every step of it contested. He is very much in the world, and the prayer for a *level path* is not for comfort but for sure progress (as a moral term it implies what is right, or straight) when the merest slip would be exploited. The word for *enemies* (as in 5:8) may contain the idea of vigilance, according to a likely derivation; hence 'my watchful foes' (NEB); *cf.* Luke 11:54. In verse 12 *the will* might be rendered 'the appetite': it is the predatory picture of verse 2 (mg.) again.

27:13, 14. Believe and wait

While some of the psalms contain an answering oracle (see on 12:5, 6) or an outburst of praise which is evidence of such an answer, whether heard inwardly or outwardly (*cf.* 28:6f.), others show the psalmist holding on in naked faith, as we may have to do.

The Hebrew of verse 14 begins with an unrelated 'Unless', which the Jewish scribes marked as a doubtful reading (the ancient versions do not have it). If it is authentic, it could be leaving the sequel to the imagination: 'Unless I believed that I should see (*etc.*)—(how could I survive!)'. *Cf.* AV, RV; and see Exodus 32:32 for this construction. It does not materially affect the sense. In the final verse the psalmist may be addressing anyone undergoing such a trial, or may be speaking to himself, as in, *e.g.*, 42:5, *etc.*, to stiffen his resolve (the *your* is singular, as are the verbs, unlike those of 31:24, where see comment); or this may even be the Lord's answering oracle. Whichever it is, the suppliant has no more to go on than the assurance that God is worth waiting for. But that is enough.

Psalm 28

The Suppliant Answered

In this psalm, which seems to be the third of a small group (see the second introductory paragraph to Ps. 26), the fear of being reckoned with the wicked and cast away, perhaps by a premature death, is very strong. But the answer is clear, and the singer takes courage to ask a similar deliverance for the people as a whole.

28:1, 2. The suppliant

The situation is probably illness or deep despair, and the fear is not a dread of death as such, but of death with unmerited disgrace. *The Pit* is sometimes a mere synonym for Sheol (on which, see on 6:5), but may also suggest the deepest confines of it, like a dungeon for the worst offenders (*cf.* Is. 14:15, 19; Ezk. 32:27 with, *e.g.*, 29f.).

2. The uplifted hands can be expressive of prayer in many moods: here as beseeching a favour, empty handed; in 63:4 as reaching out towards God Himself; in Exodus 17:9ff. as interceding, calling down the power of heaven on others. See also 1 Timothy 2:8. The word for the innermost sanctuary is *dᵉbîr* (mistranslated as 'oracle' in AV, RV), a name which first appears, apart from here, in accounts of Solomon's Temple. This need not mean that the psalm is later than David; only that the word had become the standard term for the ark's abode by Solomon's time, which suggests that it was in use well before this.

28:3–5. Justice!

Even worse than consignment to the will of the wicked, which was the fear of 27:12, is consignment *with* them to the disgrace they have earned. This was the miscarriage of justice feared in 26:9f., and while the figure there depicts a clearing away of rubbish, here it suggests the dragging of prisoners away to punishment. Nothing stings so sharply as injustice, and nothing should; so these verses are not simply vindictive, but put into words the protest of any healthy conscience at the wrongs of the present order, and the conviction that a day of judgment is a moral necessity. It is in this sense that God's elect 'cry to him day and night', and find His wrath already kindled (Lk. 18:7). See also on Psalm 10, and on 7:6–16. More fully, see Introduction, v, pp. 25–32.

28:6, 7. The suppliant heard

On the assurance of God's answer, see on 12:5, 6. The pictures of His saving power, both active (*strength . . . shepherd*) and defensive (*shield . . . refuge*), come in profusion now (6–9), enriching the praise; but the solitary metaphor in verse 1, 'my rock', perhaps outbids them all, as the urgent cry of faith under trial. Verse 7 may look back to this, if we take the tenses strictly: 'my heart trusted in him, and I shall be helped; and my heart exulted, and with my song I shall praise him.'

28:8, 9. The blessing shared

David now builds on the fact that he is more than a private citizen. As the Lord's *anointed* (a term which grew into the word Messiah) he stood for his people, and God's grace must be meant for them as well. (It was a principle that would be fully worked out in the New Testament: *e.g.* Eph. 1:3ff.) There is a small textual difficulty in verse 8, where the Hebrew has 'of them' (*cf.* AV) instead of *of his people*, through the apparent omission of one letter. The ancient versions support RSV, *etc.*, and in any case verse 9 (*thy people*) makes matters clear. This final prayer has been taken into the Te Deum, where familiarity may dull the paradox of the term *thy heritage* (for it is wonderful that God should count us His most valuable possession) and where the translation 'govern them' loses the rich content of the Hebrew '*shepherd* them', with its companion verb *carry* or sustain them, as in Isaiah 63:9. *Cf.* Isaiah 40:11, and the variations on the theme of carrying, in Isaiah 46:1-7.

Psalm 29

The King above the Storm

The towering majesty of the Lord dominates this poem, with the opening scene in heaven, where supernatural beings pay Him homage; with the violent sweep of the thunderstorm in from the sea, down the whole length of Canaan and away into the desert; and the serene climax in which, as the thunder recedes, the Lord appears enthroned in judgment over His world but in blessing among His people.

The insistent repetitions have the flavour of some of the earliest Hebrew poetry, *e.g.* the Song of the Sea (Ex. 15), the oracles of Balaam (Nu. 23 and 24) and the Song of Deborah (Jdg. 5). Early Canaanite poetry was similar in this respect.[1] Whether David was building the psalm out of an ancient fragment, or turning to a style that would recall the old battle-hymns of God's salvation,[2] the primitive vigour of the verse, with its eighteen reiterations of the name Yahweh (the Lord), wonderfully matches the theme, while the structure of the poem averts the danger of monotony by its movement from

[1] *Cf.* W. F. Albright, *Yahweh and the Gods of Canaan* (Athlone Press, 1968), pp. 4-25.
[2] The LXX adds to the psalm's title an allusion to its own translation of Lv. 23:36, indicating that it was used at the Feast of Tabernacles, which commemorated the journey through the wilderness. But it is now a psalm for Pentecost, and may well have been so used in New Testament times (see on verse 7, below). The Talmud prescribes it for this feast (Sopherim 18:3).

heaven to earth, by the path of the storm and by the final transition from nature in uproar to the people of God in peace.

29:1, 2. Homage in heaven

The *heavenly beings* are 'sons of *'ēlîm*'.[1] Probably this is not a challenge to the false gods as in 97:7, but (to judge from 89:5–7, where the term used here appears again) a summons to the angels. These two verses are quoted in 96:7f., but addressed there to humanity at large. Both of the main notes of true adoration are heard here in the words *ascribe* (or 'give') and *worship* (or 'bow down'), for the former enlists the mind—indeed 'hearts and hands and voices'—to declare the greatness of God, while the latter enlists the will to take the humble attitude of a servant. Note the words *glory* and *holy* in the angelic worship, the very theme of the seraphim's praise in Isaiah 6:3, where 'holy' speaks of what God is, and 'glory' of all that proceeds from Him. His glory as Creator fills the whole earth, as the seraphim sang, but *the glory of his name* is the explicit revelation of *who* He is, given to His servants in His words and works. True worship reflects this back to Him in love and wonder. *Holy array* is a perfectly possible translation of an expression which is literally 'the splendour of holiness' (NEB; *cf.* AV. RV).[2] It is found also in 96:9; 110:3 (mg.); 1 Chronicles 16:29; 2 Chronicles 20:21; and while it could be translated either way in all these places, the last of them tips the balance towards the 'literal' sense, understood as speaking of *God's* holiness rather than man's.[3] Here, then, we

---

[1] *'ēlîm* is the plural of *'ēl*, which is a synonym of *'elōhîm*, God. On *'elōhîm* as 'angels', see on 8:5, 6. In one composite expression *'ēl* means 'power' (Gn. 31:29; Dt. 28:32, *etc.*); hence AV, RV hazard 'the mighty'. Some MSS have an additional consonant, whereby the LXX and Vulg. understood the word as 'rams' (*cf.* PBV 'bring young rams'). But the corresponding passage, Ps. 96:7f., implies that *'ēlîm* here, like the 'families' there, are the worshippers, not the offerings.

[2] JB and Gelineau read 'his sacred court', following LXX, Vulg. But this variant reading breaks down at 2 Ch. 20:21, where LXX, Vulg. diverge from one another and from MT. More precariously still, Weiser (*cf.* Dahood) has 'when he appears in his sanctuary'. This is based on Ugaritic *hdrt*, 'dream' = ? 'vision' = ? 'theophany'—a long linguistic chain with more than one weak link.

[3] In 2 Ch. 20:21 the construction 'giving praise to the splendour of holiness' corresponds to 'give praise to the Lord', two verses earlier. Hence NEB there: 'praise the splendour of his holiness.'

should probably understand the line to mean 'Worship the Lord for[1] the splendour of (his) holiness'.

29:3-9. The path of the storm

The voice of the Lord is interpreted at once as the thunder (3); but it is emphasized as His, proclaiming its Creator's power, not merely Nature's. Out to sea, above the roar of the waves, these peals of thunder celebrate the Lord as Sovereign and Judge, as verse 10 will confirm, dominating the very element that seems the most unruly (*cf.* 93:3f.). Then as the storm bears down on the land it reveals its range as well as its force, sweeping from *Lebanon* and *Sirion* (mount Hermon: Dt. 3:9) in the far north, down to *Kadesh* (8) in the remote south, where Israel had lingered in the wilderness with Moses. With verses 5 and 6 compare Isaiah 2:12ff., which foresees the Day of the Lord when *cedars* and mountains, with everything that man finds impressive, will finally be brought low. While every display of God's power carries a reminder of this final judgment, in the psalm the dominant mood is exhilaration, voiced in the shout of acclaim in verse 9c.

In this run of verses there are some open questions of translation. *Flashes forth* (7) is lit. 'hews out', for which (or for a similar verb) LXX has 'divides' (*cf.* AV, RV). The allusion is to lightning, perhaps by analogy with the sparks that one may hew, so to speak, out of flint; or perhaps as a picture of forked ('divided') lightning.[2] It may be worth noting, in passing, the conjunction of fire, mighty wind and (in a very different form) the voice of the Lord, on the day of Pentecost (Acts 2:1–4), the feast for which the Talmud appoints this psalm (*cf.* footnote 2, p. 124). In verses 8 and 9 the words *shakes . . . shakes . . . whirl* are related, being parts of a verb which basically depicts a writhing or gyrating, either in travail or in dance: it gives a vivid picture of desert dust-storms and thrashing forests. In 9a the RSV (*cf.* JB, Gelineau) modifies the traditional vowels (which were not written in the original text) to read *oaks* instead of 'hinds'. This avoids the bewildering leap from the tremendous to the obscure and unrepresentative, which will

---

[1] The preposition is the same as in Ps. 150:1, 2a, where see comment.
[2] Dahood sees an instrumental accusative here, *i.e.*, 'cleaves (the cedars) with shafts of fire'. But this construction is attested in Ugaritic rather than biblical Hebrew, and would require verse 7 to follow hard on verse 5.

be familiar to those who have sung this psalm unprepared and somewhat mystified. Further, to bring 'kids early to birth' (NEB) may be a conceivable if tortuous translation of 9b[1], but it is hardly the crowning achievement of a storm of this magnitude. The plain rendering, *and strips the forest bare*, worthily continues the crescendo, with no hint of bathos.

The climax is the answering cry of *'Glory!'*, a response of humility, joy and understanding which reveals that, to some, the storm is not an outbreak of meaningless or hostile forces, but the voice of the Lord, heard in all His works. The Hebrew (if the text is accurate) goes even further, in that *all* is lit. 'all of it', *i.e.* everything in the temple. Some commentators refer this to the heavenly sanctuary; but the earthly one, as its 'copy and shadow' (Heb. 8:5), fulfilled the same purpose, expressing by its very pattern and ordinances the holiness and glory of God, more explicitly than the most impressive displays of power. And what was true of the material shrine is, still more, what God requires of His living temples, corporate and individual (1 Cor. 3:16f.; 6:19): that every part of such a sanctuary should cry, 'Glory!'

29:10, 11. Salvation on earth
The word for *flood* is significant, for it is found elsewhere only in Genesis 6–11, and only of Noah's flood. Here was the supreme example of natural forces purposefully unleashed. The tenses of verse 10 emphasize the decisiveness of it: 'Yahweh sat enthroned for the Flood, Yahweh sits enthoned . . . for ever' (JB; *cf.* RV, Gelineau).[2] The final verse can be taken, with RSV, as a prayer, but it is more likely to be a simple future: 'the Lord will give . . . , the Lord will bless.' So the psalm ends by showing God's power not as naked force but as the instrument of judgment (the Flood, 10) and salvation. Delitzsch puts it finely in the comment: 'This closing word *with peace* is like a rainbow arch over the Psalm. The beginning of the Psalm shows us heaven open . . . ; while its close shows us His victorious people upon earth, blessed with peace in the midst of the terrible utterance of His wrath. *Gloria in excelsis* is the beginning, and *in terra pax* the close.'

[1] *Cf.* G. R. Driver, *JTS* 32 (1931), p. 255.
[2] See S. R. Driver, *Hebrew Tenses* (Clarendon, 1892), p. 91.

Psalm 30
Mourning into Dancing

The title makes this psalm 'a Song at the dedication of the House', which was taken to mean God's House, but which RV margin interprets as David's own (2 Sa. 5:11). Either of these is possible (*cf.* the dancing in verse 11 with 2 Sa. 6:9, 14, and see the comment on Ps. 5:7), and in either case David has at last emerged from his early trials into happier days. Yet without this title the psalm would have suggested simply recovery from sickness; and this lends some colour to the theory that certain phrases in the titles should be read as postscripts to the psalms they follow (see *e.g.* 29:1, 2, 9c; but less appropriately 3–9b). *Cf.* Introduction VI. *c.* 3, p. 39.

The structure of the psalm is simple, its two outbursts of praise flanking the confession in verses 6–10 of over-confidence and its dire results. David's unaffected delight at being restored shines through every word, quite undimmed by time.

30:1–5. The rescue

The vividness of *thou hast drawn me up* is quite accurate: it is the word for pulling up a bucket from a well. That well was as deep as death (on *Sheol*, see on 6:5), and the threat had come from sickness (2b) rather than war. But in his plight David was spirited enough to be troubled most of all about leaving the enemy the last laugh (1b)—very much as Hezekiah, later, would be tantalized to see his hopes and enterprises apparently stillborn (2 Ki. 19:3). *Cf.* the positive concern of Paul in Acts 20:24, and its fulfilment in 2 Timothy 4:7.

5. This comparison,[1] marvellously expressed here, is carried even further in the New Testament, in the concept of sorrow *producing* joy (2 Cor. 4:17; Jn. 16:20–22; but *cf.* also Ps. 126:6f.) and in the contrast between the momentary and the eternal (not merely the lifelong), and between troubles that 'weigh little' and a 'weight of . . . glory which is out of all proportion to them' (2 Cor. 4:17, JB). The word for *tarry*, in

---

[1] NEB follows LXX, Vulg., Syr., which evidently read *rōḡez*, 'agitation', 'rage', for MT *reḡaʿ*, 'moment'. But MT says more, and accords better with the second half of the verse.

our verse, suggests by itself the overnight visitor; the line could be crudely translated 'At evening, weeping may arrive for the night . . .'.

30:6–10. The foolish boast

Easy circumstances and a careless outlook are seldom far apart when this Hebrew root is used for *prosperity*. *Cf.*, *e.g.*, the heedlessness in Jeremiah 22:21 and the fatal complacency in Proverbs 1:32. But the next verse in Proverbs shows the difference between the careless and the truly carefree.

7. The *strong mountain* is more accurately expressed in RV: 'Thou . . . hadst made my mountain to stand strong' (The NEB's emendation is quite unnecessary.) This striking metaphor for David's kingdom or his personal fortunes, as long as God sustained him, makes a telling contrast to the flower-like frailty (7b) of his own resources; and Psalm 104:29 applies 7b to all living things.

9, 10. *Profit* is a sharply commercial word here, and the argument is—for the moment—quite down-to-earth: 'You will gain nothing, and lose a worshipper!' The strength of this, allowing for its limited horizon, bounded by death (see on 6:5), is that it starts from God's interests, asking the question, 'What glory will God have from this?' This is the right question, though the answer is not for us to give: *cf.* John 12:27f. Then, in verse 10, argument is dropped, and David is simply a man in need, with only grace to appeal to.

30:11, 12. The celebration

The exuberance of verses 1–5 returns, enhanced by the chastened recollections of 6–10. It is all quite uninhibited, in the buoyant spirit of the David who 'danced before the Lord with all his might'. The same David, incidentally, could also show his intensity of joy by stillness: *cf.* 2 Samuel 6:14 with 7:18.

12. *My soul* is lit. 'glory' in the Hebrew text and in LXX; *cf.* 7:5 (Heb. 6); 16:9; 57:8 (Heb. 9); 108:1 (Heb. 2); in at least some of which places 'soul' or 'spirit' is evidently meant.[1] So the praise, which has the effervescence of dancing, has also depth to it, and persistence. More persistence, perhaps, than David himself could guess when he included the word *for ever*.

---

[1] Older commentators saw an allusion to man's highest powers, or to God's image. More recent ones infer an original *kābēd*, 'liver' (for *kābôd*, 'glory'), roughly corresponding to our term 'heart'. In Gn. 49:6, but not elsewhere, LXX has 'liver'. On such imagery see footnote to 16:7.

Psalm 31

Stress

This psalm impressed itself on more than one biblical character
deeply enough to come to mind at moments of supreme crisis.
Jonah's prayer draws upon it (6); Jeremiah was haunted by
a phrase from verse 13; verse 5 gave words to Jesus for His
last utterance on the cross. And in old age the writer of Psalm
71, possibly David himself, opened his prayer with the substance of verses 1-3. It illustrates the role of the Psalms in
meeting a great variety of human needs beyond the bounds of
formal worship and the original experiences of the authors.

An unusual feature of this psalm is that it makes the journey
twice over from anguish to assurance: first in 1-8 and again
in 9-24. It is hard to say whether this points to a renewed
onslaught, when 'the clouds return after the rain' (a common
enough spiritual experience), or whether the crisis of the opening verses is recalled, to be explored a second time in greater
depth. The headings suggested for the two sections leave the
question open.

31:1-8. The hunted man
  1-6. His prayer of faith. As in Psalm 18,[1] David finds
strength in remembering his early adventures and escapes, and
the reality behind the physical strongholds of those days. He
also knows that defensive strength is not enough: the right
initiatives are as vital as the right refuge: see the terms of
3b, 4a. Note the good grounds of his appeal: not his per-
suasiveness but God's *righteousness* (2), *i.e.*, God's concern to
see justice done; not so much the thought of his own good
name (*put to shame*, 1) as that of God's (3b; *cf.* 23:3); not merely
that he is innocent but that he is *redeemed* (5), and his trust is
in the only real God (6).[2] It may be significant that when the
Redeemer quoted verse 5 in His dying words He stopped short

---

[1] See note on 18:1-3, where the word for *fortress* and the two words for
rock (in reverse order) are the same as in our verses 2 and 3.
[2] Jonah 2:8 echoes 6a's description of idolaters, with their earnest futility.
In the MT our verse opens with 'I hate' (RV); but *Thou hatest* is supported
by the ancient versions and by the fact that in 6b the Heb. for *but I* is
emphatic, as if to introduce a new subject, not only a new verb.

of its second line; yet in the Old Testament the word 'redeem' (*pāḏâ*) is seldom used of atonement: it mostly means to rescue or ransom out of trouble (*e.g.* Pss. 25:22; 26:11; 44:26 (Heb. 27); 55:18 (Heb. 19); 69:18; 78:42), and only once unequivocally to 'pay the price of sin' (130:8). But see also on 34:22; 49:7, 15. The primary meaning here is either that deliverance is as certain as if it had already happened (hence the perfect tense), or that past deliverances impel David now to this act of self-committal.

7, 8. His praise. The terms for God's attitude and action in these two verses are worth pondering, together with the similar and fuller sequence in Exodus 3:7, 8. *Taken heed* is literally 'known', and *delivered* has a certain flavour of handing over into custody, which enhances the sense of liberty in 8b. This is brought out too in the contrast between the straits or pressures (the root idea of *adversities*) of verse 7 and the *broad place* of 8; *cf.* on Psalm 18:19, and see 119:32. The thought of being hemmed in recurs in 9a and especially 21b.

31:9-24. The rejected man
9-13. His isolation. The deepening demoralization of the victim, from gloom to hopelessness (12) and terror (13), shows how murderous is the impact of hatred, especially when it takes the form of rejection. In Psalm 6, which has the same rare word for *waste away*, and the same helpless grief, the root cause of the depression is left unspecified. Here it is partly guilt, according to the Hebrew text of verse 10, where *misery* should read 'iniquity' (RSV mg.); but it is man, not God, who is determined to condemn, as verses 14ff. make clear. Jeremiah knew this cruel encirclement, and borrowed the phrase *terror on every side* as a motto theme (Je. 6:25; 20:3, 10; 46:5; 49:29; *cf.* La. 2:22).

14-18. His prayer of faith. In verse 14, *I* and *thee* are emphatic (much as in 6b), as David wrests the initiative from his enemies and deliberately turns in a new direction. His prayer is all the more effective for making statements before launching into petitions, for the assertions of 14, 15a give God His true place as sovereign, and David his secure relationship of intimacy (*my God*) and dependence (*in thy hand*). The very expression *my time* (15) which faces the necessary fact of transience and change, both in one's own being and in one's surroundings, makes adversity easier to accept; while the knowledge that change is not chance (*thy hand*) can make the acceptance positive and personal. 'He (the Lord) will be the stability of your times' (Is. 33:6; *cf.* Ps. 32:6). So the prayer of committal in verse 5, 'into thy hand . . .', now reveals its practical implications. See also the comment on verses 19-24.

16. David is seeking for himself (as he did for his companions in 4:6) the familiar blessing of Numbers 6:25, now highly relevant to the dark looks or averted faces (11) which he meets on every side. *Cf.* 84:9, 11; 123:1-4.

17. NEB 'sink into Sheol' follows LXX, but the pregnant Hebrew (lit. 'be silent into Sheol') can well be translated as in RSV or JB. It is the silencing of the slanderers that David chiefly wants, as the next verse shows. On *Sheol*, see on 6:5.

19-24. His final act of praise. Each of the three pairs of verses has its own theme: the first, God's care for His own (19, 20); the second, a personal experience of it (21, 22); finally, a general call to loving trust (23, 24). Across these boundaries, verses 19 and 24 share an emphasis on biding God's time, by the mention of *goodness . . . laid up* (19), *i.e.* treasured up (a satisfying answer to our impatience) and by the encouragement to those who *wait* (24; *cf.* 15a and Is. 40:31).

19, 20. The various terms for taking cover, a metaphor natural to a former fugitive and outlaw, recall verses 1-4; see comments there.

22. *In my alarm* (or 'panic') . . .: another such cry (introduced by the same phrase) is found in 116:11, despairing now of human friendship, with as little cause as here. It underlines the need to wait (24), as pointed out at the beginning of this section (19-24), but also the need to judge by what we securely know, rather than by what we feel. What I say 'in my prosperity' (30:6) can be equally adrift. Some more fruitful declarations can be found at 16:2; 32:5; 91:2.

23. *His saints*, here, are those who are in covenant with Him and are true to it: the word is akin to *his steadfast love* in verse 21. See further on 18:25.

24. *Let your heart take courage* could equally be translated 'he shall strengthen your heart', as in AV. The latter seems the more meaningful: an assurance of help to those who dare to count on it, rather than a double exhortation. But in either case it does not promise an end to trouble: rather (*cf.* Lk. 22:42, 43) the strength to meet it.

Psalm 32
Joy of Forgiveness

To be in close accord with God is true happiness: this is the constant theme of the psalm, expressed now positively, in the opening and the close, and now negatively, in the memory of lost fellowship, in the gentle mockery of the stubborn (who should take a look at the trappings of a mule), and in the reminder of the perils (6) and pangs (10) which are the lot of those who choose to walk alone.

This is the second of the so-called 'penitential psalms', listed at Psalm 6.

32:1, 2. Sin forgiven

'Happy', a more exuberant word than *Blessed*, is the proper opening to both these beatitudes (see on Ps. 1:1). In case we over-press any one metaphor for atonement, two distinct pictures occupy verse 1: lifting or removing (*forgiven*), and concealing from sight (*covered*). The first of these corrects any idea that 'covered' means hiding what is still present and unresolved (a notion which the same verb alludes to in 5a, 'hide').

2. Leaving figures of speech aside, we now learn of being reckoned righteous and of practising the truth. Romans 4:6–8 quotes this to show that the important word *imputes* (or 'reckons') implies that, when God treats us as righteous, it is His gift to us apart from our deserts; and the rest of that chapter uses the context of this same word in Genesis 15:6 to teach that the gift is received by faith alone. Any idea, however, that we are free to 'continue in sin that grace may abound' is firmly excluded by the emphasis on sincerity at the close of our verse.

32:3–5. The deadlock broken

Even human estrangements can produce this deep unrest of mind and body—and still be doggedly kept up. If David's symptoms are exceptional, his stubbornness is common enough. Yet the relief of climbing down, and the grace which meets it

(5), altogether outweigh the cost. These verses may possibly throw incidental light on the malaise mentioned in 1 Corinthians 11:30, which may be a judgment that operates, as here, through the very tensions that are created in a Christian by his disobedience.

32:6f, 7. The timely haven

The connection with what has gone before is obscured by the emendation of verse 6b in most modern versions, to read *at a time of distress*. The Hebrew (supported by LXX, Vulg., *etc.*) has 'at a time of finding', *i.e.* 'at a time when thou mayest be found' (AV, RV), very much as in Isaiah 55:6, where it is again a question of turning to God from sin while the opportunity remains. There it stresses the day of grace, but here the day of danger, pictured in terms which inspired Charles Wesley's lines:

> 'While the nearer waters roll,
>   While the tempest still is high;
>   Hide me, O my Saviour, hide . . .'[1]

The main difficulty which the emendation would remove is the conjunction *raq* before the mention of the waters, since this usually means 'only' or 'yet'. But there are other places, notably Deuteronomy 4:6, where it has the sense of 'surely', which is appropriate here (*cf.* AV, RV). So the verse will run, '. . . prayer to thee at a time when thou mayest be found. Surely when the great waters are in flood they shall not reach him.'

7. David's first impulse was to share his discovery (6). Now he turns his face again to God, yet even so he seems aware of an encircling company of exultant fellow-worshippers—for there is no need to relegate the *shouts* (or loud songs) of deliverance to the RSV margin: they are securely in the Hebrew text.[2]

32:8, 9. The lesson to be learnt

This is the Lord's reply to David (see on 12:5, 6), and through him to the rest of us, since the command of verse 9 is in the

---

[1] Charles Wesley, 'Jesu, Lover of my soul'.
[2] LXX and Vulg. also read this word, although they vocalized it differently as 'my rejoicing'. The case for rejecting the word rests only on its rarity, coupled with the conjecture that its consonants were copied by dittography from the end of the previous word.

plural. Coming where it does, its call for a teachable spirit
drives home the lesson of verses 1–5 in a positive form. If
forgiveness is good, fellowship is better; if we have experienced
God's heavy hand (4), we should appreciate and seek His
gentler touch. But the well-known rendering in AV, 'I will
guide thee with mine eye', which suggests our responsiveness
to His glance, is not accurate, although there is a similar
thought in 123:2, where the servant watches for the master's
signal. The point here is God's vigilance and intimate care,
. . . *with my eye upon you*; our response is in verse 9.

9. This vivid picture brings out, by its contrasts, the emphasis
in verse 8 on intelligent co-operation, which God has set His
heart on eliciting from us (*cf.* Jn. 15:15); for whatever else
one can do with a horse one can hardly *counsel* it (8), or control
it without bringing pressure on it. Jeremiah 8:6 uses it to
picture a more forceful waywardness than that of the proverbial sheep: 'Every one turns to his own course, like a horse
plunging headlong into battle.' But the exact point of verse
9c is elusive. Lit. 'not to come near you', it has been taken to
mean either '(Else) they will not come near . . .' (RV) or 'That
they come not near' (RV mg.). The former is the more intelligible, though it is doubtful whether RSV *else it will not keep with
you* can rightly be extracted from it.[1]

32:10, 11. The only happiness
The opening statement has many parallels in the Old Testament, but here it is something of a testimony, in view of verses
3 and 4. But so too is the rest of verse 10, with its use of the
word *surrounds*, which is the same verb as verse 7's 'encompass'
(*cf.* NEB, 'enfold' . . . 'enfolds'). Finally, verse 11 echoes the
same promise of verse 7 by its call to *shout for joy*, expressing
in worship the 'shouts of deliverance' (7; see note) which the
psalmist had already anticipated, in faith, in the time of
trouble.

---

[1] The real difficulty is that neither sense seems to fit the theme of verse 8
or the chief use of bit and bridle. NEB omits the phrase as a marginal gloss.
To judge from its similarity to, *e.g*, 6c ('they shall not reach him'), it seems
just possible that the phrase 'not to come near you' is the surviving half of
a line which promised protection from trouble, and originally belonged
to that section of the psalm.

Psalm 33
Maker and Monarch

If the purest form of a hymn is praise to God for what **He is** and does, this is a fine example. The body of the psalm is occupied with the Lord as Creator, Sovereign, Judge and Saviour, while the beginning and end express two elements of worship: an offering of praise, doing honour to so great a King, and a declaration of trust, made in humble expectation.

33:1–3. Rejoice in the Lord

The opening call takes up the note on which the previous psalm ended. *Rejoice* is from the same root as 'shouts of deliverance' and 'shout for joy' (32:7 mg., 11), though 'Sing aloud' might be a better term, leaving the *loud shouts* of homage ('the shout of a king', Nu. 23:21) to verse 3. Note the call in that verse for freshness and skill as well as fervour; three qualities rarely found together in religious music. In due course the quiet close of the psalm will make the further point that jubilance is not the only mood in worship.

33:4–9. His creative word

His *word* and His *work* (4) are inseparable, for His words are never empty. This is the reason for the outburst of praise, above. To know that nothing came into existence but by God's command (6, 9) is to be confronted with pure creation, not iron necessity, since God acted in freedom; but confronted also with a *universe*, the work of a single, self-consistent mind. This is liberating (1–3) and humbling (8); it is also an invitation to research (111:2); but above all, the wealth of moral terms here (4, 5) makes it clear that God is far more to us than Maker. The remarkable verse 5b goes even further than Isaiah's vision of a world full of God's glory. Like Exodus 33:18, 19, it prepares us to see His glory in terms of goodness; and this goodness embraces all His works (*cf.* 145:9). It is the secret of the psalmists' enthusiasm for the created world, an enthusiasm which is increased rather than diminished by their sense of its smallness in comparison with Him (see the bold similes of verse 7,[1] and *cf.*, *e.g.*, 104:1-9; Is. 40:12), whose mastery of it is effortless.

33:10-12. His triumphant will

To speak of nature's obedient glory is to be reminded of man's blatant defiance. It is not denied or minimized here, but it is looked at in the revealing context of *for ever* (11). The standpoint of these verses is taken up and worked out at length in Isaiah 40ff. (which is the best commentary on them), where *peoples* and their *counsel* come to naught or serve God's purpose unawares (*e.g.* Is. 44:25ff.; 45:4f.), and where God's *chosen* (12) are shown the searching implications of their call (Is. 41:8ff.; 42:1; *etc.*).

33:13-19. His discerning gaze

Judgment and salvation now come into view, since God's rule, for all its formidable power, is no tyranny. It is based on perfect knowledge (13-15), perfect control (16f.), perfect love (18f.).

13-15. The insistent repetition of *all ... all ... all*, in these verses, is important for its implied contrast to the narrow basis of human judgments, with their local bias (as against 13, 14), their ignorance of what is in man (15a), and their factual uncertainties (15b). The *all* in 15a is the Hebrew word for 'together'; hence 'alike' (AV), 'all ... alike' (NEB); asserting not their uniformity but God's equal insight into all.

16, 17. Like the repeated 'all' in 13-15, the series *great ... great ... great* sets the keynote of these verses and prepares for the contrasted truth of 18 and 19. It is a familiar enough biblical assertion, but it denies a basic axiom of secular thought, epitomized in Voltaire's gibe: 'They say that God is always for the big battalions.' The place of these verses in the paragraph is to emphasize that God is not only all-discerning (13-15) but all-prevailing. Even now, in a corrupt world, force has not the last word. Where it does succeed, the Old Testament assures us that this is by divine decree, not by its own ability (*e.g.* Is. 10:15; Je. 27:5f.).

18, 19. Even the relentless scrutiny in verses 13-15 was an implied blessing in a world of injustice; here it is manifestly

---

[1] *Bottle*, or wineskin (*nō'd*), seems more suited to a creation context than MT's 'heap' (*nēd*; so AV, RV), which alludes elsewhere to the exodus. The ancient versions understood the consonants to mean 'bottle'.

'quick-eyed love', alert to danger (19a), sensitive to need (19b). The same watchful care was seen in 32:8, and it is a favourite and expressive metaphor elsewhere: *cf.* Deuteronomy 11:12; 1 Kings 8:29; 2 Chronicles 16:9.

33:20–22. We hope in thee

This is hope in its sure al finm patient (20a), confident (20b), buoyant (21a), informed (21b; the *name* of God means His revealed character: see Ex. 34:5–7); above all, focused not on the gift (though there is a place for this: *cf.* Rom. 8:18–25) but on the Giver. Such hope 'will never disappoint us' (Rom. 5:5, Phillips).

Psalm 34
Thank God!

This glowing psalm (whose darker companion-piece and prelude is Ps. 56) has all the marks of relief and gratitude for a miraculous escape. The title identifies the occasion as that of 1 Samuel 21:10ff. which had threatened to cost David his life. Other psalms that are linked with named events in his career are listed in the opening comment on Psalm 3.

It is an acrostic, its verses (all but the last) beginning with the successive letters of the Hebrew alphabet with the exception of *waw* (unless 6b in the MT supplies this). Such a scheme is simple to execute, and allows a free movement from theme to theme without an undue loss of coherence. It is no fetter to the poet's spontaneity, as the psalm itself bears witness with its lively, persuasive invitation to share the singer's joy and learn from his experience.

A substantial quotation and some distinct further echoes of the psalm in 1 Peter 2 and 3 (and in other Epistles) illustrate the indebtedness of every generation to this psalm. One of its best-known legacies is the hymn 'Through all the changing scenes of life'.

34:1–10. Rejoice with me!

The first half of the psalm alternates between personal testimony (1–2a, 4, 6) and repeated calls to join in the praise and be stimulated to fresh faith. On this sharing of a blessing see on 22:22ff.

1. The phrase, *at all times*, more exactly 'at every time', gains extra point from David's recent ordeal and its outcome (see the title and opening comments); a fresh proof to him that 'my times', however desperate, 'are in thy hand' (see on 31:15). The New Testament is still more explicit: 'Give thanks whatever happens' (1 Thes. 5:18, NEB; *cf.* Rom. 8:28, 37).

2, 3. *The afflicted* should rather be 'the humble', as in most translations. The positive side of this humility is selfless enthusiasm (*boast . . . magnify . . . exalt his name*): pure joy in Another's triumph, however poor one's own showing. Paul, in his great passage on boasting, may have remembered this saying and this episode, and so recalled his own ignominious escape from another foreign king (2 Cor. 11:30–33), and the lessons he had learnt in such straits.

4, 5. If the sequence in verses 2 and 3 was in essence 'I have reason to praise Him; join me', here it is 'This was my experience; it can be yours'.[1]

Fears, here, is a strong word akin to the 'terror' of 31:13, not the reverential fear of verses 7 and 9. It could mean either the events that are dreaded (*cf.* Pr. 10:24) or the dread itself. Probably it is the latter here, since the former are covered by the 'troubles' of verse 6, while the blessing that is shared in verse 5, flowing out of the present verse, is a change of attitude, not merely of circumstances. A celebrated statement of such release from fear, in spite of danger, is in 23:4. *Radiant* is a word found again in Isaiah 60:5, where it describes a mother's face lighting up at the sight of her children, long given up for lost. Using other terms, Exodus 34:29 tells of Moses' face shining as he came down from the mountain, and 2 Corinthians 3:18 relates this to a Christian's growing likeness to his Lord. In other words, radiance is delight but also glory: a transformation of the whole person.

6–10. The personal testimony (6) is now clearly about material deliverance; and the lesson drawn from it is on the same plane (7–10): 'God rescued me; you too are safe in His hands.'

6. NEB captures the form and spirit of this: 'Here was a

---

[1] The MT of verse 5 is 'They looked . . .', *etc.*, as in AV, RV; *i.e.* (in JB's paraphrase) 'Every face turned to him grows brighter'. The imperatives, 'Look . . .', *etc.*, have some ancient support, and apply the lesson more directly; but it is the same lesson.

poor wretch who cried to the Lord ... .' To get the force of David's words one has only to recall his peril and his abject clowning to save his life (see the title). On the word *troubles*, see on 4:1 ('distress').

7. *The angel of the Lord* is regularly a term for God Himself come down to earth (*cf.*, *e.g.*, Gn. 16:7ff., 13; *etc.*). Kirkpatrick suggests that 'perhaps, since he is "the captain of Jehovah's host" (Jos. 5:14), he is to be thought of as surrounding them with the angelic legions at his command'. Elisha may have based his certainty that 'those who are with us are more than those who are with them', on this promise by itself, when he asked that his servant might have visual proof of it (2 Ki. 6:15ff.).

8. If Elisha's servant (see above) saw and believed, it is a happier thing to believe God first and let the confirmation follow (Jn. 20:29). Both Hebrews 6:5 and 1 Peter 2:3 use this verse to describe the first venture into faith, and to urge that the tasting should be more than a casual sampling.

9, 10. Defence and supplies were David's pressing needs in 1 Samuel 21, the background to the psalm. He turns from the first of these (7f.) to the second, with the same faith as he shows in 23:1, repeating the word '*want/lack*' in 9b, 10b not only to emphasize the point by its contrast to 10a[1] (*cf.* the contrast in Is. 40:30f.) but to clarify it by the words *no good thing* (*cf.* 84:11). It is not an empty promise of affluence but an assurance of His responsible care: *cf.* the phrase 'for our good always' (Dt. 6:24) with the phrase 'and let you hunger ... ' (Dt. 8:3). See again Romans 8:28, 37. This theme is now pursued in the next section, especially verses 12-14.

34:11-22. Learn from me
The lessons of this part of the psalm are chiefly that the true good is to be in concord with God. It is the answer to the hardest times (19f.) and to the most ultimate questions (21f.).

11-14. Almost every word in the opening verse is in the style of the wisdom instructor, as in Proverbs 1-9, with his fatherly tone and his stress on *the fear of the Lord* as the beginning of wisdom. This continues with the teaching that the

---

[1] There is no need to change *young lions* into 'unbelievers' (NEB), on the basis of an Arabic root. See on 35:17.

good you *enjoy* (12) goes hand in hand with the good you *do* (14). It is an emphasis which answers the suspicion (first aroused in Eden) that outside the will of God, rather than within it, lies enrichment. David in his early days lived by the principles of these verses and urged them, as here, on others (11; *cf.* 1 Sa. 24:7; 26:9, 23), at least in his attitude to Saul; and 1 Peter 3:10–12 quotes our verses 12–16 in a similar setting, which is one of provocation and persecution. *Cf.* also verse 13 with 1 Peter 2:1, 22.

15–18. Scripture always goes beyond the half-truth that goodness is its own reward. Verses 12–14 (above) lead towards the true summit in verse 15, which is personal and a matter of grace: that God's face is turned towards us. His *eyes* see what is hidden from us, so that before we call He may answer (see also on 35:22) yet His *ears* are open to us: He takes our prayers seriously. The plight of the wicked is put in an equally personal form, in terms of the unwelcoming face of God (16). 'We can be left utterly and absolutely *outside*— repelled, exiled, estranged, finally and unspeakably ignored.'[1]

19–22. These verses reiterate the main themes of the psalm, and re-emphasize the great divide between those whom God accepts and those He rejects. The sweeping affirmation of 19b urges the mind forward to look beyond death, if such a promise is to be honoured. Verse 20 needs to be taken with 18, which admits that a godly man's suffering may be extreme; yet God never takes it lightly (18a), and never loses control (20); *cf.* the paradox of Luke 21:16, 18. The 'scripture' that was fulfilled in John 19:36 may have included this verse with Exodus 12:46. 'The promise to the righteous man found an unexpectedly literal realization in the passion of the perfectly Righteous One' (Kirkpatrick).

Condemned . . . condemned (21f.) is from the same verb as 'make them bear their guilt' in 5:10 (Heb. 11), where see comment. A case can be argued for NEB's 'brought to ruin'; but the word was strongly associated with guilt and its punishment or atonement (*e.g.* Ho. 5:15; 10:2), and the presumption is in favour of 'condemned'. So the psalm ends on a note which must lead on to questions of final condemnation (21) or, in Paul's words, 'no condemnation' (22; *cf.* Rom. 8:1, 33f.). At whatever level David himself understood his

[1] C. S. Lewis, 'The Weight of Glory', *Transposition and Other Addresses* (Bles, 1949), p. 30.

141

affirmation of 22a, *the Lord redeems the life* . . . , the whole verse is pregnant with a meaning which comes to birth in the gospel, and which is hardly viable in any form that falls short of this. The Christian can echo the jubilant spirit of the psalm with added gratitude, knowing the unimagined cost of 22a and the unbounded scope of 22b.

Psalm 35
Lord, how long?

Whether or not this psalm was written as a companion to Psalm 34, it is well placed next to it, not only because of some verbal affinities and contrasts (notably 'the angel of the Lord', 34:7; 35:5, 6, found nowhere else in the Psalter), but because it speaks out of the kind of darkness which has just been dispelled in the former psalm. The deliverance celebrated in that psalm is now seen to be not invariably swift or painless, but subject, if God wills, to agonizing delays. Yet David never doubts that his day will come. Each plea for help looks on towards that moment: the three divisions of the psalm all end in hope.

35:1-10. The scheming

The military terms of verses 1-3 are figurative, and in fact the opening metaphor is from the lawcourt (*contend*). So the psalm is matched to any situation of spite and intrigue.

3. *Javelin*, or some such weapon, is the word one expects, and some foreign terms have been adduced to support it. A similar word has come to light from Qumran, meaning the javelin's socket; but this would hardly come to stand for the whole weapon, and in fact the Hebrew makes good sense in its known form as a verb, not a weapon, as in AV, RV: 'stop the way' (*cf.* NEB).[1]

4-6. The contrast between these verses and 34:5, 7, whether specifically intended or not, is an important one, since *shame*, or being *confounded*, is of the essence of damnation (Dn. 12:2), while *the angel of the Lord* (see on 34:7) is either our salvation

[1] The socket, like a sword's hilt, acted as a stop to the blade, from which it presumably took its name, making it a still more unlikely term (*pace* Dahood) for the javelin itself.

or our doom; *cf.* Exodus 23:20–22. The dark picture in verse 6 is made even more desperate than that of Proverbs 4:19 by the almost gurgling liquidity of the word for *slippery*, and by the thought of the Pursuer close behind. Calm defiance of God will not survive the conditions that evil itself eventually produces.

7, 8. *Without cause*, twice here, and again in 19, touches the very nerve of David's pain, which will be exposed even more fully in the middle paragraph (11–18). The psalms make us specially sensitive to the hurt of injustice; it is the gospel which turns it into a situation to be redeemed, an opportunity of following in the steps of Christ (1 Pet. 2:19ff.). As for the 'poetic justice' of verse 8, the gospel accepts it, but as a tragedy to avert, if prayers and appeals can avail (Mt. 5:44; 23:37f.); not as an end to be desired.[1]

9, 10. There is an echo of the song of Moses in the cry *Who is like thee?* (*cf.* Ex. 15:11), perhaps in conscious recollection of a crisis so much greater than David's own, and of its glorious outcome. So Paul, at a time of near-despair, remembered the resurrection of the dead (2 Cor. 1:8–10), and recovered hope. *My soul* (9) and *my bones* (10) are two emphatic ways of saying 'I' or 'myself', as in 6:2, 3; *cf.* our own expression 'I know it in my bones'.

35:11–18. The mobbing

Other psalms will plumb still further depths by describing the treachery of bosom companions (*e.g.* 41:9; 55:12–14). Here the wound, which is hardly less painful, is the spite and ingratitude of men who were not close friends but had been treated 'as though' they were (14); such had been David's care for them: a concern as genuine as that of Romans 12:15 or of the Good Samaritan. In return, it is as though the Samaritan himself now fell among thieves, only to find his former protégé his chief tormentor.

13. The Hebrew does not mention *my head bowed*. The line runs literally 'And my prayer will return (or, kept returning) to my bosom', which RSV takes to be a reference to the prayer's posture, but which seems more likely to mean that the prayer would return to him either unanswered or as a blessing, as in Matthew 10:13.

[1] See Introduction, v. *d*, pp. 30ff.

15. *Stumbling* may suggest to us a sinful lapse, as in the New Testament, but the word used here is a figure for calamity, as in 38:17 (Heb. 18); Job 18:12; Jeremiah 20:10. The phrase *cripples whom I knew not* seems rather too startling to be correct, in spite of David's outburst recorded in 2 Samuel 5:6–8 (which employs a different word, whereas this one is akin to the word used of Mephibosheth whom David befriended). The same consonants for the 'smitten' (*i.e.* cripples or abjects) could probably be pronounced so as to mean 'smiters'; hence NEB 'ruffians'. This mobbing of one who has suddenly become vulnerable, whose goodness has put men to shame, was eagerly re-enacted at the trial of Jesus. But there must be few people who have never joined in some form of this sport.

16. The RSV margin ('. . . mockers of a cake') shows the awkwardness of the Hebrew at its face value. RSV text, *mocked more and more*, follows LXX, which evidently read the infinitive absolute, *lāʿōḡ* (with mockery) for *māʿōḡ* (cake?). NEB ('who would mock even a hunchback') deduces this meaning from an Arabic root 'to be crooked'. The former solution, based on a common Hebrew way of expressing intensity, seems the more probable. The second line of the verse (*gnashing* . . . ; *cf.* 37:12) reveals the fury that motivated the mockery, a fury which Stephen was to experience at his martyrdom (Acts 7:54).

17. On the word for *my life* ('my darling', AV, RV) see on 22:20, a verse which incidentally tells in favour of the straightforward translation *lions* at the end of our verse, as against NEB's 'unbelievers', here and at 34:10.

18. On the public offering of an individual's thanks, see on 22:22ff.

35:19–28. The gloating

Hatred *without cause* is so basic a response of evil towards good (already emphasized in verse 7) that Jesus saw verse 19 (and 69:4) not as David's strange misfortune but as His own predestined lot. It was 'the word . . . written in their law' (Jn. 15:25), an authoritative revelation of what must be. The pattern, pure and complete in His case, was recognizable though fragmentary with David, and is appointed for us as well (Jn. 15:18ff.).

22. *Thou hast seen* is a perfect foil to the enemy's cry, 'our eyes have seen it!' This, rather than stout denials, is the realistic answer to the triumphing of the wicked. *Cf.* the sequence introduced by 'I have seen . . . ' in Exodus 3:7; *cf.* 2 Kings 19:14ff.; Acts 4:29.

24. *Vindicate me* is lit. 'Judge me': *cf.* on 5:4–6.

25. '*We have our heart's desire!*' is a single word in the Hebrew, which is as terse and lively in this verse as a smacking of the lips.

27, 28. As in the earlier parts of the psalm, praise is waiting to break through (*cf.* verses 9f. and 18). What is more, David has remembered what Elijah in a similar crisis will overlook, that he has friends as well as enemies· 'a mighty throng' of them (18), whose *desire*, like the Lord's delight (27)—it is the same word—is only for his good.

Psalm 36
'Where sin abounded . . . '

This is a psalm of powerful contrasts, a glimpse of human wickedness at its most malevolent, and divine goodness in its many-sided fullness. Meanwhile the singer is menaced by the one and assured of victory by the other. Few psalms cover so great a range in so short a space.

Title
The description of David as 'the servant of the Lord' is found only here and in the title of Psalm 18, where see comment.

36:1–4. Abandoned wickedness
The opening words, lit. 'An oracle of transgression', make a startling heading to the portrait of this dedicated sinner. It is as though *transgression* itself were his god or prophet. Contrast this formula with (lit.) 'oracle of the Lord', 'oracle of David', *etc.* (Gn. 22:16; 2 Sa. 23:1; *etc.*). *Deep in his heart* makes easier sense than 'within my heart' (AV, RV), and is well supported by the ancient versions. But these may have been emending a text they found difficult.[1] If 'my heart' is

---

[1] Dahood however finds 'his' here, without emending the Heb., on the basis of a Phoenician form in which 'his' and 'my' are identical. But how securely one can argue from Phoenician to Hebrew is very questionable.

correct, it means that David finds himself listening intently to, and catching the meaning of, the ideas that govern such a man. *No fear* is a strong expression here, and we may contrast this attitude with that of 16:8, 'I keep the Lord always before me'. While a believer sets his course towards God Himself, this man does not take even 'the terror of the Lord' into account. This is the culminating symptom of sin in Romans 3:18, a passage which teaches us to see this portrait as that of Man (but for the grace of God) rather than of an abnormally wicked type. All men as fallen have these characteristics, latent or developed.

2. *For he flatters himself* (or perhaps, 'For it'—*i.e.* the oracle he listens to in verse 1—'flatters him') *in his* (*own*) *eyes* (those eyes that have turned away from God (1), and so have lost any true point of reference). The next phrase can be rendered, basically, 'concerning' or 'towards' 'finding out his iniquity to hate (it)'. It may mean that he is too deluded 'to detect and detest' it himself (JB; *cf.* NEB) or to think that others will (RSV); or it may mean that his optimism makes him reckless and his exposure all the more certain (AV, PBV). The general sense does not greatly vary, but the awkward and ambiguous run of the sentence suggests a damaged text.

3, 4. From the sinner's attitudes to sin, self and God in verses 1 and 2 the psalm turns to his social activities, which are assiduously disruptive (*cf.* 4a with Mi. 2:1). It is a downward path, for he is seen as one who has turned from better things (3b), not as one who never had a chance. Here again the Pauline account of man is foreshadowed (Rom. 1:28ff.). His sins of influence and action (3a, b) are the outflow of his whole being, which is corrupt in thought (4a), will (4b) and feeling (4c). A striking note in this description is the prominence of negative sins among the positive ones: *viz. ceased* . . . ; *not good* . . . ; *spurns not.* This is no anticlimax, for it shows a wholesale reversal of values, leaving good powerless to attract, and evil to repel. *Cf.* Alexander Pope on a possible series of steps towards this:

> 'Vice is a monster of so frightful mien
> As, to be hated, needs but to be seen;
> Yet, seen too oft, familiar with her face,
> We first endure, then pity, then embrace.'[1]

---

[1] Alexander Pope, *Essay on Man*, II. v. 1-4.

36:5-9. Abundant goodness
Here is a whole world to explore, a 'broad place' to be brought
into (*cf.* 18:19): unsearchable (*heavens, clouds*), impregnable
(*mountains*), inexhaustible (*the great deep*); yet, for all that,
welcoming and hospitable (6c–9). It is only man's world
that is cramping. Human fickleness makes a drooping contrast to this towering covenant-love and *faithfulness* (5);
human standards, where all is relative, are a marshland
beside the exacting, exhilarating mountains of His
righteousness (6); human assessments are shallowness itself in
comparison with His *judgments*—a term which is based on a
court's recorded decisions and therefore comes to mean not
only judgments (in both senses of that word) but Scripture,
as God's will revealed: see on 18:22; 19:7–10.

After the immensities of verses 5 and 6, a wealth of detailed
care enriches the scene in 7–9, already anticipated in 6c,
whose theme of *man and beast* is elaborated throughout Psalm
104 and taken further again in the Gospels (*e.g.* Mt. 6:25ff.).

7. The word *precious* establishes at once the change of scale
from the immense to the intimate and personal. *Steadfast love*
(see on 17:7) needs both emphases: that of verse 5 as too
great to grasp, and of verse 7 as too good to let slip. The
picture of taking *refuge in the shadow of thy wings* was used
of Ruth by Boaz (Ru. 2:12), and of Jerusalem by Jesus (Mt.
23:37); it shows an aspect of salvation which is as humbling
as it is reassuring.

8, 9. Two of David's poignant experiences as a refugee
illuminate this picture of sharing the wealth of a great house:
on the one hand the tantalizing feast of Nabal (1 Sa. 26), and
on the other, the gladdening gifts of Barzillai and his friends
(2 Sa. 17:27ff.). In the phrase *the river of thy delights* there is
possibly an echo of Eden, a name identical in sound with
'delight'; but the theme of life-giving water is developed above
all in Ezekiel 47 (*cf.* Rev. 22:1f.). *Light*, here, mainly suggests
joy (*cf., e.g.,* 4:6f.; Est. 8:16; contrast Ps. 38:10), though it
cannot be isolated from its other connotations of purity,
clarity and truth.

36:10-12. Prevailing prayer
The psalmist finds himself stationed on the disputed ground
between human wickedness (1–4) and divine grace (5–9);
so he turns to urgent prayer. Twice he has praised the *steadfast*

love of God (5, 7); now let it reach out to the place of need
(10)! There is no belittling of the enemy, though the Hebrew
and ancient versions do not support the stronger word
'crush' (11a, NEB, *etc.*) in place of *come upon* (which is itself
a hostile enough expression: *cf.*, *e.g.*, Jb. 15:21; 20:22). But
the last verse shows the victory already claimed; it speaks as
though the scene were present and clearly visible. 'There
they lie, the evildoers' (NEB). This is the faith defined in
Hebrews 11:1 (Phillips) as 'putting our full confidence in
the things we hope for; . . . being certain of things we cannot
see'.

So the early eloquence was genuine. The evil which David
portrayed in the first stanza he was ready to fight; the grace
which he praised in the second he was ready to invoke; and,
once invoked, to accept as given and as settling the matter.

Psalm 37
'Wait Patiently for Him'

There is no finer exposition of the third Beatitude (Mt. 5:5)
than this psalm, from which it is drawn (verse 11). It is a
wisdom psalm: it speaks to man, not God, and its tone and
style have some affinities with Proverbs, whose message of
the righteous man's security is the central topic here.

The framework is an acrostic, with a fresh letter of the
Hebrew alphabet to introduce each double verse (1-2, 3-4,
etc.; but our numbering falls out of step). As in some other
acrostic psalms, notably 25 and 119, this external pattern
leaves the poet free to muse on a few themes, returning to
them at will, without losing all sense of form and progress.
We owe to this psalm, among other things, the hymn 'Put
thou thy trust in God', based on John Wesley's translation
of another kind of acrostic: Paul Gerhardt's *Befiehl du deine
Wege*, each of whose twelve verses begins with a successive
word of the psalm's verse 5: 'Commit your way to the Lord . . . '

37:1-11. The quiet spirit
The advice, *Fret not yourself*, or in terms of the Hebrew verb,
'do not get heated', is virtually the refrain of the opening
passage (1, 7, 8); and the whole of verse 1 is found again in

Proverbs 24:19, apart from one synonym. (See also Pr. 23:17f.; 24:1f., on *Be not envious*.) As a bare command it would be of little use, so it is reinforced by reasoned encouragements, which could be summarized as:

(i) Look ahead! Verses 2 and 10 are unanswerably true of everything that is rooted in time and not eternity (*cf.* Is. 40:8 with 1 Jn. 2:17). And if the long view is the answer to human schemes, we can afford to *wait* God's time (7, 9).

> 'Thy reign eternal will not cease;
> Thy years are sure and glad, and slow.'[1]

(ii) Look up! See especially verses 3–7. An obsession with enemies and rivals cannot be simply switched off, but it can be ousted by a new focus of attention; note the preoccupation with the Lord Himself, expressed in the four phrases that contain His name here. It includes a deliberate redirection of one's emotions (4a, *take delight*; *cf.* Paul and Silas in prison, singing as well as praying), and an entrusting of one's career (*your way*, 5) and reputation (*your vindication*, 6) to Him. This is a liberation: see additional note on 5, below.

(iii) Be constructive! This is put positively in verse 3 (*do good*), and negatively in verse 8's warning against anger and its bitter fruit. It is both theological and psychological wisdom, not only because the aggrieved person is no longer turned in on himself, but because God's own way is to overcome evil with good; in any case 'the anger of man does not work the righteousness of God' (Jas. 1:20; *cf.* Rom. 12:21). The gospel, and indeed the Old Testament, will sharpen this advice, from doing good in general to doing it 'to those who hate you' (Lk. 6:27; *cf.* Pr. 25:21).

Additional notes on verses 1–11

3. *Enjoy security* is one of several possible translations of two Hebrew words, both of which have more than one meaning. *Enjoy* could mean 'tend' (as a shepherd), 'feed (on)' (as a sheep, *etc.*), 'be friends with', 'strive after' (assumed from the noun in Ec. 1:14). *Security* most often means 'faithfulness', but also 'faith' (Hab. 2:4), and, adverbially, 'certainly'. Weiser's 'Keep upright in heart (lit. "Tend faithfulness")' gives a parallel with 'do good' in the first line; NEB 'find safe

---

[1] D. Greenwell, 'And art Thou come with us to dwell?'

pasture' (lit. 'graze safely') finds its parallel in the second line; *cf.* RSV, AV. I incline to RV 'follow after faithfulness', but would derive the verb from the Hebrew root for 'strive after', rather than (as RV mg.) from 'feed on'.

5. The Hebrew for *commit* is lit. 'roll', as though getting rid of a burden (*cf.* Jos. 5:9). But it comes to be used simply as a synonym for 'entrust' (Pr. 16:3) or 'trust'; *cf.* 22:8 (Heb. 9).

7. *Be still* is basically 'be silent', as in 62:5 (Heb. 6). It is the stillness of waiting, not (as in AV, RV) of resting. The Hebrew root underlying *wait patiently* is probably, as Briggs suggests, not *ḥûl* 'to writhe' (hence BDB, 'wait longingly'), which suggests an anxiety foreign to the context, but **ḥûl* akin to *yāhal*, 'to wait', as, *e.g.*, 31:24 (Heb. 25).

11. The context gives the best possible definition of *the meek*: they are those who choose the way of patient faith instead of self-assertion; a way fully expounded in the foregoing verses. *The land* (rather than 'the earth') is evidently the right translation of the second noun, in view of the imperative of verse 3, which simply says 'Dwell in the land'— *i.e.* the land which God has given you. The point of verse 11 is that the wicked, who have taken more than their share, will be destroyed in the end, leaving the meek in sole possession. It is almost a refrain: see verses 3, 9, 11, 22, 29, 34. But our Lord put this promise into a larger setting: by a similar judgment the meek will inherit, not the land only, but the earth.

37:12-26. The hidden help

Up to this point the battlefield has been the mind of the believer, goaded to exasperation at the brazenness of the wicked. Now the two types of men are looked at from the outside, and their fortunes and ways compared. Nearly every verse, to the end of the psalm, names *the wicked* or *the righteous*, or has some similar set of terms.

12-15. Persecuted, but not forsaken. Resourceful minds (12a), fanatical hatred (better expressed by 'grinding' the teeth (NEB, *etc.*), as in Acts 7:54, than by the older English versions' implausible 'gnashing') and overwhelming force (14) have repeatedly combined against the godly, only to destroy their own cause sooner or later. The picture of verses 13–15 is of a defeat which the Lord *sees . . . coming*, rather than has to intervene to send. The history of the church, from Stephen and Saul to the present day, is full of such reversals.

16–20, 25. As having nothing, and yet possessing all things. While verse 16 could stand on its own, as a purely moral judgment like that of Proverbs 28:6, the righteous man, however poor he is, has better prospects as well as a better conscience than the godless. The Gospel sayings, like those of 17–19, take full account of temporal needs (*e.g.* Mt. 6:31ff.; 19:29); and in the psalm as in the New Testament the real security and wealth lie not 'in uncertain riches, but in the living God' (1 Tim. 6:17, AV). The general assurance, *the Lord upholds* (17), is heartening enough; still more the intimate exactness of *the Lord knows the days* . . . (18; *cf.* 31:15), which include all *the days of famine* (19). Verse 25 testifies to this provision, in its literal sense, from one man's experience; Job's comforters would grant no exceptions to that sense; but Paul, and others before him, knew of an *abundance* which might be material or spiritual, as God saw fit (*e.g.* Ps. 73:26; Hab. 3:17f.; Mt. 4:4; 2 Cor. 6:10; Phil. 4:12). The theme of verses 19 and 20 is close to that of Psalm 1:3f., but there have been various translations of the unusual phrase, *like the glory of the pastures*, since *pastures* can also mean 'lambs' (AV), and small alterations to the consonants offer further possibilities (*cf.* NEB). But RSV (*cf.* RV, JB, *etc.*) makes good sense if it is taken to mean 'like gay, but short-lived, flowers'.[1] The simile of *smoke* (20) is no objection to this, for in Hebrew mixed metaphors count as an enrichment.

21, 22, 26. Making many rich. This gives an important balance to the catalogue of gains—for a righteous man is no longer righteous when he grows selfish; he has joined the 'men whose portion . . . is of the world' (17:14; *cf.* 49:13–20). The element of generosity in righteousness is treated more fully in Psalm 112, and above all in 2 Corinthians 8 and 9. Further, this man's constant *giving* and *lending* (26a) is crowned by a lasting *blessing* to society, in the family he founds. Admittedly the meaning of 26b may be simply that his family will give rise to a new blessing-formula ('may you be blessed like these people'), as in Zechariah 8:13 where 'a blessing' is

[1] BDB, p. 430a.

the opposite of 'a byword of cursing'; but even this could be fruitful (*cf.* the outcome of Zc. 8:13 in Zc. 8:23). A better model of what this promise can mean is found in Genesis 12:2f., as expounded in the New Testament.

23, 24. Cast down, but not destroyed. The expression *from the Lord* is emphatic, and the Hebrew of the first line runs into the second: 'From the Lord a man's steps are established, and he delights in[1] his way.' The kind of *fall* envisaged in verse 24 is a material calamity rather than a moral plunge, to judge from the context. There will be ups and downs, but His hand is steady. The expression for *the Lord is the stay* is identical with 'the Lord upholds' (17).

25, 26. These verses are commented on at 16–20 and 21–22 respectively.

37:27-40. The long view

While this view is not a new perspective in the psalm, it dominates this section, first by the repetition of *for ever* in verses 27, 28 (emphatic), 29 (by a synonym); then by the little sketch of verses 35f., and finally by the stress on *posterity* in 37f.

27-34. The injunction to *do good* (27; *cf.* 3) is not as super-fluous as it may sound. In the first place, a conflict with evil too often tempts one to fight the enemy with his own weapons. In the second, both the Lord and the structure of life are on the side of *justice* (28, 30f.), for there is nothing capricious about His support (33), or facile about our stability (31).

On *saints* (28) see on 18:25; on *possess the land* (29, 34) see on verse 11.

35, 36. This vivid little eyewitness report has much in common with passages in the Wisdom books, with their characteristic use of experience. *Cf.*, *e.g.*, Job 5:3; Proverbs 7:6ff.; 24:30ff.; Ecclesiastes 2:1ff.; *etc*. *Towering like a cedar of Lebanon* is the reading of LXX, Vulg., *etc*. (as is the first person, *I passed*, 36), representing consonants not unlike those of the MT. The NEB preserves the latter with its translation 'rank as a spreading tree in its native soil'. But the Hebrew

---

[1] NEB 'watches over' is deduced from an Arabic root, 'to preserve'. But *delights in* makes good sense: *i.e.*, 'He takes pleasure in his progress' (JB). See also on 51:6.

of this is more awkward than the translation suggests, and RSV may well be right in following the alternative text.

37, 38. The emphasis on *posterity* is another point of contact with the Wisdom writings, with their concern to think ahead to the 'end' or the 'afterwards' of a matter. *Cf.* Proverbs 5:4 and the passages listed in the comment there. For the Christian, and perhaps even for the psalmist here (*cf.* Dahood), this extends beyond death.

39, 40. The psalm ends with calm objectivity, the answer to the fretful impatience encountered at the start. Note the *from* Him (39) and the *in* Him (40): His initiative in sending, and our response in taking shelter; the help that He gives, and the refuge that He is.

Psalm 38
The Outcast

This agonized cry (the third of the 'penitential psalms', listed at Ps. 6) shares with Psalm 70 the title 'To bring to remembrance'. Since with God to remember is to act, this word speaks of laying before Him a situation that cries out for His help. Several of the sacrifices included a 'memorial portion' to emphasize to God, in token, the gift, or means of atonement, or in one case the accusation (Nu. 5:26), that was being lodged with Him. This psalm might well be accompanied by such an offering, but RSV confuses what is secondary with what is primary by translating the title as *for the memorial offering*.

The suffering is multiple. There is a burden of guilt, made all the more crushing by a foul disease, and this in turn has estranged the sufferer from his friends, and given his enemies the chance to plot his ruin. So confession to God mingles with a sense of man's injustice, and the penitent is also a suppliant for justice.

38:1–8. The loathsome burden
The burden is both inward and outward: a torment of mind and body which is accepted as God's chastening.

1, 2. The emphasis falls on *in thy anger* and *in thy wrath*. It is not a plea to be exempt from God's discipline: only that it may be tempered with mercy (*cf.* 6:1). If there is a distinction between *thy arrows* and *thy hand*, it is perhaps between the bombardment of pains and terrors which torment the sufferer (*cf.* Jb. 6:4; 16:13), and the disquieting pressure of God's direct attention (*cf.* 32:4; Jb. 13:21).

3-8. The reiterated words *because of* (3a, b, 5) leave no doubt that this sickness was a punishment. (It would be as wrong to think that this is never so, as that it is always so. *Cf.* Jn. 5:14 with Jn. 9:3.) Whether or not it was the natural outcome of the sin, as are the diseases of lust and excess, there is no sure way of telling. What is clear is that the illness opened David's eyes to his spiritual plight. It did this, not by suggesting an analogy between the two, like that of Isaiah 1:6, but by humbling him. The guilt which a strong, successful man might have shrugged off is now *a burden too heavy*; the sins which might have seemed a mere trickle are revealed now as a flood to drown in (4). 'Before I was afflicted I went astray' (119:67).

38:9-14. The lonely victim

There is a poignant humility here, from the opening word, *Lord* (not in this case the name Yahweh, but, as in verse 22, 'my master'), to the final *no rebukes* (14) in face of the desertion of friends and the malice of enemies.

9. *Known to thee* is lit. 'in front of thee', hence NEB 'lies open before thee' (*cf.* 2 Ki. 19:14). See the introductory comments on the title of this psalm. A theorist might argue that prayer is superfluous in view of this omniscience; but our Lord points out that only faithless chatter is superfluous (Mt. 6:7ff.).

10. There is no need to exchange *my heart throbs* for RP 'my heart is bewitched' (which is a conjecture on the strength of an Akkadian root).

11. The word *plague* is perhaps chosen for its associations with leprosy (*e.g.* four times in Lv. 13:3, Heb.), for this is how his friends were treating David. Or it may have the stigma of a stroke of judgment, as in Isaiah 53:4, where the word 'stricken' is similar to this. It is ironical that the more a person needs human support, the less (by his abnormality) he naturally attracts it. It is the gospel that has done most to change this.

12-14. It is a striking contrast between the busy tongues of verse 12 and the stillness of 13f., calling to mind the supreme example of such a scene. David's silence was born partly of faith (15; *cf.* 37:7), partly of acknowledged guilt (3–5; *cf.* 2 Sa. 16:11); but on our Lord's silence, and its relevance to us, see 1 Peter 2:18–25.

38:15–22. The single hope

David is outstanding in any company for his ability to *wait* (15) for God. His fugitive years, his Hebron period and his attitude to Absalom's revolt, all proved the sincerity of his prayer in 15f., and of his advice in Psalm 37.

17–20. Fixity and infirmity are oddly mixed in the expression *ready* (or 'set') *to fall*. It may allude to nothing more than the present crisis. But it may be a confession of the sinner's chronic instability, the only consistency he displays (*cf.* NEB, 'prone to stumble'). After the penitence of verse 18 (in which concern or anxiety is implied in the word for *I am sorry*; *cf.* NEB), the claim of wrongful attack[1] in 19f. may seem surprising. But David's sins, however serious, were those of a man whose fundamental choice was to *follow after good*, and it is this choice that always rankles with the unbeliever (*cf.* Jn. 15:18f.).

21, 22. This final plea, with its pathetic urgency, shows that David's capacity to wait God's time, mentioned at the start of this section, owed nothing to a placid disposition or to a situation well in hand, but everything to the God he knew by name (Yahweh, 21a) and by covenant (*my God*), and as Master and Saviour (22b).

Psalm 39
No Fixed Abode

The burning question of this psalm is why God should so assiduously discipline a creature as frail and fleeting as man. It is an outburst like that of Job 7, and especially the cry there, 'Let me alone, for my days are a breath. What is man, that thou dost make so much of him?' (Jb. 7:16b, 17a). But the question, like that of Job, is not asked in arrogance but

---

[1] *Without cause* (*ḥinnām*) and *wrongfully* are found together at 35:19, and seem appropriate companions here. But *ḥayyîm* ('alive') stands here, somewhat ungrammatically, and we should probably read either *ḥinnām*, 'without cause', or, by a smaller change, 'the enemies of my life'.

with touching loyalty (1) and a submissive faith (7). Such 'songs in the night' reveal something of the bewilderment about man that was only finally dispelled when the Word became flesh, and when the gospel brought life and immortality to light.

Title

On *the choirmaster*, see Introduction, VI, c. 3, p. 40. *Jeduthun* was one of the chief musicians appointed by David to lead public worship (1 Ch. 16:41; 25:1-3).[1]

39:1-3. The pent-up protest

'Protest' would be too strong a word if it implied defiance; yet David's feelings were running high enough to be taken for disloyalty if he had vented them in the wrong company (1). He shows a responsible care for God's good name (*cf.* 73:15), first by his self-restraint, and then, when he can contain himself no longer, by the way he formulates his problem: as a learner (4) and as a suppliant (7).

2. The expression *to no avail* (2) is lit. 'from good', *i.e.* 'without success'; it can hardly mean 'even from good' (AV, RV), since the Hebrew could have expressed this easily enough had it so intended.

39:4-6. This fleeting life

There are mixed emotions here. The opening and the close of the psalm betray David's revulsion against the brevity of life, which has been brought home to him by suffering (10f.); yet his first prayer is that he may learn the lesson of it well (4). This seems to be a deliberate act of facing unwelcome facts as God's facts, and seeing them as He sees them (*in thy sight*, 5). How much there is to learn from this painful subject can be gauged from the word *heḇel: a mere breath* (5); *for naught* (6); *a mere breath* (11), since this was to be the key-word of Ecclesiastes (translated there as 'vanity'), to expose the fatal insufficiency of all that is earthbound. *Cf.*, *e.g.*, verse 6 with Ecclesiastes 2:18f.; *cf.* also Luke 12:20; James 4:14f.; for this is equally a New Testament emphasis.

---

[1] Mowinckel (II, p. 213) interprets Jeduthun not as a personal name but as a cultic term, perhaps 'confession', on the ground that Pss. 62 and 77 are entitled 'over (RSV 'according to') Jeduthun', as if designed to be sung 'over' a cultic action. But this preposition ('*al*) has many shades of meaning, including simply 'belonging to' (*e.g.* Nu. 36:12, Heb.).

39:7-11. This dire discipline

Certain themes here make this psalm a companion to Psalm 38, themes expressed in the words *My hope* (7, a kindred word to 'wait', 38:15); *I am dumb* (9; *cf.* 38:13); and *thy stroke* (10; the same word as 'plague', 38:11).

But while the burden of that psalm was the cruelty of friends and enemies, here it is the crushing severity of God. The only human onlooker is *the fool* (8), and he is the *nābāl* the type of fool who loves to blaspheme (*cf.* 14:1). What troubles David is the heavy-handed treatment of so ephemeral and vulnerable an offender as man (10f.); for he is looking beyond his particular case. This is the paradox that troubled Job (see the opening comments on the psalm), and like most paradoxes it concealed unexplored wealth. 'Everything difficult indicates something more than our theory of life yet embraces'[1]: in this case the fact that man is made for sonship and for eternity. The exact bearing of this fact on God's fatherly discipline was to be expounded in Hebrews 12:5-11; and the theme of treasures that are beyond the reach of any *moth* (11), actual or metaphorical, is developed in, *e.g.*, Matthew 6:19ff.; 1 Peter 1:4ff. The problem was worth wrestling with.

39:12, 13. This small petition

The *passing guest* (or 'stranger') and the *sojourner* were terms for the foreign residents in Israel, perhaps of longer and shorter duration respectively. They were to be made welcome, but could own no land. This rootlessness David sees now as his own and everyman's condition. Had not the law said as much, even of Israel? But the law said it to safeguard the inheritance, not to deny it (Lv. 25:23); and life itself had taught David the same lesson before now (16:9-11; 17:13-15). Yet for the moment, like Job or Jeremiah, he can see no more than death, and ask no more than respite. The prayer of 13a makes no more sense than Peter's 'depart from me'; but God knows when to treat that plea as in Luke 5:8ff., and when as in Matthew 8:34f. The very presence of such prayers in Scripture is a witness to His understanding. He knows how men speak when they are desperate.

---

[1] *George MacDonald: an Anthology*, ed. C. S. Lewis (Bles, 1946), para. 85, p. 49.

Psalm 40

'Glad News of Deliverance'

The theme of waiting, expounded in Psalm 37, has had its painful application in Psalms 38 and 39, but now its triumphant outcome. The rescue, pictured memorably in the opening lines, demands a fitting celebration, and David is enabled to see that no mere ritual can suffice for it: only an act of pure self-giving. This he prepares to make, with a declaration which in reality none but the Messiah will be able to fulfil, as the New Testament makes plain. His '*Lo, I come*' is the high point of the psalm.

But trouble returns, and waiting is again David's lot. The psalm ends with a prayer of distress, most of which reappears later in the Psalter as a separate psalm (70). It has a note of urgency, yet at the same time one of underlying joy, as David remembers a wider circle and a bigger cause than his most pressing needs.

40:1–10. Waiting rewarded

David's 'new song' has been echoed all the more widely for arising from a deliverance which could have been from sickness, sin, or almost any peril. We can be grateful that we know no more details of his 'desolate pit' than of Paul's 'thorn in the flesh'.

1–3. Rescue. The word *patiently* is too placid for the intensity of these opening words, better reproduced by NEB: 'I waited, waited for the Lord.' *He inclined to me* is, again, too courtly: rather, 'he bent down to me' (NEB), or 'he turned and listened to my cry' (Moffatt)—as when someone's attention is arrested and riveted.

2. A *desolate pit* is a fair translation, in spite of RSV mg.; *cf.* the related verb in Isaiah 6:11, 'until cities *lie waste*'. The further metaphor, *miry bog*, puts into two words almost all that can be suggested of horror and floundering helplessness. *Cf.* the literal plight and rescue of Jeremiah (Je. 38:6ff.). And the picture of deliverance does not end with bare extrication —as in Jeremiah's case—but with the first steps of liberty.

3. Better still, David's thoughts are not self-bound, dwelling on his ordeal: they rise gratefully to God, and flow out towards his people. There is a play on the similar words *see* and *fear*, which throws the latter into relief, for David's interest is not in attracting mere attention but in arousing fruitful awe (*fear*) and *trust*, as the next verses will confirm. Psalm 51:13 shows the same spirit.

4, 5. Reflection. *Trust* is taken up from verse 3, as David draws out for the rest of us this lesson from his experience, first by rejecting other claimants to our trust (for the *proud* he uses the term that became the nickname for Egypt, the empty blusterer, Is. 30:7), and then by enlarging on the incomparable claims of God. The past is full of His miracles (*wondrous deeds*), the future full of His plans—this is the force of the word *thoughts*. *Cf.* these two themes again in 139:13-18.

6-8. Dedication. After such a deliverance, what offering can one bring but one's heart and will? Such is the logic of this situation; yet David outruns it by speaking as if his self-offering will be the sacrifice to end all sacrifices. If this is the implication of his words, he is speaking not for himself but for the Messiah; and this is confirmed by Hebrews 10:5-10.

6. David's predecessor as king had been rebuked for insincerity in terms not unlike these (1 Sa. 15:22); but this verse, with the next, questions the very system, and anticipates the Servant prophecies and the New Covenant. The second line is difficult: lit., 'ears thou hast dug for me'. Since 'dug' may mean 'pierced' (*cf.* 22:16, Heb. 17) it could allude to the ceremony of making a slave his master's for ever (Ex. 21:6, using a different word). But the plural, 'ears', is a difficulty, and few accept this view. More probably it is a forceful parallel to the expressions used in Isaiah 50:4f.: 'he wakens my ear', 'the Lord God has opened my ear'; speaking of the Servant's training in perception and obedience. LXX, quoted by Hebrews 10:5, has 'a body hast thou prepared for me'. Whatever the origin of this reading, it carries forward the sense of dedication implied in the Hebrew text, and it is worth noting that in Isaiah 50:5f. the obedience of the 'ear' soon involves the offering of 'my back to the smiters, and my cheeks to those who pulled out the beard.'

7. For its majestic assurance, the announcement '*Lo, I come*' has only to be compared with the tentative 'Here am I!

Send me' of Isaiah 6:8. This servant is a prince. *The roll of the book* could be a reference to a coronation decree (see on 2:7; *cf.* 110:1), or, as most interpreters hold, to the book of the law, whose commands the speaker accepts as binding on him (*cf.* the end of 2 Ki. 22:13). But *written of me* refers more naturally to '*Lo, I come*', and therefore, it seems, to the conviction that his very coming is a fulfilment. This agrees closely with our Lord's assertion, 'Moses ... wrote of me' (Jn. 5:46; *cf.* Lk. 24:27) and with the New Testament's high view of this passage's significance.

9, 10. Proclamation. The positive duty to share the news of salvation is very clear in the Psalms, many of which were meant for use on such occasions. *Cf.*, *e.g.*, Psalm 116, and see on 22:22–26. An actual example of a formal thanksgiving is that of Hannah, with her offerings (and the living sacrifice, Samuel), her spoken testimony and her 'new song' (1 Sa. 1:24 – 2:10)

40:11-17. Waiting renewed
This is the first hint that trouble is still at hand. Unless this is a psalm composed for a purely hypothetical situation (and how often would such a situation arise, to call for such a composition?), it means that David has deliberately recalled and made known his past deliverance; then, with the heaped-up terms for salvation all about him (10), he turns to God with an emphatic *Thou* (11), and reaffirms them—for verse 11 is a statement, not a prayer: '*Thou* wilt not withhold ...' (*cf.* Gelineau and NEB, almost alone, but unquestionably right). In that setting he states his predicament; and he confesses it as frankly as he confessed his faith.

11, 12. 'My iniquities'. On verse 11 as an affirmation, see above. Whatever had been the 'miry bog' of verse 2, the present troubles are largely of David's own making, which are catching up with him now (notice the expression *overtaken*).

13-15. My enemies. If his sin disheartens David, his enemies rouse him: they have no right to exploit his fall. This spirited reaction to the wrong kind of pressure is part of the secret of his resilience. It is for God to bring him low, not for the mischief-maker: *cf.* Micah 7:8f.

16, 17. 'My help'. The enemies' glee (15) seems, by contrast, to put David in mind of the 'mirth that has no bitter springs'[1]: a joy which is self-forgetful (*in thee*, 16) and aroused by what is positive (not *my hurt*, 14, but *thy salvation*, 16). His overriding concern emerges in the cry 'The Lord be magnified' (16, RV, more accurately than RSV[2]), which significantly takes precedence over the personal plea 'may my Lord take thought for me' (17; *cf.* NEB mg.), and over the final cry of anguish. To compare what *I am* with what *Thou art* is a steadying thing; but to pray for God's glory is a liberation, the way of victory, and, as John 12:27f. shows, the way of Christ Himself.

Psalm 41

When a man is down

If the greater part of this psalm is plaintive, the thankfulness at the end shows that the ordeal is already over. The middle verses re-live it in all its intensity, to bring out the true value of the compassion praised in the prologue and the vindication celebrated in the epilogue. The victim's view is never quite the same as the benefactor's. Only the body of the psalm can reveal how heartfelt is the beatitude with which it opens.

41:1–3. The chance to help

It is soon clear that the word for *poor* is meant in its primary sense of 'weak' or 'helpless' (*cf.* NEB): one who is at a low ebb. The word *considers* is striking, in that it usually describes the practical wisdom of the man of affairs, and so implies giving careful thought to this person's situation, rather than perfunctory help.

What follows this beatitude is either a series of promises, as in most versions (rather than the present-tense statements of RSV), or else a series of prayers after the fashion of Psalm 20: *i.e.*, 'May the Lord deliver him . . ., protect him . . .' *etc.* Fitting in with the second view is verse 2c (Heb. 3),

---

[1] R. Kipling, 'Land of our birth'.
[2] The Hebrew of this, Yigdal Yahweh, now forms the opening of the Jewish doxology, the Yigdal, on which is based the Christian hymn 'The God of Abraham praise'.

which is a direct prayer, 'do not give him up . . . ' (*cf.* JB); but the next verse supports the notion of promises and statements. Each has its difficulty; perhaps the balance is tipped, as Perowne suggests, towards promises, since beatitudes are usually followed by these. The theme is close to that of Matthew 5:7: 'Blessed are the merciful, for they shall obtain mercy.' It is a pity that RSV tones down the simple vividness of 3b: lit. 'thou turnest all his bed in his sickness'. JB paraphrases it well (to interpret the 'all'): 'most carefully you make his bed when he is sick.'

41:4–10. The chance to hurt

David's position is all the weaker for his bad conscience (4, *cf.* 30:3); but he will get more mercy (4, 10) from God whom he has wronged than from the friend he has helped (9). Scarcely any comment is needed on the politely gloating, eagerly speculating visitors of 5–8, whose impatience for *his name* to *perish* is clarified by NEB's 'when will he die, and his line become extinct?' In verse 7 *imagine* is the same verb as 'take(s) thought' in 40:17 (Heb. 18), and as 'imputes' in 32:2; so it may refer to their evil hopes[1] and schemes, as in RSV, or to their criticisms. NEB's paraphrase allows for either, within limits: 'and love to make the worst of everything.' At this point, if not before, the reader has to ask himself whether such people should be classified as 'they' or 'we'. Such, at least, was the disciples' reaction to verse 9 (Jn. 13:18, 22; *cf.* Mt. 26:21ff.) when Jesus quoted it as due to be fulfilled at a new level. (In this, as elsewhere, He saw in the experiences of David the pattern, writ small, of His own calling. See Introduction, IV *d*, p. 22.)

10. This verse belongs to the account of David's plea for help, which began in verse 4 and should be read throughout as the appeal he had addressed to God on that occasion. The quotation marks in verse 4 should not be closed until the end of verse 10; the words of his enemies (5, 8) were part of his report to God. The emphatic *But . . . thou*, in the present verse, corresponds to the emphatic 'My enemies' (5), and

---

[1] Verse 8 is an example of these, with its diagnosis of the trouble as, lit., 'a thing of Belial'. Belial, a word for which various derivations have been suggested, always has connotations of evil or destruction, and is synonymous with death and Sheol in Ps. 18:4f. (Heb. 5f.). It emerges as a name for Satan in 2 Cor. 6:15 and in later Judaism, where it is also spelt Beliar.

resumes the request of verse 4. The plea *that I may requite them* is unusual, in that the psalms mostly pray that God Himself will do this. David, however, as king, had authority to act judicially, a power which he used in fact with great restraint. But the contrast between his personal reaction and our Lord's to enmity and betrayal remains very striking: the contrast between punitive justice and atoning grace.

41:11, 12. The last word

David knew his imperfections well enough (*cf.* verse 4) not to imagine himself always in the right, as his meekness towards Shimei made very plain (2 Sa. 16:11). So his relief at being vindicated is heartfelt. What is equally revealing is the chief ingredient of that relief: the sense of renewed fellowship, *that thou art pleased with me.* And his ambition confirms it, being centred not in himself but *in thy presence for ever.* 'For ever' is not always as absolute an expression as it sounds to us; but whether David was looking beyond this life (*cf.* 16:11) or not, the answer would not disappoint him.

41:13. Doxology to the First Book of Psalms

Each of the five books ends with an outburst of praise, clinched by a double Amen (here and at 72:19; 89:52), an Amen and Hallelujah (106:48) or, finally, what is virtually a double Hallelujah (150:6), indeed a whole psalm of doxology. For all its fluctuations of mood, the Psalter constantly returns to its keynote, identified in its Hebrew title, 'Praises'.

Book II: Psalms 42–72

Psalms are brought together here from various sources: the Sons of Korah, who were temple musicians (42–49); Asaph, the founder of another temple group (50); David (51–65; 68–70); Solomon (72). There are also three anonymous psalms: 66, 67, 71. For further discussion see the Introduction, II, pp. 4ff.; vɪ, *b*, pp. 33ff.

Psalms 42 and 43
Far From Home

While each of this pair of psalms can be sung by itself, they are in fact two parts of a single, close-knit poem, one of the most sadly beautiful in the Psalter. Not only does one title serve for the two psalms, but the soliloquy 'Why go I mourning . . .' is heard in both (42:9; 43:2), and the refrain which closes the two parts of Psalm 42 at verses 5 and 11 comes a third time at 43:5 to round off the whole. It is the lament of a temple singer exiled in the north[1] near the rising of the Jordan, who longs to be back at God's house, and turns his longing into resolute faith and hope in God Himself.

42:1–5. The drought
The metrical psalm, 'As pants the hart for cooling streams', adds the touch 'When heated in the chase'. But the psalmist seems to have had in mind the slower agony of drought (*cf.* the similar Joel 1:20), a condition grimly depicted in Jeremiah 14:1–6 with its withered landscape and dazed, dying creatures. His long spiritual ordeal shows itself in the pathetic *When?* of verse 2, and the emptiness of his landscape is revealed by the onlookers' taunts of *Where?* (3).

Before men, he is vulnerable because he has declared his faith; he can be ridiculed when God's ways become

---

[1] *Cf.* perhaps such a situation as that of 2 Ki. 14:14. Mowinckel's suggestion (I, p. 242) that this is a psalm for the king, away on campaign, would be much more suited to, *e.g.*, Ps. 61.

165

inscrutable. Inwardly he is vulnerable because his thirst is for God; he will not settle for less: note the reiterations in verses 1b and 2.[1] This 'stricken deer' is no camel, desert-dwelling and self-sufficient. He has chosen the blessedness of those who hunger and thirst after righteousness, not the deceptive ease of 'you that are full now'.

4 For the psalmists the heart of the matter in public worship was undoubtedly God Himself (1, 2), but the comrade-ship and stirring ritual of a great occasion were an added delight: *cf.*, among others, Psalms 48, 68, 84, and the Songs of Ascents (120–134). Whether this singer *led* the worshippers *in procession* or only took his place among them depends on the meaning of a rare word[2] which the ancient versions read differently from the Massoretic Text (see the variations in NEB, JB).

5. This self-communing is the major refrain of the two psalms: see verse 11 and 43:5. It is an important dialogue between the two aspects of the believer, who is at once a man of convictions and a creature of change. He is called to live in eternity, his mind stayed on God; but also in time, where mind and body are under pressures that cannot and should not leave him impassive. *Cf.* 'Now is my soul troubled . . .' (Jn. 12:27f.). The psalmist's refrain teaches us to take seriously both aspects of our existence. There is no hint that his distress was avoidable on the one hand, for it arose out of his love; or unendurable on the other, for it did not shake his faith.

42:6–11. The depths

This is a totally different figure. The poet's thoughts are set in turmoil by the alien scene in which he stands, where the river Jordan, not far from its source on the slopes of *Hermon*,[3]

[1] Verse 2b (Heb. 3) with the traditional vowels reads 'and appear before God' (AV, RV). But the same consonants can be vocalized to read '*and behold the face of God*' (RSV), which is an easier construction. *Cf.*, *e.g.*, Ps. 27:8.

[2] MT *'eddaddēm*; *cf.* Is. 38:15; see BDB, 186b. The LXX ('wonderful') evidently read *'addîr(îm)*, 'majestic', and interpreted the previous word as a variant of 'booth'; hence, 'thy wonderful tabernacle'. Dahood proposes 'when I cross the barrier, and prostrate myself . . .', basing the latter verb on an Ugaritic root.

[3] The hill *Mizar* ('smallness') was evidently part of the range which Hermon dominated, but is so far unidentified. Or conceivably it could be an ironic reference to the mighty Hermon itself ('the little hill!'), in the spirit of 68:15f. where the great peaks are made to feel insignificant beside Mount Zion, God's abode.

rushes among boulders and over falls. Something of its booming and hissing seems to be echoed in the Hebrew of verse 7 (Heb. 8): *t^ehôm-'el-t^ehôm qōrē' l^eqôl ṣinnôrèḵa*; and the first of these words (the *deep*) has the formidable background of Genesis 1:2.

Here is the picture of all that is overwhelming: his footing gone, and wave after wave submerging him. This is the very language that Jonah takes up in the depths (*cf.* 7b with Jon. 2:3)

Yet his faith keeps asserting itself. In 6a, his *I remember thee* is an advance on the nostalgia of 'These things I remember' (4)—things that, unlike God Himself, were no longer within reach. Again, the deep waters are seen as *thy* cataracts, *thy* waves, *thy* billows. Above all, verse 8 is as deeply assured of God's presence as verses 9f. are hurt by His 'absence' (*cf.* the comment on verse 5). There is no easing of the stress, but the emotions now have the background of strong convictions. So there is a telling contrast between the mentions of *day . . . and . . . night* in verse 8 and verse 3.

Three refrains meet here, unobtrusively binding the whole composition together. Verse 9b ties in with 43:2b; 10b with 42:3b; 11 with 42:5 (where see comment) and with 43:5.

43:1-5. The release

Throughout Psalm 42 there has been a growing reliance on the things that cannot be shaken, although the storm of suffering has given no sign of abating. The process continues here. The dark moods (2b, 5) alternate with increasingly affirmative praying. *Vindicate me* (1) is a more resilient opening than the confessions of dryness and bewilderment in 42:1f., 6f., necessary as they had been. And the ordeal of darkness and insecurity is apparent to us now only through a positive request, a plea for the *light* and *truth* (*i.e.*, divine faithfulness) that will dispel them (3).

This prayer of verse 3 is worded in such a way as to raise the question whether it looks forward to a necessarily literal homecoming or not. To be led home by God's light and truth could mean being brought back from exile by the One who displays these qualities; but it is a rather indirect way of saying it. It seems at least a possible meaning that, given this light and truth, the psalmist knows he can enjoy even in exile the very blessings of God's *holy hill* and *altar*. The Psalms often speak of such spiritual equivalents of the outward means of worship: *e.g.* 50:13f.; 51:17; 141:2.

So the chief refrain (5), at its third appearance, can take up the brave words of 42:5, 11 with a different tone, confident rather than doggedly defiant. Homeward bound or not, the poet can praise God as his 'exceeding joy' and—not merely his *help*, which is too weak a word—his 'salvation'. Outwardly nothing has changed: but he has won through.

Psalm 44
National Defeat

The innocent sufferer goes through many heart-searchings in the Psalms. But the larger unit, the nation, is less often sure of its innocence: its sins can all too easily account for its sufferings. This psalm is perhaps the clearest example of a search for some other cause of national disaster than guilt and punishment. It comes within sight of an answer at the point of its greatest perplexity: 'Nay, *for thy sake* we are slain . . .' (22). Momentarily it sees that God's people are caught up in a war that is more than local: the struggle of 'the kings of the earth . . . against the Lord and his Anointed' (2:2). The New Testament, with more of the pieces in position, will see the persecuted church foreshadowed here, and diagnose not defeat but victory (Rom. 8:36ff.).

The scattering among the nations (11) and the people's clear conscience about idolatry (17ff.) seem at first sight to indicate post-exilic times for the composition of the psalm; but there were deportations before the Exile (*cf.* Am. 1:6, 9), and such a psalm as the Davidic Psalm 60 (with strong similarities to the present one) is a reminder that defeat was not unknown in the reigns of loyal kings. The inclusion of this psalm in the Second Book of the Psalter makes a pre-exilic date more likely than not.

44:1-8. The glorious past
When Cranmer's Litany brought together the first verse of this psalm and the last (26), as declaration and petition, it was treating the prayer as a Christian inheritance, not merely an Israelite relic. Romans 8:36 does the same (see above);

and the psalm itself rests its case on the continuity to be expected down the generations of God's people.

1-3. The link with the past is all the stronger for the fact that the fathers' exploits were not their own but God's; there is no question here of looking back to a race of heroes that has since degenerated.

4-8. Nor has their secret of success been lost. If the king is the speaker in verse 4, he is declaring that Israel is still as surely a theocracy as ever. The cry, *Thou art my King, O God* (RSV mg.), is his act of homage, followed at once by prayer (the Heb. has 'Ordain victories . . .'; *cf.* RSV mg.) and by words of trust. The strong emphases in verse 6, *not in my bow . . .* , *nor can my sword . . .* , clearly echo those of verse 3: 'not by their own sword . . . , nor did their own arm . . .'. Nothing in their battles has changed, it seems, except the results, which are disastrous. This is the theme of the next paragraph.

44:9-16. The disastrous present

Verse 9b would be better translated by the present tense: 'and dost not go forth with our armies', exactly as at 60:10. If this is true, the rest is no surprise; but much depends on the sense in which it is true, which will be explored in verses 17ff. Meanwhile the distress of God's people deepens with every line of verses 10-12, with rout, spoil, slaughter, scattering and slavery; but worse than any of these is their inner defeat described in verses 15f.: a complete loss of confidence, through accepting the world's valuation of them in 13f. They are more than defeated; they are demoralized.

But they are not so demoralized as to give up trying to make sense of what has happened. In the next paragraph this will lead them, and us, to the brink of the New Testament's answer.

44:17-26. O Lord, why . . . ?

In the heart-searching of verses 17-22, the important fact begins to emerge that disaster is one thing, and disgrace quite another. The defeats which seemed to prove God's withdrawal in wrath, now suggest only His refusal to be hurried (23ff.) or to do what everyone has expected of Him. The psalm is exploring the baffling fluctuations that have their counterpart in Christian history: periods of blessing and barrenness, advance and retreat, which may correspond to no apparent changes of men's loyalty or methods. Although its picture of the sleeping Lord may seem naïve to us, it was acted out in the New Testament, to teach a lesson which we still find relevant; *cf.* verse 13 with Mark 4:38.

But the crux is in verse 22, with the phrase *for thy sake*. The psalm does not develop it, but it implies the revolutionary thought that suffering may be a battle-scar rather than a punishment; the price of loyalty in a world which is at war with God. If this is so, a reverse as well as a victory may be a sign of fellowship with Him, not of alienation. So Paul quotes verse 22 not with the despair of the 'more than defeated' (see on 9–16, above), but with conviction that 'in all these things we are more than conquerors through him who loved us' (Rom. 8:36f.). The divine sleep, aloofness and inattention of verses 23f. are the appearances; the reality behind them is given the last word in the psalm: *thy steadfast love.*

Psalm 45
Royal Wedding

This wedding benediction is as dazzling as the occasion it graces. The outward splendour of the event is evoked in every line, and beneath the surface we can sense the momentous event that it is for the two central characters: both an end and a beginning (10f., 16f.), pivotal not only for them but for the kingdom, whose future is bound up with the sons they will produce. Above and beyond this, the psalm is Messianic. The royal compliments suddenly blossom into divine honours (6f.), and the New Testament will take them at their full value.

This last point has possible implications for another example of wedding poetry, the Song of Songs, since by its language and its title, '*a love song*', the psalm comes as clearly into the category of literal wedding verse as does the Song, yet speaks undoubtedly of Christ. It is proof enough that the one level of meaning need not exclude the other. But Ephesians 5:32f. puts the matter beyond doubt.

Title

According to Lilies, or 'set to Shoshannim' (RV): see Introduction, VI. *c*. 3, p. 42. On *Maskil* and *choirmaster*, see pp. 38, 40.

45:1. Prologue: Verses for a King

This is one of the rare occasions when a psalmist allows us a glimpse of the process of composition; *cf.* 2 Samuel 23:2; perhaps Psalm 36:1 (see comment); Psalms 39:1-3; 49:3f.; 73:2ff.; 78:2f. The present verse tells of a theme almost clamouring to be heard; the poet's heart is 'astir' with it (*cf.* NEB), and the words come fluently. In the other passages different aspects of inspiration appear, and yet others in the Law and the Prophets.

45:2-5. Kingly stature

This king is no figurehead but the embodiment of all that gives kingship its unique glory: its claim to combine immemorial continuity (2c, 6a) and compelling personal glory (2ff.) in one man. The portrait could be discounted as conventional flattery were it not for the one king of whom similar things can soberly be said: that he is 'chiefest among ten thousand' (*cf.* 2a), that 'no man ever spoke like this man' (*cf.* 2b), that he is 'meek and lowly', yet rides forth 'conquering and to conquer' (*cf.* 3-5), and that he 'is called Faithful and True' (*cf.* 4a, b).

2. The phrase *God has blessed you for ever* may have prompted the last words of Romans 9:5. If so, the fact that the psalm later addresses the king as God (6f.) may have a bearing on the vexed question of Paul's meaning at that point.

4. This verse inspired the magnificent hymn, 'Ride on! ride on in majesty!', whose third line, 'O Saviour meek, pursue Thy road', derives the thought of meekness from the AV, *etc.*, as in the Hebrew text. But the Hebrew reads lit. 'because of truth and meekness-righteousness', which the older versions ease by adding an 'and', and most newer versions by bolder changes.[1] On the whole, the simplest solution still seems to be 'meekness *and* righteousness', as in LXX, Vulg., *etc.*

---

[1] More moderately, Dahood suggests '. . . and defend the poor' (*weʿānāw ḥaṣdēq*), for MT's *weʿanwâ-ṣedeq*. This involves no change of consonants, and is similar to 82:3. It does however involve a change of vowels and of word-division.

45:6–9. Kingly state

Throne and *sceptre* introduce the array of formal splendours and symbols of the king, for whose honour and retinue no rarity is too costly and no person too exalted.

But these are incidentals beside the astonishing words addressed to the king in verses 6 and 7. The RSV, NEB and NT (but not JB nor Gelineau) have sidestepped the plain sense of verse 6 (which is confirmed by the ancient versions and by the New Testament) by reducing the words 'Thy throne, O God' to something less startling. But the Hebrew resists any softening here, and it is the New Testament, not the new versions, which does it justice when it uses it to prove the superiority of God's Son to the very angels (Heb. 1:8f.). Added to this, verse 7 distinguishes between *God, your God*, and the king who has been addressed as 'God' in verse 6. This paradox is consistent with the incarnation, but mystifying in any other context. It is an example of Old Testament language bursting its banks, to demand a more than human fulfilment (as did Ps. 110:1, according to our Lord). The faithfulness of the pre-Christian LXX in translating these verses unaltered is very striking.

8. *Ivory palaces* were so named for the inlays of ivory in their panelling and ornamentation. The implication here is that their contents would be of equal excellence. Ahab's palace was so adorned (1 Ki. 22:39), as were other great houses (Am. 3:15; 6:4). Some fine examples of this ivory work have been recovered.

9. The climax of the setting of the scene is reached with the place prepared for *the queen* herself, who will be the subject of the next part of the poem. Not only at the wedding but in the affairs of state her place will be at his side: *cf.* Nehemiah 2:6 (and, by analogy, Eph. 2:6).

45:10–12. The bride's allegiance

A royal wedding emphasizes with special clarity the parting and new beginning which are fundamental to all marriage.[1] Here the brunt of it falls on the bride, as a king's daughter (13; *cf.* AV, *etc.*), whose old loyalties must not compete with the new. This verse stands as an important counterpart to

[1] See Tyndale Commentary on *Genesis* (on 2:24); see also W. Trobisch, *I Married You* (IVP, 1972), especially ch. 2.

Genesis 2:24, which stressed the husband's corresponding break with his former home, to give himself to his wife. His side of the matter is glimpsed here too, not only in his desire for his bride (11a) but in his new orientation to the future, to be a parent rather than a son (16).

12. The bride's submission to her partner as both husband and king (11b; *cf.* Sarah's use of the word *lord*, Gn. 18:12, AV, RV) goes hand in hand with the dignity she also derives from him. His friends and subjects are now hers; she is the gainer, not the loser, by her homage. *Tyre* is mentioned as the last word in wealth (*cf.* Ezk. 27) and at the same time an old trading partner of David and Solomon. The Hebrew has 'the daughter of Tyre', which RSV is probably right in taking to mean *the people* (*cf.*, *e.g.*, Is. 47) rather than an individual. Whether the first phrase of verse 13 (*with all kinds of wealth*) should be joined to verse 12, as in RSV and most moderns, or to the rest of verse 13, is a moot point and of small importance.

45:13-15. The bridal train

The AV is unforgettable with 'The king's daughter is all glorious within'; but since the word for 'within' usually means inside a building, RSV is probably right in seeing this as *in her chamber*, the point from which her procession now sets out towards *the palace of the king* (15). For the expression *virgin companions*, JB has simply, and preferably, 'bridesmaids'.

This escorting of the bride, *led to the king* in her finest attire while he awaits her in full state, is no superfluous formality: it is the acted equivalent of Paul's phrase 'to present you as a pure bride to her one husband' (2 Cor. 11:2), and brings out the emphasis of the first wedding, in which God 'brought' the woman to the man, and of the last, in which the church comes 'prepared' as a bride 'adorned' for her husband. To do away with these elements of a marriage is to trivialize it, playing down the honour due between bridegroom and bride, and the place they both occupy in a wider circle.

45:16, 17. Sons for the throne

It is the king who is addressed now; the *you* and *your* are masculine. It is his turn to be pointed towards the future rather than the past (16; *cf.* 10 above), with the promise of new glories. These words could be simply the formal good wishes appropriate to a king, like the greeting 'live for ever'.

But the Messianic oracle of verses 6f. prepares us to take them as a foretaste of God's bringing 'many sons to glory' (Heb. 2:10, 13), who will 'reign on earth' (Rev. 6:10) with their master, whose praise will be as endless as this benediction makes it.

Psalm 46
A City Unshaken

Luther's battle-hymn, *Ein' feste Burg*, took its starting-point from this psalm, catching its indomitable spirit but striking out in new directions. The psalm for its part proclaims the ascendancy of God in one sphere after another: His power over nature (1–3), over the attackers of His city (4–7) and over the whole warring world (8–11). Its robust, defiant tone suggests that it was composed at a time of crisis, which makes the confession of faith doubly impressive. But as the crisis is left unidentified, and the psalm ranges far beyond any local situation, there is little to be gained by historical speculation. On the theory that its origin is to be sought in a cultic drama, see Introduction, III, pp. 9ff.

Title
See Introduction, VI. *c.* 3, pp. 40f.

46:1–3. God in the tumult
Until recently, man has had few thoughts to spare for the possibility of a world catastrophe. But this psalm can face it unafraid, because its opening phrase means exactly what it says. Our true security is in God, not in God *plus* anything else. Both this confidence and the threat to it are now spelt out.

1. *Refuge* gives the defensive or external aspect of salvation: God the unchanging, in whom we find shelter. *Strength* probably implies the dynamic aspect: God within, to empower the weak for action. Both are summarized in the words *a very present help in trouble*, where the term *very present* has implications of His readiness to be 'found' (as the root is used in, *e.g.*, Is. 55:6) and of His being 'enough' for any situation (*cf.* the Heb. of Jos. 17:16; Zc. 10:10).

2, 3. This is not only a powerful word-picture, built up of the two things that are most immutable[1] and impregnable, *the earth* and *the mountains*, over against the symbol of what is most restless and menacing, *the sea*; it begins to contemplate the end of the whole created scheme, by which the earth, the mountains and the waters were set in place, as described in, *e.g.*, 104:5–9. This ultimate undoing, glimpsed darkly here, is made explicit in 102:25ff., where the final security of God's servants is made equally clear.

46:4–7. God in His city

From the upheaval of nature the psalm turns to the raging of man, and a city under siege.

4. With God the waters are no longer menacing seas but a life-giving *river*; *cf.* the seas and floods (rivers) of 98:7f., welcoming their Maker; *cf.* too the picture of God's help as the quiet water-supply of the besieged, in Isaiah 8:6. *The city of God* is one of the great themes of the Old Testament, and especially of the Psalms, where the present psalm and the next two form a memorable group.[2] God's choice of Zion, or Jerusalem, had been as striking as His choice of David, and the wonder of it keeps breaking through; for it is only as God's abode that it is either strong (5) or of any consequence; yet as such it will be the envy of the world (68:15f.) and the mother-city of the nations (87). Indeed the Old Testament already points towards the New Testament's vision of Zion as a heavenly community rather than a mere locality on earth (*cf.* on 48:2).

5. The promise *she shall not be moved* gains special force from the repetition of the same word, *moved*, used of the mountains (2; RSV 'shake') and of the kingdoms (6; RSV 'totter'), impressive as these are in comparison with little Zion. Also the words *right early* (lit. 'at break of day'; *cf.* NEB) set up an echo of the greatest deliverance of all, the moment when 'at break of day' the Red Sea turned back to engulf the armies of Egypt (Ex. 14:27).

6. As in some other places, judgment is seen here in both its aspects: first the outworking of the inherent instability of

---

[1] Note, by contrast, the word *change* (2a), the same word as in 15:4c.
[2] See also, among others, Pss. 65; 68; 76; 84; 87; 99; 122; 125; 132–134; 137.

evil, where the fitting sequel of to *rage* (or be in tumult) is to be insecure (to *totter*, on which see also on 5, above); and secondly the intervention of God, whose *voice* will be as decisive in dissolving the world as it was in creating it (*cf* 33:6, 10).

7. The first line of this stirring refrain speaks of might (whether the *hosts* are the armies of Israel, as 1 Sa. 17:45 may suggest, or those of heaven, as in 1 Ki. 22:19), and the second line speaks of grace, by the mention of *Jacob*, God's chosen. The word *refuge*, here and in verse 11, is distinct from that of verse 1, and implies inaccessible height: hence NEB 'our high stronghold'.

46:8–11. God exalted in the earth

This is a vision of things finally to come, although the victories of the present are a foretaste of them. The word for *behold* is generally used for seeing with the inward eye, as a 'seer' or prophet sees.

Although the outcome is peace, the process is judgment. The reassuring words, *he makes wars cease* . . . , are set in a context not of gentle persuasion but of a world devastated and forcibly disarmed (8, 9b).[1] This sequence, with tranquillity on the far side of judgment, agrees with Old Testament prophecy and apocalypse, and with the New Testament (*e.g.* Is. 6:10–13; 9:5; Dn. 12:1; 2 Pet. 3:12f.).

10, 11. So, too, the injunction *Be still* . . . is not in the first place comfort for the harassed but a rebuke to a restless and turbulent world: 'Quiet!'—in fact, 'Leave off!' It resembles the command to another raging sea: 'Peace! Be still!' And the end in view is stated in terms not of man's hopes but of God's glory. His firm intention 'I will be exalted' (so AV, RV, more accurately than RSV) is enough to arouse the resentment of the proud but the longing and resolve of the humble: 'Be exalted, O God, above the heavens' (57:11). But also their renewed confidence. The refrain comes back with added force, if such a God is 'with us', and if one so exalted is 'our high stronghold' (NEB).

---

[1] The word translated *chariots* (9) normally means 'carts', which makes LXX's 'shields' look more probable (*cf.* NEB, JB, Gelineau). 'Shields' represents the same Heb. consonants as 'carts', with one vowel-change.

Psalm 47
'The Shout of a King'

From the first word to the last, this communicates the excitement and jubilation of an enthronement; and the king is
God Himself. A strong school of thought holds that this psalm
and others, notably 93, 95-99, arose out of an annual festival
which dramatized God's power over His foes and His kingship
over creation.[1] But given the notion of God as King, it is a
short step to creating the poetry that exploits the analogies
it suggests, festival or no festival. And more than poetry: this
is prophecy, whose climax is exceptionally far-reaching.

47:1-4. Our king, their conqueror

The opening summons to *all peoples* sets the scene truly: the
vision is world-wide. 'Peoples', 'nations' and 'all the earth'
are words that dominate the psalm. The note of *joy* (1) will
be dominant too, for this king is no tyrant; but the first
stanza establishes His awesomeness, and makes no bones
about His judgments and His right of choice (3f.), which will
have the look of favouritism until the final verse brings the
dénouement. Meanwhile, *Jacob* can unashamedly delight in
his conquests and in his privilege of knowing God by name
(*the Lord*, 2; *i.e.*, Yahweh) as well as by title.[2] *Cf.* 147:19f.

4. *The pride of Jacob* is a brief way of saying 'Jacob's glorious
land'. The phrase, *Jacob whom he loves*, may provoke the
question 'Why?'—which is equally unanswerable whether the
object of the love is 'Jacob' or 'me' or 'the church' or 'the
world' (*cf.* Gal. 2:20; Eph. 5:25; Jn. 3:16). The Bible's
concern is, instead, to deal with our wrong answers (Dt. 7:7),
doubts (Mal. 1:2ff.) and betrayals (Ho. 11:1f.).

47:5-7. Royal march and royal welcome

The clue to verse 5 is its allusion to 2 Samuel 6:15, where the
ark was brought up to the city of David to make that city
God's abode. In the words, *with a shout, . . . with the sound
of a trumpet*, the two passages (2 Sa. and the Ps.) are identical

---

[1] See Introduction, III, pp. 9ff.
[2] *Most High* (Elyon) was a term used also by the Canaanites.

in the Hebrew. So God is pictured here ascending His earthly throne, whether or not this was dramatized anew by a periodic procession with the ark. The perfect tense, *God has gone up*, may mean that the allusion is to the single great event in David's day.

6, 7. The insistent repetition, *sing praises* (a single word in Heb., with therefore a swifter, livelier impact) suggests something of the sound of a crowd shouting their acclamation. The final word is *maśkîl*, which is found as a title for certain psalms (32, 42, *etc.*; see Introduction, VI. *c.* 2, p. 38), and so is translated by RSV here as *with a psalm*. But it comes from a root containing the idea of wisdom and skill—hence NEB 'with all your art', and AV, RV 'with understanding'. The last of these contributes most to the sentence, and is the interpretation given by LXX, which Paul seems to have had in mind in I Corinthians 14:15, 'I will sing with the mind also.'

47:8, 9. One throne, one world

The vision of the psalm takes in a whole new area in the final verse. So far, God's relation to the world at large has been presented as that of a 'great king' (2), *i.e.*, an emperor, whose own people are distinct from the outer circle of his subjects (3f.). Now, with a single word, the real end in view comes into sight. The innumerable *princes* and *peoples* are to become one *people*; and they will no longer be outsiders but within the covenant: this is implied in their being called *the people of the God of Abraham*. It is the abundant fulfilment of the promise of Genesis 12:3; it anticipates what Paul expounds of the inclusion of the Gentiles as Abraham's sons (Rom. 4:11; Gal. 3:7-9).

But characteristically the psalm relates this to its theme, the kingly glory of God. Its comment is not 'the nations will be at peace', true though it would be, but instead, *he is highly exalted*. This was, in different words, the climax of 46:10, above and beyond 46:9. It is the point to which everything is moving. Meanwhile the gospel will reveal the unexpected kind of 'exaltation' which will begin the process of 'gathering' the peoples: 'I, when I am lifted up . . . , will draw all men to myself' (Jn. 12:32).

Psalm 48
City of God

There is much in common here with Psalm 46, and not least
with its atmosphere of elation after a great deliverance. Here
too, whatever the occasion that immediately inspired the
psalm, we are conscious of a bigger setting than the hills of
Judah. Zion is more than a local capital; the struggle concerns
the whole earth and the whole span of time. The outlines of
'the Jerusalem above', with its great walls and foundations
which are 'for ever', are already coming into view.

48:1–3. The King in residence
If this is a 'Zion psalm', it is so simply because of *the great
King* who reigns there, as our Lord pointed out in quoting
verse 2 (Mt. 5:35). It sees the city as it will be when 'all the
nations flow to it' (Is. 2:2ff.)—for it is certainly not yet *the
joy of all the earth*. By an effective turn of phrase it portrays
the literal Zion in terms of the heavenly one—the community
whose king is God—by identifying it with *the far north* (2), of
all places. (Geographically one could as soon speak of Rome
or London in such a way!) This was a traditional expression,
in Israel and among her neighbours,[1] for God's royal seat:
in Isaiah 14:13 it is equivalent to 'heaven'.

3. But Zion is also very much on earth and within history.
It has need of fortifications (*citadels*, as verses 12f. confirm
by their parallel terms, rather than purely decorative 'palaces'),
though it is God who effectively mans them; and it looks
back on particular emergencies in which God has revealed
Himself in power (*cf.* JB 'God proved to be her fortress').
There is the same mingling of mundane precautions and
miraculous help as in the church's experience.

48:4–8. The kings in rout
The kings (4), in the plural, and *the ships of Tarshish* (7), *i.e.*,
the great ocean-going craft, seem to indicate a wider struggle
than any of the attacks on Jerusalem in the Old Testament.[2]

---

[1] *Cf.* Baal's Mount Zaphon ('north') in, *e.g.*, *ANET²*, p. 136, c. 27ff.
[2] But the disaster at sea may conceivably be no more than a metaphor
for the sudden overwhelming of an army. *Cf.* our figurative use of the expression 'sunk without trace'.

The scene is more like the world-wide conspiracy of Psalm 2, though it could well have been initially suggested by the great army of Assyria, whose commanders were 'all kings' (Is. 10:8), as Kirkpatrick and others point out, and whose people God promised to 'break', using the same basic verb as *shatter* here (Is. 14:1ff.). The language is sweeping enough to only limit the great victories in 'the wars of the Lord', and to anticipate the end itself. The church can sing this psalm with the triumphs of the gospel in mind, and with an eye to the final rout. Verse 7 is echoed in Ezekiel 27:26, where *the east wind* wrecks the treasure-ship of Tyre; and this in turn becomes the symbol of the world's end in Revelation 18 (*cf.*, *e.g.*, Rev. 18:17ff. with Ezk. 27:29ff.).

8. The sequence, *heard* and *seen*, is made much of in the Bible, with its emphasis on believing, since faith rests on testimony (Rom. 10:17) and is content for proof to follow. The hardship of only hearing is poignantly shown in 44:1, 9ff.; the subsequent 'seeing' may be exhilarating, as here, or overwhelming as in, *e.g.*, Job 42:5f.; John 20:28f.; perhaps always, in some degree, both together.

48:9-11. The chorus of praise

The basic meaning of the verb translated *we have thought on* is to picture or formulate. Most versions, ancient as well as modern, take this as happening purely in the mind (*e.g.* 'reflect on', JB; 'ponder', Gelineau), but NEB sees here a dramatic ritual, and translates it 'we re-enact the story of . . .'. This is possible but precarious; the evidence for anything in Israel's worship more dramatic than a procession (see on verses 12ff.) is indirect and ambiguous. See Introduction, III, pp. 14ff. Some instances of celebrating God's acts of love at the Temple are found in, *e.g.*, 2 Chronicles 5:13; Nehemiah 8:13-18, where psalms and readings were the chief means to this end.

10, 11. This world-wide vision agrees with verse 2 and is more explicit, since the *name* of God stands for His self-disclosure (*cf.* Ex. 34:5-7, and see on Ps. 20:1), and His *praise* is both the renown He deserves and the response it awakes. In other words, there is a glimpse of a revelation for the whole earth. In view of this, the translation *victory*, in the last line, is unduly narrow, since it basically means 'righteousness' and so has reference to what issues from God's character, not simply from His power. *Judgments* (11) are similar, and speak of His fair decisions: a boon to the oppressed, if a terror to the wicked; cf. Isaiah 11:4; 42:4.

The daughters of Judah are its cities and villages: cf., e.g., Judges 1:27, Heb.

48:12-14. The ramparts reviewed

When Nehemiah finished the wall of Jerusalem he had two processions counter-marching round the top of it for the dedication (Ne. 12:31ff., 38ff.). After the lifting of a siege it would be equally appropriate to do the rounds of the defences, singing such a psalm as this; so too at one of the pilgrim feasts. But again, the march could be pictured in the mind (as perhaps in 84:5); there is no sure means of telling. For the Christian singer of the psalm there is a corresponding encouragement to review the towers and ramparts of the church, a community as indestructible, essentially, as a fortress (Eph. 2:20-22; Rev. 21:10ff.), yet as vulnerable, undefended, as a flock of sheep (Acts 20:29).

13b, 14. But the psalm is not in praise of Zion except as God's abode. Verse 14 is almost a non-sequitur: when we are expecting a crowning glory of the city, we hear no more of it: only of God ('Such is God', NEB). But it is God as *our God*; and this relationship is permanent because the covenant that established it was primarily of His making (Gn. 17:2, 8). Three different words express this permanence, and RSV's third *ever* is an emendation of the Hebrew *'al-mût*,[1] 'unto dying' ('unto death', AV, RV).

---

[1] The consonants of this, if joined into one word, can be revocalized as *'ōlāmôt*, 'evermore', as in LXX, Vulg. Another view is that they are a musical direction appended to this psalm or introducing the next: cf. the title to Ps. 9 or (assuming haplography) Ps. 46. On this, see Introduction, VI. c. 3, p. 40 ('According to Alamoth'). The chief objection to the sense 'unto dying' is that the psalm's interest is corporate rather than individual; but this is hardly a conclusive point. A. R. Johnson would overcome this objection by making 'death' a term for Israel's national enemies, with the translation 'God . . . is our leader against "Death"' (*Sacral Kingship in Ancient Israel* (University of Wales Press, 1955), p. 81). Yet it seems enough to point out that 'unto death' is simply the strongest expression one can use for constancy.

Psalm 49
'This World's Empty Glory'

The language of the prelude, the call to mankind, uses many of the terms which open the book of Proverbs, and proclaims this a wisdom psalm, offering instruction to men rather than worship to God. Its theme of the futility of worldliness, summed up in the refrain (12, 20), is close to that of Ecclesiastes. But it brings out into the open the assurance of victory over death which Ecclesiastes leaves concealed. The great *But God . . .* (15) is one of the mountain-tops of Old Testament hope.

49:1-4. To all men everywhere
Like most of the Wisdom writings, this psalm speaks to men in their common humanity, not only to Israelites in their special bond of covenant with God. It brings a revelation from Him, and by its concern to catch the ear of the world it implies the crucial importance of what it has to say. So these initial verses play their part towards the interpretation of, *e.g.*, verse 15, by preparing us to take it at its full value rather than in some weaker and less epoch-making sense.

2. Each of the words *low* and *high* represents the phrase 'sons of man' (using the general term *'āḏām* and the individual term *'îš*). They are more convincingly translated by NEB: 'all mankind, every living man'.

4. *Solve* is lit. 'open', and could therefore mean either answering the problem or expounding it. The former is more likely in view of the summons to the world to listen. NEB paraphrases it well: 'and tell on the harp how I read the riddle.'

49:5-9. Brief triumph
With a teacher's thought-provoking technique, the psalmist's *Why?* invites a fresh look at a closed question—which is a fruitful approach, even in a situation as bad as this, with the enemy everywhere (5b), and overbearing (6), and as unscrupulous as an unregenerate Jacob (whose name, in its bad sense of 'overreacher', is akin to RSV *persecutors* here, or those who are 'at my heels' (5, RV); *cf*. Gn. 27:36).

7-9. Even before the answer, the question itself has offered a clue in verse 6, with the words *who trust in their wealth*—since wealth is notoriously unstable (Pr. 23:5). But now comes the full absurdity: that of living for what always fails, and must do so at the point where failure undoes everything.

The *ransom* picture is doubly appropriate, since being held to ransom is as much the hazard of the very rich as redemption is the need of the very poor. At this stage the point is simply one's inability to buy one's way, or that of anyone else,[1] out of dying. The question of ransom as atonement (*cf.* Mt. 20:28) will not be glimpsed until verse 15, and indirectly at that.

49:10–12. Total loss

Verse 10 gives merciless clarity to the fact that the answer to the question 'How much did he leave?' is 'Everything'. It is hardly softened by the grim exception allowed in verse 11, if the right reading is that *their grave(s)*[2]—in contrast to the *lands* they named—are the one permanent piece of 'real estate' a man can own.

12. There will be a telling change (which RSV and other recent versions iron out[3]) when this refrain is heard a second time in verse 20. In the Hebrew text its two forms sum up the two halves of the psalm. Here it drives home the point that at the end there is no 'overnight lodging' (the common meaning of this word for *abide*) that money or position can buy. (*Pomp* has connections with both: *cf.* 'precious', Pr. 20:15; 'honour', Est. 6:3.)

Yet, for both better and worse, homelessness is not the end of the story. This now continues, soon to reach its climax.

---

[1] Instead of 'a brother' (*'āḥ*; *cf.* AV, RV), some MSS have *truly* (*'ak̠*, RSV), which would then be followed by the reflexive verb *ransom himself*, a difference of vowels, not consonants. But the reading, 'brother', is attested by LXX, *etc.*, and makes good sense ('None . . . can by any means redeem his brother', AV, RV). NEB 'Alas! no man can ever ransom himself' involves the same vowel-change as RSV in the verb, but takes the word *'āḥ* to mean 'Alas', as it does in Ezk. 6:11.

[2] The ancient versions are united in reading *their grave(s)* (*qibrām*), as RSV, rather than 'their midst' (*qirbām*), *i.e.*, 'their inward thought'. The italics in AV, RV show how hard it is to make sense of the latter, which is the MT reading. There seems little doubt that a copyist has transposed the two middle consonants, as RSV assumes.

[3] The ancient versions read 'understand' in both places, whereas MT has *yālîn*, 'abide', here, and *yābîn*, 'understand', in verse 20 (Heb. 21). NEB's change from *pomp* to 'oxen' (*bāqār* for *yᵉqār*) is purely conjectural.

49:13-15. The great divide

So far, although the stress has been on the mortality of the arrogant, since the problem started with them in verse 5, death has been seen as the common lot of all men. Now a distinction begins to emerge between these worldlings (together, perhaps with their admirers; but the meaning of 13b is obscure[1]) and on the other hand the men of God.

14, 15. *Death* personified is an unusual poetic figure in the Old Testament; this passage ranks for sinister effect with Jeremiah 9:21, where death climbs in at the windows to carry off the living. Now he is no intruder; he is on his home pastures. But the text as we have it (supported by the ancient versions) sees another conquest as well. 'The upright shall have dominion over them in the morning' (RSV mg., AV, RV; *cf.* JB).[2] This may simply promise that the victims will turn the tables on their oppressors in the long run, after the manner of, *e.g.*, Habakkuk 2:6ff. But it may look on to the resurrection morning of Daniel 12:2; *cf.* the words 'when I awake' in Psalm 17:15.

What can certainly be found in this verse up to this point is the contrast between the finally helpless and the finally victorious. But the rest of verse 14 leaves no doubt of the ultimate contrast, completed in 15, which is between corruption and salvation. The corruption is described impersonally, as an unmaking (*waste away*) and a dispossessing,[3] but the salvation is personal from start to finish. God, instead of demanding a ransom as in verse 7, pays it Himself (15)—in which fact there is at least a hint of atonement in view of the context, whereby Sheol has the custody of the sinner. And the *he* and *me* confirm that this is not salvation at arm's length

[1] Lit. 'and after them with their mouth they are pleased'—where 'after them' could mean 'afterwards' or refer to those who follow them; 'their mouth' could mean their sayings (AV, RV) or their portion, and 'they' could be these men or their followers. NEB, JB, Gelineau revocalize the consonants of 'they are pleased', to yield 'they run', and take this verb with either the present verse or (NEB) the next. This makes easier Hebrew and leaves the consonants intact; it may well be right. *Cf.* JB 'with men to run after them when they raise their voice'.

[2] RSV assumes that 'morning' (*bōqer*) is a mistake for 'grave' (*qeber*). But a new miscopying of the latter, so soon after verse 11, is hardly probable, and it also involves changes in the vowels and word-division in the rest of the line. NEB is even more speculative at this point.

[3] The most probable meaning of this difficult sentence is 'And their form (or show) is for Sheol to consume, without a place for it'.

but face to face. The word *receive* is more positive than it may sound to us; it is Enoch's word: 'God took him' (Gn. 5:24); it will recur in a setting like this in Psalm 73:24. Whether this vision reached as far as resurrection or not, it tells us the first thing that matters beyond death, that nothing can separate the servant from his Master, whose concern for him is loving and active.

49:16-20. The great illusion

We return to the question that was put in verse 5, now with even stronger grounds for the answer. Instead of *Be not afraid* we might have expected 'Look not (with envy)', a rather similar word (*cf.* NEB). But verse 5 explains the fear, for the kind of rich man who is in mind is ruthless. Notice that there is no promise here that he will not have the upper hand: only the reminder that his glory cannot last. Its rewards, such as they are, are faithfully summed up in verse 18. There is nothing more.

20. So the call is to courage and clear-sighted faith; and the closing refrain drives home the lesson by a pointed change from its earlier form. The Hebrew text, which RSV and NEB reject in spite of ancient testimony, is preserved in AV, RV: 'Man that is in honour, *and understandeth not*, is like the beasts that perish.'

Between the first refrain (12) and the second there has come the great promise of 14b, 15, but also the great gulf between the destinies of men. It is a sombre ending, but its purpose is made clear by the opening call: that 'all peoples' may 'hear' (1) and find the 'understanding' (3) which alone leads to life.

Psalm 50
The Judge Breaks Silence

In this powerful psalm the imagined scene is a theophany, God appearing in fire and tempest at mount Zion to summon the entire world to His judgment seat. But if all eyes are on Him, His eyes are on Israel. The whole psalm is addressed to the covenant-people, speaking first to the unthinkingly religious, and then to the hardened and hypocritical, to bring them a sharp breath of reality. It is the message which the prophets and finally Jesus had to put to a church that had forgotten that its dealings were with the living God.

The features that recall mount Sinai and the covenant (1–5), the allusions to the Ten Commandments (7, 18 an), and the reference to reciting them and to professing allegiance to the covenant (16), combine to give the impression of a ceremony of covenant remembrance and renewal as the setting of the psalm. See Introduction, III, pp. 13ff.

50:1-6. The Judge appears

The array of titles, El Elohim Yahweh—two general words for God together with the special name revealed to Israel—make a majestic and appropriate opening to a passage which brings together the world at large and the small circle of the chosen people. Everything at first points to a diatribe against the heathen, who are summoned to Zion (its beauty still untouched by judgment; contrast 2a with the nostalgia of La. 2:15), where sinful man must meet the impact of deity at its most dazzling and overwhelming (2, 3). Suddenly—for it emerges with the last word of verse 4—the tables are turned. Israel has appealed to God[1], only to find that she is herself the one on trial. The rest of mankind, with all heaven and earth (1, 4), has been assembled to witness the charge (cf. Dt. 30:19), not to answer it. Judgment must 'begin with the household of God' (1 Pet. 4:17). Her special calling is not played down: it is emphasized three times over in verse 4, where the words my faithful ones (ḥasîḏāy) and covenant and sacrifice recall the great ceremony of Exodus 24:3–8. Because of this, not in spite of it, she will be brought to strict account. It is the same point which is made with startling effect in Amos 3:2 and is explained in the saying about those 'to whom men commit much', in Luke 12:48. The Christian may reflect on the demanding implications of enjoying a still 'better covenant' (Heb. 7:22; 10:22ff.).

50:7-15. Plain words to the religious

It soon appears that the judgment scene is not for passing sentence but for bringing truth to light and sinners to repent-

---

[1] Verse 3 should run, 'Let our God come, and not be silent!' (cf. JB).

ance. Verses 8ff., by their very reassurances,[1] give a more damning picture of mindless religion than would any accusation. What caricature of God does Israel picture to itself? Is He a celestial 'poor relation', grasping, dependent and reproachful? And why, at the first sign of His displeasure (7), do their thoughts fly to points of ritual, not of relationship? Verses 14f. are equally revealing, by their implication of prayers and promises made in adversity and forgotten in prosperity. But the truth is meant to heal, not only to convict. The speech has opened (7) with reminders of the covenant (*my people . . . your God*) in words that recall both the Shema ('Hear, O Israel . . .', Dt. 6:4f.) and the Decalogue (Dt. 5:6ff.); and it presents God as the great Provider (*cf.* 11 with Mt. 6:26; 10:29) and great Deliverer (15), who looks for the warm response of gratitude and trust. These are the sacrifices (*cf.* Heb. 13:15) and this is the glory—not pomp but love—which He most desires.

50:16–21. Plain words to the hypocrites

These men are not the heathen but the nominally orthodox, those who combine 'wickedness and worship' (to borrow G. A. Smith's translation of Is. 1:13). If the mechanically pious folk of verses 7–15 needed reminding that God is spiritual, the hardened characters of 16–21 must face the fact that He is moral. It is now the second half of the Decalogue that becomes the touchstone.

16. This verse may well refer to the public law-reading commanded in Deuteronomy 31:10ff. One of the greatest of such occasions was Josiah's covenant-renewal (2 Ki. 23:1–3); yet Jeremiah was to suffer lifelong persecution from the very nation that had professed it. He appropriately looked for a new covenant (Je. 31:31ff.), of the heart, not simply *on your lips.*

17. To *hate discipline* is evidently not as modern a trait as it seems. The importance of accepting it is a constant theme of Proverbs (where it is usually translated 'instruction': *e.g.* Pr. 1:7), because wisdom is a quality of character, and character is hard-won. The New Testament fully endorses this. In the present verse its association with *my words* shows

---

[1] There is no reason to turn verse 8 into a question ('Shall I not find fault . . .?' NEB). In verse 9 the similar construction is clearly a statement.

that it refers to the training of mind and conscience through Scripture (as in, *e.g.*, 2 Tim. 3:14 – 4:5), rather than the chastening effects of hardship (as in, *e.g.*, Heb. 12:3–11).

18–20. Three of the Ten Commandments, so glibly recited (16), are called in to expose men's rebellious affections and actions. It hardly needs saying that the friendship mentioned in verse 18 is that of boon companions, not of compassionate befrienders. The New Testament enlarges on this distinction in, *e.g.*, Mark 2:15–17; Luke 15; 1 Corinthians 5. In the present verse there may be an implication, too, of the hypocrisy of enjoying sin at second-hand while keeping out of trouble oneself; and this would be in character with the deviousness portrayed in 19 and 20. In the latter, the clause *You sit and speak* is legitimately translated in NEB 'You are for ever talking'.[1] But it could be meant literally, as a further vivid glimpse of this man in different settings: standing at worship (but in verse 16 JB 'standing there' is only an assumption, however valid), hobnobbing with his dubious friends (18), and holding forth at leisure to an interested circle (20).

21. Part of the value of God's silence is that it allows us to be ourselves—and to reveal ourselves. The middle line of this verse (which could be the epitaph of theologians, in their sphere, as well as of libertines in theirs) has its truth confirmed by the rash appeal of verse 3 that God should break His silence (see the footnote there).

50:22, 23. The parting charges

The two groups are addressed in reverse order. Verse 22 displays the twin characteristics of God's wrath: that it is reluctantly unleashed, but irresistible once that point is reached. In verse 23 the word *way* is simply 'a way', not 'his' or 'my way'; and there is much to be said for the RV margin's translation, after Delitzsch: '. . . glorifieth me, and prepareth a way that I may show him the salvation of God.' Whether in this translation or in the more familiar version ('who orders (his) way (aright)'), it again dismisses any notion of our doing God a favour. The phrase (lit.) 'he who sacrifices a thanksgiving', while it leaves room for a literal sacrifice, is suggestive of an offering of pure praise, such as that of

---

[1] D. W. Thomas, *TRP*, *ad loc.*, draws attention to this sense of 'sit' as 'continue' in the Heb. of Gn. 49:24; Lv. 12:4f.; 1 Ki. 22:1.

Hosea 14:2; Hebrews 13:15. The giving—the *salvation*—is on His side; ours is to receive it with the delighted thanks and obedience it deserves.

Psalm 51
Whiter than Snow

This is the fourth, and surely the greatest, of the seven 'penitential psalms' (see on Ps. 6). It comes from David's blackest moment of self-knowledge, yet it explores not only the depths of his guilt but some of the farthest reaches of salvation. The last two verses show that the nation, in its own darkest hour, found words here for its own confession and its re-kindling of hope.

The psalm can be studied for its themes, as well as in its progress from pleading to assurance. Much is to be learnt about God, sin and salvation in the course of it. It is rewarding, as well, to study the varieties of speech: the imperatives of request, the present and past tenses of confession, and the futures (more than appear in most translations; see comments) which thankfully take hold of saving grace.

David's name, reappearing here, will be found in all but four titles of the remaining twenty-two psalms of this Second Book.

Title
The story of David's sin and repentance is told in 2 Samuel 11 and 12. Between the David of this psalm and the cynical tactician of 2 Samuel 11 there stands simply (on the human scene) Nathan the prophet. The power of God's word is nowhere more strikingly evident than in this transformation.

51:1, 2. Appeal
The opening plea, *have mercy*, is the language of one who has no claim to the favour he begs. But *steadfast love* is a covenant word. For all his unworthiness, David knows that he still belongs; *cf.* the paradox of the prodigal's words, '*Father*, . . . I am no more worthy to be called thy son.' Coming closer still, he appeals to God's tender warmth, in the second word for *mercy*, an emotional term, used in, *e.g.*, Genesis 43:30 when

Joseph's 'heart', or inmost being, yearned for his brother. It is akin to the New Testament's visceral word for being 'moved with compassion'.

1b, 2. But there is more to forgiveness than a tender spirit. The accusing record of the sin remains, and the pollution clings. The plea, *blot out*, means 'wipe away', like the writing from a book (*cf*. Ex. 32:32; Nu. 5:23). Only the gospel could reveal at what cost 'the bond which stood against us' could be blotted out (*cf*. Col. 2:14). The companion metaphor, *wash me thoroughly*, uses a verb normally connected with the laundering of clothes, as if David is comparing himself to a foul garment needing to be washed and washed. The thought is still primarily of the guilt that makes him unfit for God's presence or God's people (*cf*. the potent object-lessons in Lv. 15). He will dwell on the more inward aspect of cleansing in verses 6–12.

51:3-5. Confession

In a new image, his sin looms up as an accusing presence: *cf*. NEB 'my sins confront me all the day long'. But this is not all.

4. His sin was treason. To say '*Against thee, thee only, have I sinned*' may invite the quibble that adultery and murder are hardly private wrongs. But it is a typically biblical way of going to the heart of the matter. Sin can be against oneself (1 Cor. 6:18) and against one's neighbour; but the flouting of God is always the length and breadth of it, as Joseph saw long before (Gn. 39:9). Our bodies are not our own; and our neighbours are made in God's image. Notice the immense contrast here to the self-absorbed outlook of 2 Samuel 11, where David's only question was, in effect, 'How do I cover my tracks?' Now it is, 'How could I treat God so?'

His complete acceptance of God's verdict (4b) is matched in the New Testament by the penitent thief (Lk. 23:41), and quoted in Romans 3:4 in its LXX form ('when thou art judged'). In that form it makes the point with maximum force, but it is still the same point as in the Hebrew here (*i.e.*, as in RSV, *etc.*): that no-one could find fault—even if it were our place to do so—with God's judgment on the sinner.

5. The new perspective on his sin, as self-assertion against God, opens up a new self-knowledge. This crime, David now sees, was no freak event: it was in character; an extreme expression of the warped creature he had always been, and of the faulty stock he sprang from. Similarly Isaiah saw his people's corruption as well, when he caught sight of his own (Is. 6:5). David is, of course, not speaking against his mother in particular, nor against the process of conception. Nor is he excusing himself. It is the climax of the facts that he is facing: that his sins are his own (the fivefold *my* in verses 1–3), and inexcusable (4); worst of all, they are the very element he lives in (5).

51:6–9. Restoration

This crescendo begins at an ominous point, at the gulf between what God desires[1] (6a) and what David has just confessed. But God's wishes are intentions: desiring *truth* He will *teach . . . wisdom*, not deplore its absence. A series of futures, not imperatives, begins with 6b (Heb. 8b; lit. 'thou shalt teach me . . .'), to the end of 8. Coverdale's version, in the Prayer Book, is almost alone in reproducing them as the affirmations which they are.

7. *Thou shalt purge me with hyssop* alludes to the cleansing of the leper, sprinkled seven times with the sacrificial blood into which the bunch of hyssop was dipped as a sprinkler (Lv. 14:6f.); or it may refer to the ritual for cleansing those who had come into contact with a dead body (Nu. 19:16–19). In either case it ended with the forthright pronouncement, 'and he shall be clean'—a promise which David takes up in the first person. He also knows from that context the special word for *purge*, to which the nearest equivalent would be 'de-sin' (Lv. 14:49; Nu. 19:19), and he pictures the final sequence in the ritual, the washing of clothes and body. But the descriptive touch, *whiter than snow*, is all his own: a flash of realization that with God there are no half-measures. *Cf.* Isaiah 1:18.

8. There is no need to substitute *Fill me* (RSV; *cf.* JB) for the Hebrew text 'Thou shalt make me hear . . .', by which David seems to picture the outcast's return into society, greeted by the sounds of welcome and festivity. For the climax, NEB rightly takes the basic meaning of the verb *rejoice* (*gîl*):

---

[1] In spite of verses 16 and 19, NEB and RP reject the common meaning of this verb in the present verse, in favour of one inferred from an Arabic root 'to keep, or guard'. This is improbable (16, 19), unnecessary and, in NEB, irrelevant to the context. *Cf.* on 37:23.

'let the bones *dance* which thou hast broken.' Once again, he looks for no half-hearted help.

9. This verse, with its echo of verse 1, completes the first part of the psalm, in which the emphasis has been mostly on guilt and its cleansing. Now the centre of gravity will move to salvation.

51:10-13. Inward renewal

The depth of self-knowledge seen in verses 3-5 might have led to despair. Instead, it has enlarged David's praying. (*Cf.* Rom. 7:18-25.) With the word *Create* he asks for nothing less than a miracle. It is a term for what God alone can do; but it can refer to a sustained process as well as an instantaneous act (*cf.* Gn. 2:3), and evidently does so here. Both David's early history and the language of 11b, 12a show that this is not an unregenerate man's request, but a prayer for holiness (*cf.* 11b). It covers, so to speak, all seven days of creation, not simply the first.

With the words *heart* and *spirit* he goes to the 'springs of life' (Pr. 4:23), and relates his own spirit to the Spirit of God. The prayer of 10b is given more accurately in the older versions as 'Renew[1] a right (or, steadfast) spirit within me'. It is parallel to the plea '*Restore* . . .' in verse 12: the prayer of a backslider who has found repentance.

11. The likely background to this fear of being a castaway was the example of Saul, from whom the Spirit of the Lord had departed (1 Sa. 16:14). This verse is not concerned with the bare doctrine of perseverance but with the practice of it, as was Paul in 1 Corinthians 9:27, and our Lord in John 15:6. The word *holy* is, or should be, a reminder of the magnitude of such a request; *cf.* 1 Samuel 6:20.

12. While the prayer of verse 10 for steadfastness was obviously fitting, after so great a fall, the earnest plea[2] for a *willing* spirit may strike us as less relevant. The word suggests the enthusiast and volunteer, with his eager and generous outlook. But on reflection, such a spirit is God's own antidote to temptation: that positive delight in His will (40:8) which David had largely lost in his prosperity.

---

[1] This is the regular meaning of this verb in the Old Testament. See, *e.g.*, Ps. 104:30; Is. 61:4; La. 5:21. The only apparent exception is Jb. 10:17.

[2] It is an emphatic imperative: 'O restore . . .'. *Cf.* the opening of verse 13.

13. 'O may I teach . . .'—for there is a similar eagerness here to that of verse 12, as if already the prayer of that verse is being granted. We may note the close connection between a joyous faith and an infectious one, and between experiencing restoration and leading others to that knowledge. 'When you have turned again, strengthen your brethren' (Lk. 22:32). The words *restore* (12) and *return* (13) are parts of the same verb. But above and beyond this, the psalm itself is the richest answer to the prayer, since it has shown generations of sinners the way home, long after they had thought themselves beyond recall.

51:14-17. Humble worship

The enormity of his sin continues to horrify David. He has none of the glibness of Isaiah's contemporaries, who were oblivious of the blood on their praying hands (Is. 1:15), and had never wrestled with the realities of worship (Is. 1:11). For *bloodguiltiness* the Hebrew has 'blood(s)'; hence the possible alternatives, 'death' (RSV mg., JB) or 'bloodshed' (NEB). But these alternatives seem too self-regarding to match David's contrition. Nowhere in this psalm is he concerned to escape the material consequences of his sins: it is the guilt of them that burdens him. Even *deliverance* is too narrow a word: in reality he wants to praise God's 'righteousness' (14c, lit.; Heb. 16), whose crowning work is to make the sinner himself righteous (*cf.* 6ff.).

15. In the light of verse 14b, the prayer *open thou my lips* is no mere formula but the cry of one whose conscience has shamed him into silence. He longs to worship freely, gratefully again; and he believes that by the grace of God he will. Seen in its true setting, this heartfelt, humble plea leads the worshipper in one step from confession to the brink of praise.

16, 17. The Old Testament has a way of saying 'not that, but this', where we should say, 'this rather than that' (*cf.* Ho. 6:6), or 'not that without this'. Verses 18f. with their praise of sacrifices remind us that the early singers of this psalm understood these verses so. God is not rejecting His own appointed offerings, still less saying that we can be self-atoning. What He is emphasizing is that the best of gifts is hateful to Him without a contrite heart. And the reference is not simply to atonement (for which only the blood of another can suffice: Lv. 17:11; Heb. 9:22) but to the whole range of worship, not in token but in personal reality, since the peace-offering (*sacrifice*, 16) expressed communion, and the *burnt offering* dedication. In all this, God is looking for the heart that knows how little it deserves, how much it owes.

> 'Myself my gift: let my devotion prove,
> I'm given greatly, how I greatly love.'[1]

51:18, 19. A people's prayer

Conceivably, David could have added these words himself, picturing Zion's spiritual plight in physical terms. But it is far more likely that the generations between the Captivity and the Rebuilding made David's penitence their own, adding these verses to make their prayer specific. As pointed out above (on 16, 17), they do not contradict, but rather interpret, verses 16f. For the glorious answer to the prayer see Nehemiah 12:43, where the walls are completed: 'And they offered great sacrifices on that day. . . . And the joy of Jerusalem was heard afar off.'

Psalm 52
The Troublemaker

The title links the psalm with one of David's bitterest experiences. In flight from Saul, he had talked Ahimelech the priest into giving him a few provisions; and now Ahimelech has been denounced to the king, and his whole community massacred. The informer was the Edomite Doeg, and it was he who carried out the slaughter.

We have two of David's utterances on this. One is his outcry to Abiathar, Ahimelech's son: 'I have occasioned the death of all . . . your father's house. Stay with me . . .; you shall be in safe keeping' (1 Sa. 22:22f.). The other is this psalm, where he reflects first on the kind of man that Doeg is, who carves out his career by slander and intrigue; but then, too, on the brevity of such success. Finally he renews his trust in God, who stands by His own as surely as he, David, has promised to stand by Abiathar.

52:1–4. Destructive tongue

The word *boast* does not necessarily imply an outward show:

[1] S. J. Stone, 'Weary of self and laden with my sin'.

the real point is the man's self-satisfaction.[1] He thinks himself clever, he is absorbed in his intrigues, he has given himself to evil—for the repeated *you love . . . you love* implies choice as well as attraction.

1. In their context (see title, and opening comments), the insinuations against Ahimelech had been well-timed to ingratiate Doeg with the king, who was now fancying himself friendless. Perhaps, too, there is irony in David's military term, *O mighty man* (1), as if earned by Doeg's exploit in butchery. How valiant the big herdsman (1 Sa. 21:7, Heb. 6) has shown himself!

(In the same verse, the phrase *against the godly*, *'el-ḥāsīd*, is based on the probability, supported by the Peshitta, that two Hebrew words have been transposed in the copying. As it stands, the Hebrew text has *ḥesed 'ēl*, 'the steadfast love of God'; *cf.* AV, RV. This can make sense, but it is abrupt, and anticipates the contrast to be made in verse 8.)

52:5–7. Short shrift
Violent verbs jostle one another in verse 5 with increasingly radical effect; for if it is distressing to be broken down (5a), it is worse to be made homeless, as David well knew (5b); and there is final disaster beyond that (5c), to which the wicked have no answer (*cf.* 49:13–15).

6. The sequence of *see* and *fear* (two similar verbs), or in other words 'look on, awestruck' (NEB), came in 40:3 as the response to God's deliverance, which can be as striking as His judgments. But here the final stage is laughter, which is the wholly devastating penalty for the high and mighty.

7. The word *refuge* brings out the insecurity of even the strongest. The thruster, for all his aggressiveness, is partly spurred on by fear. The last line, however, does not reiterate the point in the Hebrew, which reads 'became strong through his craving'[2]—for this is the dominant part of his motivation.

52:8, 9. Safe keeping
As we suggested earlier, David may have seen the parallel between the protection he offered (1 Sa. 22:23) and the pro-

---

[1] *Cf.* 49:6 (Heb. 7) where it is parallel to 'trust'; see also, *e.g.*, Je. 9:23 (Heb. 22).

[2] *Cf.* BDB, which however prefers the reading 'wealth' (LXX, Targ.), which is a different word. For the translation 'craving', *cf.* Pr. 10:3.

tection he found. The *olive* is one of the longest-living trees;
here the point is doubly reinforced, for he pictures an olive
'in full sap' (Weiser), and one that grows in a sacred court-
yard (was this another reminiscence of the sanctuary at Nob?),
where no-one will tamper with it, still less 'uproot' it (*cf.* 5c).
Certainly there is a pointed contrast between the object of
his trust (8b) and that of Doeg (7b): the one tangible but
transient, the other unseen but *for ever and ever*.

9. The thanks are, it seems, still part of the trust, since the
Hebrew text (confirmed by the ancient versions) does not
say 'I will proclaim', but 'I will wait on, or hope for, thy
name'—and this not privately but openly, where failure, if
God were to fail him, would be obvious. *Cf.* his open refusal
to force God's hand in 1 Samuel 26:8–11. His final words in
the psalm are excellently rendered in JB: '. . . and put my
hope in your name, that is so full of kindness, in the presence
of those who love you.'

Psalm 53
Serpent's Brood

Apart from a few details, and the greater part of verse 5, this
is identical with Psalm 14, where see comments. The title adds
the note *according to Mahalath* (see Introduction, VI. *c.* 3, p. 42);
it occurs again at Psalm 88. Throughout this version of the
psalm the divine name is simply *God*, as it is almost invariably
in this Book of the Psalter (see Introduction, II, p. 5),
whereas in Psalm 14 the name Yahweh (the Lord) occurs four
times. In this collection, incidentally, this meditation on the
arrogant fool, the *nābāl*, is placed, like the story of Nabal
himself (1 Sa. 25), between material relating to Doeg (Ps. 52;
1 Sa. 22) and to the Ziphites (Ps. 54; 1 Sa. 23 and 26).

The following are variants from Psalm 14:
1. Iniquity ('*āwel*): *cf.* '(evil) deeds', 14:1 ('*ᵃlîlâ*).
3. *They have all fallen away* (*kullô sāḡ*): *cf.* 'they have all gone
astray', 14:3 (*hakkōl sār*).
4. *Those who work evil*: this is prefaced by 'all' in 14:4.
5. *In terror such as has not been*. While this is a possible trans-

lation, it is more straightforward to take it as 'where no terror was' (*cf.* AV, RV, JB). This in turn could mean either 'where previously they were not afraid', or, more probably, 'where there was no cause for fear'. The phrase is absent from Psalm 14, and introduces the considerable change in the rest of the verse, where instead of RSV *the ungodly* we should read, as in the Hebrew text, 'him who encamps against you', or 'your besieger'. This may well give the clue to the change: *i.e.* the psalm in this form celebrates a miraculous deliverance through a sudden panic descending on the enemy (*cf., e.g.*, 2 Ki. 7:6f.). For further details of the variants in this verse, see on 14:5b, 6.

Psalm 54
My Helper

This psalm arose out of testing experiences that followed those of Psalm 52. To be betrayed by Doeg the Edomite had been hardly a surprise (1 Sa. 22:22), but now David finds himself rejected by men of his own tribe (1 Sa. 23:19ff.; 26:1ff.), in spite of his rescue of one of their border towns from the Philistines (1 Sa. 23:1ff.). In this dangerous and disillusioning situation he turns again to God.

54:1-3. My prayer

Against the background of treachery there is added force in appealing to God's *name* and in the prayer *vindicate me*. Those who had betrayed David were opportunists, standing for no principle, suiting their colour and shape to the moment. God, by contrast, has declared Himself, and stands by His good name: *cf., e.g.*, 23:3; 48:9f. And David, for his part, is concerned for justice, not only safety. *Vindicate*, here, is a judicial term, although the verdict will have to be pronounced in saving deeds, not words. The slur on David's character is that he is no more than a traitor. His words to Saul reveal the hurt of it: 'For what have I done? What guilt is on my hands?' (1 Sa. 26:18).

3. *Insolent* (or 'arrogant', JB) is the reading of several Hebrew MSS and the Targum, and is probably right, as against MT's 'strangers'.[1] *Cf.* the almost identical 86:14. Its companion word, *ruthless*, can be studied especially in Isaiah 25:3–5. The last line of our verse has a typically biblical emphasis on what is *lacking* in a man's attitude, as a point of special significance. Here it is the climax of the description; *cf.* the last lines of 36:1, 3, 4; and of 53:1, 3, 4.

54:4, 5. My helper

If in verses 1–3 David was bringing himself and then his enemies to God's attention, he now brings God before his own attention. In 4b the ancient versions, followed by most modern ones, seem to have found the Hebrew text too startling, where it numbers God 'among' *the upholders of my life*. But this is not belittling Him; it is seeing His hand behind the human help—the 'six hundred', the 'thirty', the 'three', of 1 Samuel 23:13 and 2 Samuel 23:8ff.—whose faithfulness was David's support and delight. On the theme of requital verse 5, which leaves the matter to God, is in full accord with Romans 12:19, though it has not gone the second mile to which the next two verses in Romans are a signpost.

54:6, 7. My thank-offering

The point about a *freewill offering* was that no vow had been included in the prayer for help; there had been no question of saying, in effect, 'If You will do this, I will give that.' The thanks and the sacrifice were spontaneous (*cf.* 51:12); and while Psalms 50 and 51 point out that an offering is valueless in itself, yet rightly offered it gave access to God's presence through atonement, gave visible expression to one's love, and brought a company together to share the feast and hear the story (*cf.* Dt. 12:6f.). So David re-lives the anguish of his initial prayer (1–3) and the faith to which it led (4f.), as the prelude to the thanks—tangible and articulate—which he now presents. And in bequeathing the psalm to us he makes 'straight paths for our feet', for a similar progress, if need be, from near-despair to liberation.

---

[1] In the consonantal text the difference is between two very similar letters.

Psalm 55
Betrayed

Such a cry as this helps to make the Psalter a book for the extremities of experience as well as for its normalities. The person who is driven to distraction finds a fellow-sufferer here; the rest of us may find a guide to our intercessions, so that we can pray with our brethren 'as though in prison' (or other distress) 'with them' (Heb. 13:3). Further, the heart-rending passages on the betrayal (12ff., 20f.) give us added insight into the sufferings of Christ, and at the same time into His self-mastery and redemptive attitude, in such a situation as gave David every reason to appeal for judgment.

55:1-3. The intolerable strain

A recurrent phrase in the law of Deuteronomy 22:1-4 (RSV mg.) lights up the plea, *hide not thyself*, by using this very expression to forbid the ignoring of a neighbour's predicament, however inconvenient the moment. So the allusion makes David's prayer an appeal to God's self-consistency as well as to His mercy.

2. While the ancient versions support RSV in reading *I am overcome* ('*ûraḏ*), the standard text has a rare word ('*ārîḏ*) which appears to mean 'I am restless' (RV; *cf.* NEB, JB), giving a more vivid description of his plight, which chimes in with the next expression, *I am distraught*, a word used of the confusion of a demoralized army (*cf.* Dt. 7:23).

3. Now comes the cause of this agitation: a hostile group which feels itself very much in the ascendant. RSV is somewhat colourless here. The rare word translated *oppression* is more likely to match *the noise* of the first line with 'the stare' (Dahood)[1] or 'the shrill clamour' (NEB; *cf.* JB, RP, Gelineau)[2] of the second. Again, a more graphic word than *bring* should follow this: it pictures something tipped over (*cf.* RSV mg.), as in JB's phrase, 'they bring misery crashing down on me'.

---

[1] Conjectured from Ugaritic '*q*, 'eyeball'.
[2] Conjectured from Arabic '*ayyaḵa* ('*āḵa*): G. R. Driver, *JBL* 55 (1936), p. 111, cited by D. W. Thomas, *TRP*, *ad loc.*

55:4-8. The urge to escape

It is some comfort to us to know that there are spiritual giants who have had this urge, whether they have succumbed to it like Elijah (1 Ki. 19:3ff.) or withstood it like Jeremiah (Je. 9:2; 10:19).

6. RSV rightly resists the influence of the popular aria, and preserves the good sense of the Hebrew which says *like* (not 'of'[1]) *a dove*.

55:9-11. The forces of anarchy

While any good citizen is distressed at social breakdown, David as king is directly challenged. His prayer is perceptive, and a lesson to us: he remembers how God dealt with Babel (9a), another arrogant city, by exploiting the inherent divisiveness of evil. He prayed a similar prayer when the too-clever Ahithophel became the counsellor of Absalom (2 Sa. 15:31). In this part of the psalm, further, David's personal trials make way for his public concern. This is God's city, whose *walls* should be the reassurance of His people (48:12ff.), not the parade-ground of rebels and terrorists (10), and whose *market place* (11) should be above reproach (144:14). The prayer is on strong ground.

55:12-15. The false friend

We need not try to name the traitor from our limited knowledge of David's circle; it is the description that matters. For *my equal* JB has, still more exactly, 'a man of my own rank'; cf. NEB 'a man of my own sort'. But what David was unwittingly describing in this moving passage was also the essence of his own treachery to Uriah, one of his staunchest friends (2 Sa. 23:39).

15. Note the plurals in this sudden outburst. Rather characteristically, David's chief reaction to the personal betrayal was grief (12-14), while his wrath flamed out against the collective threat to his authority—though this of course would fully include the ringleader. The phrase, *let them go down to Sheol alive*, is a clear echo of Numbers 16:30, where Moses had called for proof that in resisting him the rebels of his day were resisting God.

---

[1] As Churchill might have remarked, some dove!

On a point of detail, the consonantal text of 15a (Heb. 16a) is most easily translated 'Desolations (*yᵉšîmôṭ*) upon them!', but the traditional vowels change this to 'Let death deceive them'—*i.e.*, come on them unawares. It is a small difference, taken with the rest of the sentence. At the end of this verse the variation between RSV and AV is due to (a) the existence of two roots of identical form but different meanings, where RSV decides for *terror* and AV for 'dwellings'; and (b) RSV's conjecture that the consonants of 'among them' should be transposed, to read *their graves*. This conjecture is unsupported by the ancient versions.

55:16–19. The God who hears

In driving God's servant to prayer the enemy has already overreached himself; a fact worth remembering in such a situation. It is the turning-point of the psalm.

17. While the 'seven times a day' of 119:164 are doubtless a round number, these three points of time have the look of a regular pattern, to which David committed himself during the crisis. Others, from Daniel onwards (Dn. 6:10), have been moved to adopt disciplined counter-measures such as these, against pressure from the world. NEB is too defeatist with 'I nurse my woes': the word means basically 'I meditate' (*cf.*, *e.g.*, 77:6, 12 [Heb. 7, 13]), and is coloured by its context, which includes here the prayer of faith (16, 17b).

18. *The battle* is an unusual word, but since it comes again in verse 21 ('war') it is gratuitous to emend it with NEB to 'they beset me'.

19a. A number of words with more than one possible meaning have tempted NEB to an ingenious re-translation of 19a,[1] which is unnecessary (since the obvious translation makes good sense), irrelevant (since there is no need to bring in distant enemies) and contrived (since the text must be modified for the purpose).

19b. The translation, *because they keep no law*, is derived rather remotely from the lit. 'to whom are no changes' (*cf.* AV, RV, RSV mg.), through interpreting '(ex)changes' as 'respect for mutual obligations' (*cf.* K-B). This is presumably possible; but the basic meaning, 'changes', is hardly obscure enough to call for it. In its literal sense it will mean that

---

[1] Based on G. R. Driver, *HTR* 29 (1936), pp. 171ff.

these men are either too set in their sins or materially too
secure to worry about God. *Cf.* the complacent Moab in
Jeremiah 48:11, 'settled on his lees; he has not been emptied
from vessel to vessel.'

55:20, 21. The smooth talker

The depth of this perfidy was that it broke specific pledges:
it stabbed sworn allies in the back, not merely companions.
The sacredness of a *covenant* comes out in the word for *violated*,
which means profaning something holy. God would have been
invoked as witness to such a bond.

55:22, 23. The long view

We, if not David, can see that his suffering was, after all,
hardly too much to have to pay to bequeath verse 22 to the
world. The word *burden* is too restrictive: it means whatever
is given you, your appointed lot (hence in NEB 'your fortunes').
And the promise is not that God will carry it, but that he will
sustain *you*. It is the verb used of Joseph the provider (Gn.
45:11, *etc.*), and of various human patrons; above all, of
God's inclusive care for Israel in the wilderness (Ne. 9:21).

23. From the expression, *not live out half their days*, it seems
that David is simply pointing to the cut-throat's precarious
career, though he does not forget that this is of God's appoint-
ment, whose world this is. At other moments he can see
still further (*e.g.* 16:10f.; 17:13–15); but what counts is that
God has the whole matter in hand, and that David's choice
has been made. The *I* is emphatic, dismissing the preoccupation with the enemy. In effect, there are two parties involved,
not three. 'As for me, I will trust in the Lord.'

Psalm 56

'What can man do to me?'

To have fled from Saul to Gath of all places, the home town
of Goliath, took the courage of despair; it measured David's
estimate of his standing with his people. And now this has
failed, and he is doubly encircled. So far, his own followers
were very few; the four hundred of 1 Samuel 22:10 were yet
to be gathered. The psalm is the first of two which flowered

from this crisis. It breaks through into thanksgiving at the end, which was to become the unclouded theme of Psalm 34.

Title
See Introduction, vi. *c.* 2, p. 38; vi. c. 3, pp. 42f.

56:1–4. Pressure and promise

While rsv may be right in its translation *men trample upon me*, here and in verse 2, it suits the situation better to take it as 'men pant after me', as if in hot pursuit (*cf.* Jb. 5:5). They are closing in (see the opening comments, above), but David is not yet crushed.

2. *Proudly* is lit. 'height', which AV takes as a term for God: 'O thou most high'. Because of its abruptness, NEB and JB alter it, turning it into an imperative ('Appear on high'; 'Raise me up'), and take it with the next verse. On balance, since nouns are often used adverbially, 'proudly' (RV, RSV) begs the fewest questions.

3. The Hebrew expression here for 'When' is '(In) the day (when)', much as in verse 9. *Cf.* the old translation 'What time I am afraid'—which brings a certain vividness to the phrase. Faith is seen here as a deliberate act, in defiance of one's emotional state. The first line might too easily have run, 'When I am at peace . . .'.

4. This striking verse becomes a refrain, enlarged and repeated in verses 10 and 11, and quoted in 118:6 and Hebrews 13:6. It adds to the delineation of faith already given in verse 3, by showing where faith rests, *i.e. in God*, and where it finds its content, *i.e.* in His *word* (a point which will be made twice over in verse 10). The further phrase, *without a fear*, is better in its more literal form: 'I will not be afraid' (RV), since it matches and answers verse 3a, as the outcome of the act of trust. The last line, with its sturdy reasoning, shows how much the proportions of the scene have changed since verses 1 and 2, where enemies were looming up around their victim. Now, over against God, they are seen as frail *flesh* (*cf.* Is. 31:3). They can still do much to hurt God's servant, as the next verses (especially verse 8) will confirm; but nothing to defeat him. *Cf.* the context of suffering and thanksgiving in which Hebrews 13:6 quotes these words.

56:5-7. The oppressors' zeal

The unremitting pressure is the worst part of the ordeal. It was the first thing David emphasized: *all day long . . . all day long* (1, 2); and now he tells of it again (5). Whether the attack was by misrepresentation ('they twist my words', JB; *cf.* AV, RV) or a more general harassment (RSV) it is difficult to be certain.[1]

But the probing watchfulness of verse 6 was a test which David's Lord would also undergo (Lk. 11:53f.). Incidentally the present context for the word *waited* illustrates the eager expectancy which is always implied in it: it is never a placid word; see, *e.g.*, the comment on 40:1.

7. The Hebrew has 'Rescue' (*pallēṭ*), which AV, RV take to be ironical (hence, 'Shall they escape?'), but which looks more likely to be an early miscopying for *pallēs*, 'weigh out (to them)'; *cf.* RSV. The dative, 'to them,' also tells in favour of this.[2] The second half of the verse leaves no doubt of the main thrust of the prayer, and we may trace part of David's resolve to subdue the Philistines to this period of his life. He was to see his prayer answered: *cf.* 2 Samuel 5:17ff.; 8:1.

56:8-11. The Protector's care

For no good reason, RSV alters the Hebrew text from 'wandering' to *tossings*. No doubt both were true, but 'wandering' was David's special lot, and the word for it (*nōḏ*; *cf.* Gn. 4:16) evidently brought to mind the similar sound of *n'ōḏ*, flask or *bottle*, just as the expression *kept count* suggested the related word, *thy book*.[3] So, it seems, this poignant verse took shape, marked vividly with its author's affectionate trust as well as with his restlessness and melancholy. Our Lord had equally striking terms for God's attention to detail: *cf.* Matthew 10:29f.

9. *In the day when I call* is a similar expression to 'the day when I am afraid', in verse 3, to which it makes a good companion. Paul was to echo the triumphant end of this verse (or 118:7a), and cap it with 'who is against us?' (Rom. 8:31).

---

[1] Of two possible verbs, one means 'to vex' and the other 'to shape'; while the noun can mean either 'words' or 'affairs'.

[2] NEB, with support from LXX, keeps the MT's verb ('escape') and finds the missing negative behind the word for 'crime' (*'ayin* for *'āwen*).

[3] The ancient versions vary considerably from the MT's first line. NEB simply omits it, diagnosing the word-play as a garbled repetition.

10, 11. This takes up verse 4 (where see comment) as a refrain, emphasizing its first line by virtual repetition, a favourite device in this psalm. Here the name Yahweh (*the Lord*) makes one of its rare appearances in the Second Book (42–72) of the Psalter.

56:12, 13. The danger past

Now comes the explicit point of the psalm: it is being sung to celebrate the answered prayer and keep the promise made in adversity. *Thank offerings* can be a term for literal sacrifices (*e.g.* Lv. 7:12) and for songs of gratitude (*e.g.* Ps. 26:7); here, doubtless, both are meant, and the psalm would serve many a subsequent worshipper with words to accompany his offering. We can in fact see the last verse borrowed, and actually enhanced, in the perfected form of 116:8f., where the sufferer's tears are not merely taken to heart, as here (8), but taken away.

Psalm 57

Saved to Sing

The end of the psalm's heading gives the setting of this song as 'in the cave'; and we can sense the same realistic but adventurous spirit, spurred instead of cowed by danger, in the psalm as in the story. This is the David who could say 'there is but a step between me and death' (1 Sa. 20:3), yet win the initiative from his pursuer and still keep humble faith with God (1 Sa. 24:1–15).

The stirring refrain of verses 5 and 11 punctuates and binds the psalm together, and verses 7–11 will reappear as the opening to Psalm 108, which brings together this act of praise and the battle-hymn from Psalm 60.

Title

The terms in the title which are found frequently in the Psalter are discussed in the Introduction, VI. *c.* 2, p. 38). On the words *Do Not Destroy*, see Introduction, VI. *c.* 3, p. 43.

57:1–3. The refuge

The repeated plea, *be merciful*, is identical with the opening of Psalm 56, 'Be gracious', which is simply a translator's variation, equally valid. As for David's *refuge*, it was characteristic that where most men would have named the cave as this, David saw beyond it. Solid rock, by itself, could be a trap as easily as a stronghold (*cf.* 1 Sa. 23:25ff.); the living protection symbolized by *wings* would not fail: *cf.* 61:4 and the sequels to Ruth 2:12 on the one hand, Matthew 23:37 on the other.

2. The two titles for God in this verse show the enrichment which can be given to a prayer by the way in which it addresses God. On the name *Most High*, see on 7:17; it could well have brought memories of God's good hand on Abram, another homeless man; certainly it prepared for the thought of help from on high, voiced in 3a. The second line, while we cannot match its brevity (three words in Hebrew), says enough in a few syllables to turn despondency into thankful, expectant certainty.

3. God's exaltation as 'Most High' (2) does not make Him remote: only unhampered in sending help—a fact which the opening of the Lord's Prayer should also bring to mind. We should probably translate *those who trample upon me* as 'those who hotly pursue me': *cf.* on 56:1. The next part of the psalm will enlarge on this.

57:4-6. The ring of enemies

The more recent translations have accepted the argument that the expression 'set on fire' (4a, AV, RV) means here 'consuming' or 'swallowing': hence NEB's terse summary, 'man-eaters'.[1]

5. Here is the other and chief aspect of God as Most High: not, now, that He is all-powerful (*cf.* on verse 3), but that He is all-important. David, wonderfully, looks up from his own urgent interests to his overriding concern: that God should be exalted. In such a crisis, this equivalent to 'hallowed be Thy name' was both a victory in itself (*cf.* Jn. 12:27f.) and a weapon against the enemy.

6. The fight had almost gone out of David (6a), perhaps until he prayed the God-centred prayer of verse 5; now at the last moment the tables are turned, with evil characteristically bringing its own judgment.

---

[1] *Cf.* G. R. Driver, *JTS* 33 (1932), p. 39.

57:7-10. The paean of praise

The cry, *my heart is steadfast!* stands in happy contrast to 6a:
'my soul was bowed down'. *Steadfast* is not the same word as
in the expression 'steadfast love' (10), which translates a
single Hebrew noun, *ḥeseḏ*, but is a quite common adjective
for things that are steady or well prepared. The singer is going
to give his whole attention to his offering of praise.

8. For *my soul*, the Hebrew text has 'my glory' (*cf.* AV, RV);
but see the footnote to 30:12. In the last line RSV rightly keeps
the lively metaphor of awakening the dawn. J. W. McKay[1]
has pointed out that although *dawn* is a masculine noun and
regarded in the Old Testament as a natural phenomenon, it
is sometimes personified for poetic effect: here, as someone
asleep; in Song of Solomon 6:10 as one who 'looks forth';
cf. further Psalms 110:3; 139:9; Jb. 3:9c; Is. 14:12.

9. It is easy to overlook the breadth of this vision, forgetting
that the shelter of a cave and the withdrawal of the enemy
would have satisfied most men in the hard-pressed situation
of David. But his thoughts had already soared 'above the
heavens' (5); and his *Lord* was no local ruler. These words,
or their near-equivalent in 18:49, are taken with full serious-
ness in Romans 15:9 as a prophecy which had to be fulfilled.

10. *Cf.* 36:5, in very similar words. Here NEB is probably
right in taking *great* to mean 'wide', leaving the idea of height
to the second line.

57:11. God above all

The refrain rounds off the whole, sung now not with the
defiant faith of verse 5, but with grateful love.

Psalm 58

Tyrants on Trial

With its passion for justice, the Psalter does not allow us to
get used to the scandal of evil in high places. David's outcry
against human despots is matched by Asaph's in Psalm 82
against principalities and powers. The two realms are coupled
in Isaiah 24:21, where both are faced with judgment: 'On

[1] *VT* 20 (1970), pp. 451-465.

that day the Lord will punish the host of heaven, in heaven, and the kings of the earth, on the earth.'

A change of form marks off each stanza from its fellows, as the tyrants are first addressed (1f.), then described (3–5), prayed against (6–9), and finally, at their downfall, rejoiced over (10f.).

Title

For the phrase *Do Not Destroy*, see Introduction, p. 43. The other terms are discussed in the Introduction, vi. *c.* 2, p. 38.

58:1, 2. The challenge

The question and answer, using the simplest of ethical terms, *right* and *wrongs*, may seem politically naïve, but remain the most searching of all. David himself, for example, had to be faced with this quite unnoticed aspect of his dealings with Bathsheba and Uriah. Notice, too, the true sequence, *your hearts . . . your hands*. Here is a calculated ruthlessness, thought out and meted out (*deal out* is lit. 'weigh') with businesslike efficiency. Micah describes this unsleeping eagerness for domination in Micah 2:1f.

In verse 1a the various translations reflect the many possible meanings of the Hebrew consonants *'lm*.[1] Probably they should be pronounced *'ēlīm*, and taken to refer to rulers (NEB), either from a word for 'rams', which is sometimes used for leaders (*e.g.* the Heb. of Ex. 15:15; Ezk. 17:13), or from one of the words for 'gods' or 'mighty ones', used in the same way.[2] But these are human rulers; *cf.*, *e.g.*, verse 3. In Psalm 82, where the word *'ĕlōhîm* is used, the context points to angels.

58:3–5. The charge

The tyrants are no longer addressed but portrayed. Yet the difference between such people and David himself, as he confessed in 51:5, was one of degree rather than kind. He too was a sinner *from the womb*. And the description in verses 3ff. is close enough to what is quoted in Romans 3:10ff. to warn

---

[1] RV ('in silence') keeps the traditional vowels but makes no sense. AV, PBV have 'congregation' (inferred precariously from a verb 'to bind'). LXX, Vulg. took the word to be *'ūlām*, 'but indeed?'

[2] *Cf.*, *e.g.*, Jb. 41:25 (Heb. 17); Ezk. 32:21, where, however, some MSS use a spelling which would indicate the meaning 'rams'.

the reader that he faces a mirror, not only a portrait. If he, unlike these as yet, has been 'granted repentance unto life' (*cf*. Acts 11:18), he has only God to thank.

Towards man, *lies* and *venom*; towards God or any voice of reason or persuasion, a *deaf* ear; this is the sinner who has followed his principle of self-regard to the bitter end. He is a menace—this is the emphasis of the psalm—he is also an unhappy creature, isolated by his aggressive-defensive spirit. In the simile of the serpent the word translated *adder* should rather be 'cobra', whose characteristics are indicated by the other occurrences of the word *peṭen*. *Cf*. K-B; also G. S. Cansdale, who writes: 'The cobra is the main subject of snake-charmers. . . . It is now agreed that all snakes are deaf, . . . and the charmer holds their attention by the movement of his pipe, not its music.'[1] It is sad, incidentally, that modern translations can do nothing to match Coverdale's engaging line, 'charm he never so wisely'.

58:6-9. The curse
This prayer is motivated by a sense of outrage that brutal men should roam and ravage in God's world. On its violent rhetoric, see Introduction, p. 27. It prompts the question whether an impassioned curse of tyrants is better or worse than a shrug of the shoulders or a diplomatic silence. The New Testament (*e.g.* Mt. 23) leaves us in little doubt, even while it moves the matter on to fresh ground by labouring to overcome evil with good.

6. The aggressiveness of the *young lions* supplies an element missing from the lurking figure of the serpent (4f.).

7. The second line of this verse has suffered in the copying, and yields no sense as it stands; witness the italics in AV. Most modern versions agree in substance with RSV's conjectured restoration: *like grass let them be trodden down and wither*, whereby the final verb is derived from *mālal* (wither), as in LXX, Vulg., rather than *mûl* (circumcise). But the remaining three Hebrew words have had to be rearranged and altered.[2]

8. As G. R. Driver pointed out,[3] the translation *snail* is doubly inappropriate, first because a snail does not in fact

---

[1] G. S. Cansdale, *Animals of Bible Lands* (Paternoster, 1970), p. 206.
[2] For details, see *TRP*.
[3] *JTS* 34 (1933), pp. 40-44.

perish in its trail of slime, and secondly because the sense
'miscarriage' matches the second line and is attested in the
Talmud, where it evidently refers to a miscarriage at too early
a stage to be called an abortion. The Greeks made a similar
distinction. Hence he translates it 'Like a miscarriage (which)
melteth away' (*cf.* NEB).

9. In the same article Driver conjectures a copying error
which gave rise to the word *your pots* out of a verb 'he pulls
up', plus the word 'like'. In the second line he argues for the
meaning 'weed(s)' where RSV has *green*, and for the normal
meaning 'wrath' where RSV has *ablaze*. His result is: 'Ere they
perceive (it), he pulleth them up like thorn(s), like weed(s
which) in (his) wrath he sweepeth away' (*cf.* NEB). This is
but one attempt to unravel what seems to be a thoroughly
tangled text, on which no two versions reach the same answer.

58:10, 11. The purge

If verse 10 is hot-blooded, the context has already shown that
this is the fierceness of men who care about justice. The point
is reinforced by their being named *the righteous*, and by the
fact that the *vengeance* (or, less emotively, retribution) is from
God, as the foregoing prayer anticipated and the final verse
confirms. What might appear as ghoulishness in 10b takes on
a different aspect against the rebuke of Isaiah 63:1–6, where
God is appalled that none will march with Him to judgment.
These are warriors, not camp-followers. The New Testament
will, if anything, outdo this language in speaking of the day
of reckoning (*e.g.* Rev. 14:19f.; 19:11ff.), while repudiating
carnal weapons for the spiritual war (Rev. 12:11).

11. The scene now widens. Mankind will witness at last
what the righteous have always known by faith. In the
Hebrew a small turn of phrase confirms that these speakers
are the heathen, for their words treat *'elōhîm* (God) as a
plural; whereas Israel always treats it as a singular in speaking
of the true God.

So this verse drops a clue towards one answer to the problem of the psalm. If tyranny is given formidable scope, so is
faith. The righteous will see their harvest; but its glory will
be, not least, that it was sown in tears and awaited (as Jas.
5:1–11 points out in such a context as this) with indomitable
patience.

Psalm 59
Scatter our Enemies

David's night escape from an upper window of his house
(1 Sa. 19:11ff.) gives the psalm its urgency, its sense of outrage—'for no fault of mine' (4)—its scorn of the nocturnal
prowlers who would trap him (6f., 14f.) and its fierce delight
in God's deliverance. But the adventure and its song have
flowered into something greater, so that 'all the nations' (5, 8)
and 'the ends of the earth' are in view in the completed psalm,
which must be dated after David's accession, when he can
speak of 'my people' (11) and of the world-wide repercussions
of his enemies' defeat (13). The psalm has, in fact, much in
common with Psalm 2, just as David the outlaw showed all
the promise of David the king.

Title
For the phrase *Do Not Destroy*, see Introduction, VI. *c.* 3, p. 43.
For the other terms see pp. 38, 40, 43ff.

59:1-5. The ring of foes
For the peril that David faced, and the foretaste of a bigger
conflict, see the opening remarks above. The word protect (1),
like the kindred word 'fortress' (9, 16, 17), contains the thought
of what is set high up, out of reach: hence NEB's phrase 'be
my tower of strength'. By contrast, David's house was no
protection, but a death-trap, as he realized (1 Sa. 19:12).
Cf., as an extension of this comparison of refuges, Proverbs
18:10, 11 (mg.).

2. The Bible refuses to reduce human conflicts to mere
clashes of interests. If verse 1 only goes as far as this, the
present verse goes deeper, to look at the mentality that adopts
evil and violence as a way of life. (On *those who work evil*, see
footnote to 6:8.) David himself was later to be accused of
this (2 Sa. 16:7f.), and unconsciously to refute the charge at
once by the way he took it.

3, 4. The context of this protestation of innocence, in the
psalm and in the story, throws light on other passages where
the claim may sound exaggerated, as if it were absolute (see
further on 5:4-6). But the gospel has brought a new angle to

the question of unfair treatment, which is set out in 1 Peter 2:18ff.

5. Here the picture widens as David, now king, applies the personal prayer of 4b to a larger situation. But it was the kind of prayer he was already capable of praying in his youth, as his far ranging words to Goliath show in 1 Samuel 17:45f.

59:6, 7. The prowling pack

This contempt could well be David's spirited reaction to the night ambush (1 Sa. 19:11). A fit time for scavengers! Job 24:13-17 develops the same kind of theme with a fine scorn for the murderer and the adulterer, whose day, like theirs, shamefully begins at nightfall.

7. *Bellowing* is hardly appropriate. The root idea is of bubbling up or bursting out; so in terms of dogs JB has 'See how they slaver at the mouth', and in human terms NEB translates it 'From their mouths comes a stream of nonsense'. *Cf.* its use in Proverbs 15:2, 28. But 'nonsense' is too mild; the second line (lit. 'swords in', not *snarling with*) implies destructive talk, and the final line blasphemy.

NEB gratuitously inserts verse 15 between 6 and 7, and abolishes verse 14. This tells us no more than how the translators would have written the psalm themselves.

59:8-10. Triumphant trust

For God's formidable derision *cf.* 2:4-6, and the laughter of Wisdom in Proverbs 1:24ff. But the picture must be balanced by His grief (Gn. 6:6; Lk. 19:41ff.), even though it is no less a sign of coming judgment.

9, 10. These verses, celebrating the turning-point which has now been reached, are repeated in brief at verse 17 to round off the psalm. But the Hebrew text has the difference between hope and fulfilment in the two places. Here it reads 'O my Strength (or, Stronghold), I will *watch* for thee' (9, mg.), as against '. . . sing praises to thee' (17); and likewise the 'futures of verse 10 stand over against the past of 16b.

The word *meet* (10a) is vivid: it is based on the idea of what is 'in front' of someone, usually in the sense of confronting them by coming to meet them, as in the beautiful phrase of 21:3 (where see note). But it can alternatively imply going in front to lead the way, as in 68:25; hence AV, RV, 'prevent' (*i.e.* precede) and, freely, NEB 'be my champion'. Either sense would serve; what matters is that God, rather than the enemy, fills the foreground before David's eyes.

59:11-13. Slow decline

By the reference to *my people* and to *the ends of the earth* this stanza applies the lessons of David's early life to the great affairs of state and, beyond these, to the world-wide glory of God (13b).

11. The realism of the phrase *lest my people forget* is typically biblical; it is one of the chief concerns of Deuteronomy (*e.g.* 8:11ff.), and dominates Psalms 78 and 106 in their review of history. In face of His people's waywardness and inattention God uses hostile powers in various roles: as scourges (Is. 10:5f.), as tests of loyalty (Jdg. 2:22), as hardeners (Jdg. 3:2), and in this passage as object-lessons. In view of verse 13, the prayer *Slay them not* is not absolute: it asks only for the unhurried course of judgment to the bitter end. There is no need to read it as a question ('Wilt thou not destroy them?') with NEB, and no warrant for removing the word 'not', with JB. The Old Testament frequently uses one uncompromising remark to interpret another, where we should use a modifying clause (*e.g.* Ex. 20:4f. in the light of, *e.g.*, Nu. 21:8; 2 Ki. 18:4b).

The remainder of the verse (with 68:1) evidently inspired the controversial lines 'Scatter her enemies, And make them fall' in the British national anthem. Here, 'wander' is a better rendering than *totter*; the root reappears in verse 15a (Heb. 16), and David himself was to experience this humiliation (2 Sa. 15:20).

12. A classic example of a whole community destroying itself by *pride . . . cursing and lies* is the story of Shechem in Judges 9. Each one of these sins is fatal to community, and brings its natural punishment; but pride is also a straight challenge to God.

13. David's great words to Goliath in 1 Samuel 17:46b, which are very close to 13b, confirm that the final phrase should be taken with *know* rather than with *rules*. The longing to see God acknowledged is a mark of the true servant (*cf.* 1 Ki. 18:36; Jn. 12:27f.); and while David may have implied 'God—not Saul' (Perowne) when he first sang the psalm, his subsequent enlargement of its scope gives it the meaning 'God—not David', for he is praying for a clear intervention from heaven.

59:14, 15. The hungry pack

At its second appearance, the refrain is altered by David's certainty of triumph. Back come the prowlers, but where is their arrogance now? *Cf.* verse 7 with 15.[1] There is some uncertainty over the word *growl*, which is the expression used for the Israelites' 'murmuring'—one might almost say 'whining'—in the wilderness, and makes excellent sense. It is understood so in the ancient versions; but the traditional Hebrew vowels suggest an alternative meaning 'they stay for the night', which some commentators prefer. The rendering *growl*, however, with its reminiscence of the hungry rebels in the desert, seems the right way of reading the consonants, and this impression is clinched by the telling contrast that immediately follows.

59:16, 17. Triumphant praise

After the first sinister refrain (6f.) there was a strong anti-thesis, 'But as for Thee . . .' (8). At its second appearance there is an equally pointed sequence from an emphatic 'As for them' (15) to the words 'But as for me . . .' (16); and it is followed by the further contrast between frustrated grumbling and exuberant singing. Three different words are used for this, which might be rendered 'I will sing . . . I will shout . . . (16); I will raise a psalm' (17).

17. Just as the dark refrain came back changed (6f., 14f.), so too the song of trust. In verse 9 the theme was patient waiting: 'I will watch for thee' (see the comment there). Now David looks back in gratitude for prayer already answered (16b), and changes 'I will watch' to '*I will sing praises*', or (NEB) 'I will raise a psalm to thee'. And he no longer needs to complete the sentence whose counterpart in verse 10 began with the phrase, 'the God who loves me' (JB). The line can break off there,[2] bringing the psalm to a perfect conclusion with the refrain (in JB's version):

---

[1] NEB, with surprising insensitivity, abolishes this refrain by deleting verse 14 and uprooting verse 15 to make it follow verse 6.

[2] NEB, however, deletes it.

'My Strength, I play for you,
my citadel is God himself,
the God who loves me.'

Psalm 60
Vain is the Help of Man!

But for this psalm and its title we should have had no inkling of the resilience of David's hostile neighbours at the peak of his power. His very success brought its dangers of alliances among his enemies (*cf.* 2 Sa. 8:5) and of battles far from home. At such a moment, when his main force was with him near the Euphrates (2 Sa. 8:3), Edom evidently took i chance to fall upon Judah from the south.

The setting of the psalm, then, is the deflating news of havoc at home (1–3), and of a defeat, apparently, at the first attempt to avenge it (10). But the sad tale and the closing prayer are dominated by the startlingly boisterous rejoinder of God (6–8).

There are links with other scriptures. Verses 6–12 are reproduced in 108:7–13, and verse 10b uses the language of 44:9b. Three men, David, Abishai and (here) Joab are credited with the slaughter in the Valley of Salt (*cf.* 2 Sa. 8:13; 1 Ch. 18:12), a fact which may reflect the chain of command or, as 1 Kings 11:15f. suggests, different outbreaks of fighting. The variation between the figure of 12,000 here and 18,000 in Samuel and Chronicles may arise from different ways of summarizing the long campaign or from copyists' errors, a minor example of which is found in the Hebrew text of 2 Samuel 8:13 (where see margin).

Title
For the terms *Choirmaster* and *Miktam*, see Introduction, pp. 40, 38. *According to Shushan* may be a musical direction,[1] perhaps the name of a tune. Its plural, *shoshannim*, 'lilies', is regularly translated into English in RSV (*cf.* titles of 45, 69, 80), and at Psalm 80 the word *Eduth* is also given its English equivalent, *A Testimony*. By this term, and the phrase '*for*

---

[1] See, however, Introduction, VI. *c*. 3 (p. 42) for another view.

instruction', we are reminded that the psalm, with its heartfelt plea from man and its resounding word from God, is no museum-piece but a forceful message to every generation.

60:1-4. The trail of havoc

The pronouns *thou* . . . *thou* . . . *thou* . . . are not emphatic, but they are embedded in the verbs which come thick and fast, characteristically tracing the *hard things* (3) right back to God, not merely to some intermediate point in the chain of causation. So David sees the chaotic picture as, in principle, intelligible and under a single ultimate control.

1. *Rejected* must be coupled with the expression at the opposite extreme, *thy beloved (ones)*, in verse 5. So this is not final repudiation; none the less it is formidable anger. It is the first thing to be mentioned, for it matters more than all the rest. Nothing cuts so deep as estrangement.

2. The earthquake imagery confronts us with God's unsparing handling of what we think secure, 'that what cannot be shaken may remain'. This was not an isolated blow. Unlike the prophets of peace who would plaster over the cracks of society (Ezk. 13:10-16), God would continue to shake down what was not fit to stand, and to split open what was not 'at unity in itself' (as in, *e.g.*, 1 Ki. 12). The process would persist in the New Testament (*cf.* Rev. 2 and 3) and in the history of the church.

3. NEB may be right in seeing a drunken state in both lines of the verse,[1] but the more obvious translation of 3a, 'Thou hast shown . . . hard things', makes sense enough. With 3b, in either case, the plight is desperate, the outward crisis matched by inward confusion and shock.

4. Some of the words in verse 4 have more than one possible meaning. The verb in the second line seems to echo the word *banner* (hence RSV, JB *rally*, and AV, RV 'displayed'), but it could equally be from a root meaning to flee (*cf.* NEB). Again, *from* can mean 'because of' (*cf.* Heb. of Dt. 28:20; Ne. 5:15), and *the bow* should perhaps be translated 'the truth' (Pr. 22:21) or 'justice' (*cf.* NEB).

So the meaning may be either a first gleam of encouragement, *e.g.* 'to rally to it on account of the truth' (or 'from the

---

[1] See G. R. Driver, *JTS* 36 (1935), pp. 152f., deriving the first verb irregularly from *rāwâ*, 'be saturated', rather than regularly from *rā'â*, 'see' (here causative, *i.e.*, 'show', as in AV, RV).

bow'), or else the heaviest blow yet: the order to retreat. On balance the latter seems slightly more probable: the ancient versions understood it so (*e.g.* LXX: 'to flee from the bow'), and the *Selah* at the end of verse 4 suggests that the tale of disasters continues to that point, leaving verse 5 to speak the first word of hope. We may note that Jeremiah 4:6 gives an instance of a banner as a rallying point for flight instead of attack: 'Raise a standard toward Zion, flee for safety, stay not.'

60:5-8. The dwarfing of man

5. However desperate were the straits, this verse is a prayer of faith, which shines out in the single expression *thy beloved* (*ones*). The Hebrew word belongs to the language of love poetry; it appeals to the strongest of bonds, the most ardent of relationships. It is not disappointed: the response is immediate and overwhelming.

6-8. On the divine answers that break into some of the psalms, see on 12:5, 6. Here, the words *in his sanctuary*[1] suggest to most modern interpreters the scene of a festival such as that of Deuteronomy 31:10ff., to commemorate and realize God's gift of the promised land to Israel. Whether David was quoting from such a ritual or whether the words came to him new-minted in the crisis, the proclamation is magnificently apt. It is as though, at the height of a children's quarrel which has come to blows, there could be heard the firm tread and cheerful voice of the father.

Verses 6 and 7 proclaim the inheritance of Israel; verse 8 puts her neighbours in their place. Like a colossus, God dominates the scene: it is no longer a matter of rivals fighting for possession, but of the lord of the manor parcelling out his lands and employments exactly as it suits him.

6, 7. *Shechem* and *Succoth*, on either side of the Jordan, were the first parts of the promised land to be occupied by Jacob after his years with Laban. *Gilead* was the Israelite territory east of Jordan, the tribe of *Manasseh* straddled the river, and *Ephraim* and *Judah* were the principal tribes to the west of it. So in a few bold strokes the early history and distinctive areas of Israel are called to mind, and the chief agents of defence and rule (*helmet* and *sceptre*) are named. But note the

[1] But the meaning may be 'in his holiness': see RSV mg., NEB mg.

repeated *mine* and *my*, for everything is His, not theirs, and those to whom He gives it are His tenants and stewards. Yet it is theirs all the more securely for that.

8. After the honourable posts, the menial ones; but they are still His to allot, and they have their uses: *cf.* 2 Timothy 2:20f. There is probably no special reason to make Moab rather than Edom the *washbasin, etc.*, except possibly that Edom, who is the enemy here, has the lowest place of all. Both of them were noted for their pride (Is. 16:6; Ob. 3). Delitzsch's suggestion, that to *cast* a *shoe* was to claim a property, is unnecessary; the picture is of a man returning home and flinging his shoes to a slave or into a corner. As regards *Philistia* and the *shout*, the Hebrew text has 'Philistia, shout over me!' (*cf.* AV, RV), which could be either an ironical taunt to them or a call for homage (*cf.* 'the shout of a king', Nu. 23:21). But Psalm 108:9 (Heb. 10) has 'over Philistia I shout', as RSV has here, which is probably the true text for both psalms.

60:9–12. The fight resumed

It is one thing to glory in the might of God, another to venture forth in it. The task is not belittled; *the fortified city* is beyond David's resources (*cf.* 2 Cor. 10:3f.) unless God goes with him —indeed, unless He goes before him (*bring me . . . lead me*). And this is not taken for granted (10); the humbling lesson of God's withdrawal is frankly faced. (For another situation like this, and the questions it provoked, see on 44:9–16, 17–26.)

But note the new spirit of attack, for all David's self-mistrust. The enemy is no longer the invader, as in verses 1ff., but the one to be invaded. Finally prayer turns into affirmation, and the lonely venture into a partnership. For our part, there will be valiant deeds; for God's part, there will be not only His hand on ours (*with God*, 11a) but His foot on the enemy (11b).

Psalm 61

'The Rock that is Higher than I'

In the broadest terms, this is first a prayer for security, and then, after the *Selah* in verse 4, a thanksgiving for the assured answer, and a constructive request for lasting grace. But verses 6 and 7 may be an inspired interjection for the use of later worshippers, making David's plea a prayer for the current occupant of his throne. If so, it reminds us to use the psalms as intercessions for our contemporaries as well as prayers for ourselves.

But this may have been a cry for help when David was away on campaign (*cf.* the first comments on Ps. 60) or driven out by Absalom. Equally, he could have adapted it during his kingship from an earlier petition made in his years of flight from Saul. What he could hardly have foreseen was the abundant answer to the prayer for the king (6f), destined to be granted, in Christ, above all that he asked or thought.

61:1–4. 'To be safe . . . !'

The Old Testament abounds in examples of men who trusted God when far from home, where all would have seemed alien and precarious (*e.g.* Abraham, Jacob, Joseph . . .), and where other gods ostensibly held sway (*cf.* 1 Sa. 26:19). Here David had the added trial of depression or exhaustion (2); *cf.* the same word *faint* in the title of Psalm 102, where the condition is subsequently described at some length.

2b. This unforgettable petition is reduced to something far less striking in LXX, which evidently had a slightly different Hebrew text.[1] NEB follows suit, exchanging the text that we possess for the conjectured one, almost as if the former were too good to be true, and so losing the reference to what is *higher than I*. On the theme of a high refuge, using a different word, see on 59:1.

3, 4. God's safe keeping is viewed here in increasingly personal terms, as the aloof ruggedness of the high crag of verse 2 gives place to the purpose-built *tower* of verse 3, and this in turn to the hospitality of the frail *tent* (4) with its implication of safety among friends; and finally the affectionate, parental shelter symbolized by *thy wings*. This, against all appearances, is the best security of all: *cf.* on 57:1. And, in spite of RSV, it is more than a fond wish: verse 4b is as confident a prayer as 4a.

61:5–8. Better than safety

5. While the sudden note of certainty could mean that the whole psalm is a thanksgiving piece to accompany the payment

---

[1] Presumably (*cf. BH*) *tᵉrômᵉmēnî* instead of MT's *yārûm mimmennî*.

of a vow, and the opening verses simply a recollection of the prayer that had been made in trouble, it seems better to take verse 5 as following hard on the petition, as God's assurance dawns on David. The content of it may seem vague, but in fact it is all-embracing, since *the heritage*, or appointed possession, of God's followers is **unlimited** and **inalienable**. See 37:11, 29, the equivalent of 'all things are yours'. It must be waited for, but it is certain. Using different language, David goes even further in 16:5f.

6, 7. Whether David offered this prayer as king, claiming the promises of, *e.g.*, 2 Samuel 7:16, or whether it was added for use in public worship (see the opening paragraphs), it was to be fulfilled to overflowing in the person of *the* king, the Messiah. Through Him His people share the kingly blessings (Eph. 2:6; Rev. 22:3-5) and can pray this magnificent petition on their own behalf.

8. The psalm has rung the changes on the words for what is lasting, in contrast to the insecurity expressed at the beginning. Here the word *ever* carries the mind illimitably forward, while *day after day* directs it first to what lies immediately ahead, and on to a practical response. *Vows* were usually discharged in a single ceremony, but David is conscious of a debt that can never be paid off. As George Herbert expressed it elsewhere:

> 'Surely Thy sweet and wondrous love
>   Shall measure all my days;
> And as it never shall remove,
>   So neither shall my praise.'[1]

Psalm 62

All My Hope

This psalm stands high among the many fine fruits of adversity in the Psalter, for it was evidently composed while the pressure was still intense (3), and it shows the marks of growing confidence and clarity as it proceeds. The secret that David learnt alone (1) he impressed again on himself (5, see comment) and urged on others (8), drawing out finally the

---

[1] George Herbert, 'The God of love my Shepherd is'.

lessons of experience and revelation for our benefit and God's honour. It has the immediacy of a prayer that still awaits an answer, and of convictions newly confirmed and deepened.

Title
Jeduthun is discussed at the opening of Psalm 39. See also Introduction, VI. *b*, p. 35, and (for *the choirmaster*), VI. *c*. 3, p. 40.

62:1-4. Stillness under stress
The first two verses will return to bring in the second stanza (5f.), with a subtle change of tone which will be noted there. Here the opening phrase has a telling simplicity in its literal form: 'Truly (or, Only) towards God my soul is silence'; captured best by NEB: 'Truly my heart waits silently for God.' The words have all been said—or perhaps no words will come—and the issue rests with Him alone. It may even be that, as in 39:2, David dare not trust himself to answer his tormentors. It is the kind of situation that is caught to perfection in 123:2. (For silence as a climax of another kind, see on 65:1.)

Not only these opening words but the bulk of the first two stanzas (1–8) are given extra force by the exclamation *'ak*, 'truly' or 'only', which introduces five out of the eight verses. It is an emphasizer, to underline a statement or to point a contrast; its insistent repetition gives the psalm a tone of special earnestness.

2. The thought of God as *rock* and *fortress* (the latter word implying a refuge set high up, as in, *e.g.*, 18:2; 144:2; see on 59:1) is understandably a favourite with David, whose psalms are seldom free from some shadow of an enemy. Almost as an afterthought he qualifies the assurance, *I shall not be moved*, with the word *greatly*, which comes last in the verse. But when the refrain comes back in verse 6 it is unqualified—a revealing touch which NEB and JB obliterate.

3, 4. Evil, being ruthlessly competitive, is attracted to weakness, to give a last push to whatever is *leaning* or *tottering*.[1] It is also attracted to strength, the target of its envy and duplicity ('to topple him from his height', NEB). It is a total

---

[1] We follow here the tradition, supported by the ancient versions, by which the word for *shatter* is vocalized as an active verb (so most modern translations) rather than a passive (so AV, PBV, RV mg.). The Heb. MSS vary as to the vowel concerned.

contrast to the goodness which spares the bruised reed, is glad 'when we are weak and you are strong', and achieves its ends by 'the open statement of the truth'.[1]

62:5-8. Stillness held and shared

Verses 5 and 6 repeat the opening refrain, but modify its tone of voice by three small nuances. First, David now urges on himself the silence which he simply stated in verse 1. (Is this a self-recall after the agitation of verses 3 and 4?) So 5a should read 'For God alone, my soul, wait in silence' (lit. 'be silent'). The second change is simply one of style, substituting *hope* for 'salvation' in 5b (*cf.* 1b) and thereby avoiding a repetition in the next verse. The third is very positive: strengthening the partial confidence of 2b ('not . . . greatly moved') to become the unqualified assurance, 'I shall not be moved' (RSV *shaken* is a translators' variation; the word is the same as in 2b).

7. It was right to speak frankly of the traitors and their plots in the first stanza; now it is David's wisdom to brood on them no longer. He fills his thoughts with God. They are mostly reflections he has already put into similar words; but they hold his mind to its course, and there is one new point to emerge: that *on God rests . . . my honour*. It is something more than the need of refuge and rescue which had first come to mind, and which could arise conceivably from some other quarter. This has only one source, and without it the rest is worthless: *cf.* Jeremiah 9:23; Mark 8:35-38. The worthlessness will be spelt out in the final stanza.

8. Meanwhile his experience is something to share. What he has found in one crisis will avail *at all times*; what God has been to him He can be for others. We may notice here, in the expression *pour out your heart*, the opposite pole of prayer to the silence which reigned in verses 1 and 5. Together there could hardly be two better expressions of the spontaneous unburdening of oneself which is one side of the matter, and the disciplined expectancy which is the other side.

62:9-12. Shadows and substance

The two pairs of verses draw out the wider lessons that have emerged about life, in terms of man (9f.) and God (11f.).

---

[1] *Cf.* Is. 42:3; 2 Cor. 4:2; 13:9.

9. The words *low estate* and *high estate* are only an inference; the Hebrew simply has two parallel expressions for 'sons of man', using for 'man' the generic word *'ādām* and the specific word *'īš*, as at 49:2. In both these places NEB is probably right in taking them as a poetic way of saying 'all men'. *Breath* is the word translated 'vanity' in Ecclesiastes, where, as here, it might well be rendered 'a puff of wind' (NEB, JB, here). The New Testament speaks in such terms in James 4:14. The word for *a delusion* is 'a lie'. The point, then, is not so much that we have nothing to *fear* from man (as in 27:1ff.), as that we have nothing to hope from him. Both thoughts are present in 118:6ff. His treachery was seen in verses 3ff., and now his evanescence —together with 'this world's empty glory'—in the present couplet. Since the Hebrew word for honour (7) is based on what is weighty or substantial, the picture of the *balances* is particularly apt, especially in JB: 'Put (them) in the scales and up they go, lighter than a puff of wind.'

10. True to the theme of the psalm, the accent is so firmly on the right and wrong objects of faith, that absorption with *riches* counts as no less perilous than a life of crime. The Gospels make the point with equal boldness, and 1 Timothy 6:17ff. may be alluding to this verse in its own careful treatment of the subject. *Set . . . vain hopes* is a single word, a verb formed from the contemptuous term for 'breath' discussed at verse 9. The word *increase*, applied to riches, is based on fruit-bearing, which points to part of the fascination of money-making. *Cf.* NEB 'though wealth breeds wealth . . .'.

11, 12. After the pathetic shadows we are brought back to solid reality, and this at two levels, practical and moral. NEB takes these to be the two lessons of *twice have I heard this* ('two things I have learnt'), but it is more likely that the *once . . . twice* is an emphatic way of saying that the whole oracle was reiterated.[1] It makes little difference to the sense.

The first saying, *power belongs to God*, casts its light in two directions: towards the pretended power of man, which has just been dismissed, and towards the trusting servant, who will be reminded both of God's ability to save, and of the earthly power which He delegates to whom He will.

The second attribute used to be translated 'mercy', but

---

[1] Jb. 33:14 may be an example of the former sense, and Jb. 40:5 an example of the latter. There are various examples of the idiom in Pr. 30.

verse 12 makes it particularly clear that this word (*ḥeseḏ*) has
its basis in what is true and dependable. It is closely linked
with covenant-keeping, hence the modern translations, *steadfast love* or 'true love'. Here it is the steadfastness that pre-
dominates, and the glance at retribution is a grateful one,
not so much preoccupied with final judgement (if that is in the
picture at all) as with God's fair dealing in general, which
has none of the duplicity or moral cynicism which the psalm
has deplored.

For such a God David can well afford to wait in silence (1);
and the psalm ends by offering back to God in worship (*thee
. . . thou*) the revelation He has given of His character.

Psalm 63
All My Longing

Once more the worst has brought out David's best, in words
as it did in deeds. The title in the canonical text identifies
the desolate scene which set these thoughts in motion, and the
mention of *the king* in verse 11 points to the time when Absalom
rather than Saul had made him take to *the Wilderness of Judah*
on his way to the Jordan (*cf.* 2 Sa. 15:23). Not only is the
weariness of the way emphasized in the narrative (*e.g.* 2 Sa.
16:14) but, as Kirkpatrick points out, the strong faith evident
in the psalm has its counterpart there as well, in that David
was prepared to part with the ark itself (2 Sa. 15:25) in his
certainty of God and his commitment to His will. There may
be other psalms that equal this outpouring of devotion; few
if any that surpass it.

63:1-4. God my desire
The longing of these verses is not the groping of a stranger,
feeling his way towards God, but the eagerness of a friend,
almost of a lover, to be in touch with the one he holds dear.
The simplicity and boldness of *Thou art my God* is the secret
of all that follows, since this relationship is the heart of the
covenant, from the patriarchs to the present day (Gn. 17:8c;
Heb. 8:10c), and its implications are endless—indeed literally
so, as Jesus pointed out in Matthew 22:31f. Here its reality
shows itself in the love it has awakened in *soul* and *flesh, i.e.*

in David's whole being (*cf.* 35:9f.), which is deeply restless and unsatisfied without God. *Cf.* the unrecognized thirst experienced even by the unbeliever, which Jesus diagnosed in John 4:13f.

There is no compelling reason to abandon the familiar translation, *early will I seek thee*, which is based on the derivation of *seek* from the word for 'dawn', suggesting an eagerness which chimes in with the thought of 130:6 and the language of 57:8.[1] In Psalm 143:6 the *weary land* is itself the picture of David's thirsty soul, but here there is no direct comparison. The comparison may of course be implied, but it is not stated. The word *as* is not in the text of verse 1 (Heb. 2), which simply says that David is praying in parched and cheerless surroundings (which the title defines as the Wilderness of Judah). The implication is that the longing which this desolate spot arouses is only the surface of a much deeper desire. But his explicit comparison, introduced by the *So* of the next verse, gives a fresh turn to the matter.

2. The NEB clarifies the *So* by expanding it to 'So longing'.[2] With the same intense desire (in other words) David had worshipped God in happier days at Zion, and God had revealed Himself. It would be the same now, desert or no desert, for God is not the prisoner of His sanctuary. David speaks the same language here that his actions had spoken when he sent away the ark (see the opening comments to the psalm); and the thought would come to perfect expression in Psalm 139. On the vision of God, see on 11:7.

3. Now he goes a step further. How much further, any reader of his words may judge by considering whether his own unprompted estimate would have taken such a form as this. But it is a true estimate, vouched for by the whole army of martyrs, and put into similar words by Paul in Acts 20:24 (AV): 'Neither count I my life dear unto myself, so that I might finish my course with joy.'

4. The inwardness of David's devotion was completed by what was outward and corporate, as verse 2 has shown, the

---

[1] RSV and JB omit 'early', presumably on the grounds that the etymology of a word tends to recede into the background, or that a cognate Akkadian root means 'turn towards' (*cf.* K-B). But NEB retains 'early', and Pr. 13:24 (*cf.* RV) supports the view that this element in the verb was prominent in Heb.

[2] But NEB departs from the Heb. text by continuing, 'I come before thee'.

one reinforcing the other. To *lift up . . . hands* or eyes (Jn.
17:1) to heaven was to give the body its share in expressing
worship (*cf.* 134:2) or supplication (28:2; *cf.* 1 Ki. 8:54). The
New Testament speaks the same language (1 Tim. 2:8).

63:5–8. God my delight

The new stanza sees the faith and persistence of verses 1–4
abundantly rewarded.

5, 6. The contrast to 'my soul thirsts for thee' (1) is unexpectedly strong with *My soul is feasted*—as if the mere slaking
of thirst would be too weak a metaphor. The praise is now
exuberant: the Hebrew word for *joyful* (5), like 'sing for joy'
in verse 7, has a full-throated ring: *cf.* NEB 'I . . . wake the
echoes'. Yet the chief difference is one of mood. In both
stanzas it is to God Himself, not some lesser goal, that David
is drawn; in both he praises Him, and in both he is humbly
dependent. If the wilderness of verse 1 sharpened his appetite
for God, his wakefulness through *the watches of the night* (an
expression which stresses the slow progress of the hours)
enlisted time and thought for the same Lord. Both kinds of
hardship yielded 'streams in the desert' and 'honey from the
rock'.

7, 8. On *thy wings* see comments on 17:8; 61:3, 4. The two
halves of verse 8 make one of the most vivid statements of the
two facets of perseverance. The word *clings* is familiar to us
elsewhere in the Old Testament as 'cleaves' (*e.g.* Gn. 2:24,
in marital devotion; Dt. 10:20, in loyalty to Yahweh); *cf.*
Ruth 1:14 for an outstanding example of it. In the present
verse it is strenuous: lit. 'clings after thee', as if in hot pursuit.
The old translation remains the best: 'my soul followeth hard
after thee.' But it is God himself who makes this possible, and
the firmness of His upholding grasp is implied in the allusion
to the *right hand*, the stronger of the two; *cf.* Isaiah 41:10. There
is the same divine-human interplay in Philippians 3:8–14.

63:9–11. God my defence

David's enemies, ever present in his psalms, only now come
into view, so intense has been his absorption. But the threat
is real enough, and its dark shadow brings out the solidity of
his faith, which has nothing 'fugitive and cloistered' about it.
He knows that the 'steadfast love' of God, which he praised

in verse 3, is strong with justice (*cf.* 62:12). The New Testament will not dissent: *cf.* Romans 2:4–6.

10. *Jackals* make sense here, rather than the 'foxes' of some older translations (one Hebrew word serves for both). They are the final scavengers, consuming the remains of the kill rejected by the larger beasts.[1] The wicked are, in other words, the very leavings of mankind.

11. We have already noticed David's term for himself, *the king*, as a clue to the circumstances of the psalm (see opening comments). But it is surely more than a synonym for 'I'. If this is written from his banishment at the hands of Absalom, the royal title becomes a reassertion of his calling, which was from God, and an avowal that this cannot fail. A Christian parallel, one of many, can be found in the doxology of John the prisoner, who praises God even from Patmos for the liberty and royal priesthood which are his birthright and ours (Rev. 1:5f.). If David's faith in his kingly calling was well-founded, still more is the Christian's.

Psalm 64
Measure for Measure

While Psalm 63 was focused on God, with the enemy on the edges of the picture, here the composition is reversed, although the outcome is the same. In fact the brevity of God's countermeasures, after the elaborate scheming of the wicked, tells its own decisive tale.

64:1–6. Insidious attack

Everything in these verses emphasizes the cunning and perfidy of the opposition, who fight from concealment, not of necessity like an outnumbered army, but of choice, as those whose cause is shameful and their tactics indefensible.

1. *Complaint* is a word with a somewhat querulous tone, to our ears. Basically it is a man's musing on his situation, whether good (104:34) or bad (*e.g.* Jb. 10:1). Perhaps 'troubled thoughts' would be nearer the mark here. In the second line,

---

[1] *Cf.* G. S. Cansdale, *Animals of Bible Lands* (Paternoster, 1970), pp. 124–126.

note the word *dread*, which is paralysing, whereas fear can be sobering and healthy. Weiser remarks on the good sense of asking first for deliverance from the state of mind which would put an end to clear thought and firm resistance.

2. Now the thought moves to the enemy's camp. Rather than its *scheming*, it is its 'turbulent mob' of which the second line speaks (*cf.* NEB, JB), *i.e.* the outer circle of rebels who carry out the ringleaders' designs; for the word translated *secret plots* means both the plans and the planners. It is the word used in a good sense in 25:14, of an intimate company of friends.

3. Next, their weapons, from which it emerges that these men are plotters from within the realm, sowing doubts and discord. (On the theory that their words were spells, see footnote on 6:8. It needs no magic to spread havoc with the tongue![1] *Cf.*, *e.g.*, Pr. 16:27f.)

4. Now their methods, which cannot afford to be those of honest opposition ('the open statement of the truth', 2 Cor. 4:2; *cf.* 'I opposed him to his face', Gal. 2:11). In the context of this war of lies and innuendo the *ambush* will be either the prepared situation which 'frames' an innocent man, or the shelter of anonymity from which a rumour can be launched *without fear*. (There is no need to emend the latter words, as in NEB, JB, although these changes would be slight in the Hebrew.)

5. Finally, their thoughts. It is an open question whether the beginning of verse 5 means 'they encourage themselves' (AV, RV; *cf.* JB) or *they hold fast* (RSV); but the latter seems a slightly more direct expression.[2] Their delight at having covered their tracks sets the scene perfectly for what will follow; meanwhile the movement of the psalm pauses for the pointed comment of 6b on human nature[3]—akin to our own saying, 'deep as a

---

[1] The word translated *aim* is usually found in the expression 'bend (lit. tread) the bow', which seems to have been transferred here from the bow to the arrows, as also at 58:7 (Heb. 8) if that is the correct text. For a bold, but more logical, use of the same verb see Je. 9:3 (Heb. 2). NEB 'wing . . . like arrows' is an emendation, using an expression which can find some support from Is. 49:2; Je. 51:11, and from the lack of the word 'like' in our present text; but it remains a conjecture.

[2] NEB somewhat high-handedly transposes the next words to 8a, where the context gives them a different sense. But the verb translated *they talk* in 5b (RSV) can have the meaning which RSV gives it: *cf.* 59:12 (Heb. 13); 73:15.

[3] NEB removes this by substituting the word 'evil' for *man*.

well'. It is a remark which warns the reader that the deception (and self-deception) which he has just observed may have their counterparts much nearer home.

64:7–10. Exemplary punishment
Everything speaks of the swiftness and aptness of the judgment. It is all over in a verse and a half (7, 8a), in contrast to the long, laborious scheming which it frustrates; and the conspirators are despatched by their own weapons. Note the *arrow*(s) (3, 7), the attack that comes *suddenly* (4, 7), and the use of their own sharp *tongue* against them (3, 8; *cf.* mg).

8b, 9. The theme is summed up in Isaiah 26:9: 'For when thy judgments are in the earth, the inhabitants of the world learn righteousness.' In the Old Testament the expression 'shake the head' may speak of derision (Je. 48:27) or of shocked concern (Je. 31:18). It could be either of these here,[1] but more probably the second, in view of verse 9 with its chastened reaction to what has happened.

10. So the prayer of verse 1, to be preserved from panic, is more than answered. The judgment is still future, but joy can break out already. It is a sober joy, with the facts faced at their worst, but also at their overwhelming best.

Psalm 65
This Bounteous God

The climax of this psalm, a stanza as fresh and irrepressible as the fertility it describes, puts every harvest hymn to shame as plodding and contrived. Here we almost feel the splash of showers, and sense the springing growth about us. Yet the whole song has this directness, whether it is speaking of God in His temple courts (1–4) or in His vast dominion (5–8) or among the hills and valleys which His very passing wakens into life (9–13).

The occasion of it has been variously identified: *e.g.* an autumn festival which looks ahead to a coming year of plenty, and perhaps includes rituals that call down the expected

---

[1] NEB ('take fright') derives this from the root *nādad*, to flee, rather than *nûd*, to move to and fro. Although BDB supports the former, the latter is equally possible and more appropriate.

blessing; or, in view of the lush pastures it describes, it could be a spring celebration such as the offering of first fruits at Passover; or again, a national deliverance after famine (note the opening allusions to prayers heard and sins forgiven). Whatever event or season it first celebrated, its grateful delight in God as Redeemer, Creator and Provider makes it a rich and many-sided act of praise, not merely a psalm for a harvest festival.

65:1-4. God of grace

This opening suggests a throng of worshippers at the Temple,[1] celebrating a renewal of God's mercy and the answer to their prayers. Perhaps, to judge from the way the psalm ends, His displeasure had been shown by drought and shortage; but their first joy is that they are now reconciled, and welcome at His house.

1. The translation, *praise is due to thee* (*cf.* NEB, JB), follows that of LXX, Vulg. and Syr., and is certainly appropriate enough; there is a similar thought in 147:1 in different words. But it involves a vowel change and, even so, the resultant verb does not easily have this meaning.[2] Therefore we should leave the text unaltered, as in the familiar version, 'Praise waiteth for thee' (AV, RV): lit., 'Praise is silence for thee', or (Delitzsch) 'Silence is praise'; and compare 62:1 (Heb. 2). It may sometimes be the height of worship, in other words, to fall silent before God in awe at His presence and in submission to His will.

2, 3. The mention of *vows* (1) and of answered *prayer*, in this context of sin and forgiveness, suggests that this is a psalm to celebrate a renewal of God's favour; see above. But there is an abruptness in the Hebrew of 3a (Heb. 4a), which reads lit. 'Words (or matters) of iniquities prevail over me; as for our transgressions . . .'. This can be made smoother by re-punctuating it to make it part of the previous verse, either by interpreting the opening phrase adverbially, *i.e.*, *shall . . . come on account of sins* (RSV), or by a small change in the verb *come* (2), to make it causative: 'shall *bring* words of iniquities', somewhat as in Hosea 14:1f. *Cf.* NEB here: 'All men shall lay

---

[1] On the use of this term in the psalms of David, see note at 5:7.

[2] *I.e.*, *dōmiyyâ*, Qal participle fem. of *dāmâ*, 'to resemble' (*e.g.* Is. 46:5). This has the same consonants as *dūmiyyâ*, 'silence', which is the word in the Heb. text (supported by Targ., Aquila and Jerome).

their guilt before thee.' Either way, it leads to a striking statement of grace, which abounds all the more where sin abounded. The acknowledgment of transgressions that are too great to deal with, has the same outcome as the phrase in the parable, 'When they had nothing to pay . . .'.

4. If forgiveness brings man over the threshold, the pattern of God's courts and of His rites made it clear how much remained to be explored beyond that point. By confining to a chosen few (4a) the hereditary right to count themselves at home in His house, God emphasized the pure grace of such a welcome. It remains no less an honour now that all believers are invited in (Heb. 10:19ff.). And the sacrifices that made atonement also made provision (4b), supporting the priests and in some cases feasting the worshippers (*cf.*, *e.g.*, Lv. 7:7-16). Some of the very tithes were earmarked to provide banquets for the givers and their poorer neighbours (Dt. 14:22-29). The expression 'poor as a church mouse' would never have arisen in those precincts! If verse 3 anticipates Romans 5:1, verse 4 has its counterpart in Romans 5:2 and indeed 2 Corinthians 9:8.

65:5-8. God of might

The emphasis now falls on God as Lord of nature and of man, whose power to put the unruly in their place is as welcome as it is formidable.

5. *Deliverance* is more strictly 'righteousness'. Admittedly, God's righteousness is dynamic, righting what is wrong or disordered, and so bringing deliverance; but its motive is moral, and its ends and means are just. On other nuances of this term and its kindred expressions, see on 24:5.

There is breadth of vision here. The *us* and *our* have the ring of personal experience, but not of pride.

> 'The arms of love that compass me
> Would all mankind embrace.'[1]

The word *hope* is more exactly 'trust' or 'confidence'—not to imply that all men have this, or even seek it, but that all men should. There is no other rest for us. For its ultimate implications, see on 47:8.

6, 7. While *mountains* are to all appearance massively secure, and *seas* menacingly wild, the psalmists know better than to

---

[1] C. Wesley, 'Jesus! the name high over all'.

think of them apart from their Creator, as objects of either trust or terror in their own right; *cf.*, *e.g.*, 46:2; 104:5–9; 121:1f. So, too, the sea of humanity is subject to its Master (7b; *cf.* Is. 17:12–14)—an analogy which makes the miracle of Mark 4:35ff. at the same time an acted parable.

8. The phrase *earth's farthest bounds* would be more literal as simply 'the farthest bounds'. But *the outgoings* are a puzzling expression, apparently borrowing the poetic term for the east (where the morning sun 'goes out' on its journey) to serve also for the west (as if to portray darkness setting out from the place of sunset). What is pictured, then, may be either the glory of day and night (*cf.* 19:1f.; Jb. 38:7, 19f.), or the whole expanse of earth from east to west, praising the Creator.

65:9–13. God of plenty

It would be hard to surpass this evocative description of the fertile earth, observed with loving exactness at one moment and poetic freedom at the next, culminating in the fantasy of hills and fields putting on their finest clothes and making merry together.

9, 10. The word, *thou visitest*, expresses a characteristically biblical thought, that God who is always present and active has nevertheless His decisive times of drawing near to bless or judge (*e.g.* Gn. 50:24f.; Ex. 32:34; Lk. 1:68). The word for *waterest* is rendered better in NEB by 'dost . . . give it abundance'; *cf.* the overflowing vats of Joel 2:24. The end of verse 9 puts great emphasis on the sureness with which He works, repeating the same verb in *providest* and *prepared* (and possibly the same root again in the word *so*, with in that case the meaning 'surely'). The last word, *it*, refers back to the 'it' of the first two lines, *i.e.*, the earth. Verse 10 shows more exactly, and almost tangibly, how He makes it ready for the crops it is to bear.

11. Strictly, the first line speaks of 'the year *of* thy bounty'— for its whole course is a gift from God, to which spring and summer add the crowning touch. The *chariot* should rather be the farm waggon; the line is literally 'thy cart-tracks drip fatness'—picturing a 'richly-laden cart dropping its contents in its track' (BDB); a poetic figure for God's pouring out the 'latter rains' as He passes by, bringing abundance in their wake.

12, 13. The *wilderness* is mentioned as a place which is ordinarily drab and sparsely clad; probably the *hills* likewise (*cf.* the paradox of 72:16); but even these are quickly gay with grass and flowers after the rain. *Meadows* and *valleys* have even richer clothes. So the whole landscape has turned out in its best, as if to sing and keep festival. This joy is seasonal and the scene local; but it is no far cry from this to the glimpse in other psalms (*e.g.* 96; 98) of a final coming of God, and a welcome from the whole creation.

Psalm 66
God of All—of Many—of One

This is a thanksgiving psalm, in which the focus sharpens from corporate praise, to which the whole earth is summoned (*Come and see . . .*, 3) by an Israel celebrating its redemption, down to the thanks of one individual, who brings his offerings and summons the faithful (*Come and hear . . .*, 16) to listen to his story, a miniature of theirs. We may picture the scene of public worship, perhaps at Passover or at a victory celebration, in which the corporate praise gives way to the voice of this single worshipper, who stands with his gifts before the altar, and speaks of the God whose care is not only world- and nation-wide, but personal: *I will tell what he has done for me* (16).[1]

66:1–4. A world's homage
God's universal sway, which should and shall be acknowledged, is no exceptional theme in the Psalter, where we need look no further, for a start, than the psalms on either side of this.

1. Apart from the term for God, this verse is identical with the opening of the Jubilate (Ps. 100). The *joyful noise*, in such a context, is a homage cry like that of 1 Samuel 10:24, when all the people 'shouted' to acclaim their king.

2. This verse, which may seem to say little, lays down the

---

[1] It is also possible that this speaker is the king or leader, acting for his people. But the tone of his testimony, and the allusion elsewhere to paying one's vows in public (*e.g.* 40:9f.; 116:14), make it more likely that this is a psalm designed to give a private worshipper a public setting for his votive offering.

first principles of singing in worship: what is its chief content or concern (2a) and its proper quality (2b; *cf.* av, rv 'make his praise glorious'; similarly neb). The gloriousness will be that of 'spirit and truth'. The psalms themselves show the grandeur and vitality of worship that has this character: never trivial, never pretentious

3. It is typical of Scripture not to gloss over the harsh realities of salvation, in which judgment is always an ingredient, and to which God's undisputed sway is fundamental. On the word *cringe*, see footnote at 18:44.

4. The tenses allow a present sense but prefer a future one, as in av, rv. The future also does more justice to the facts: it is a promise which is yet to materialize.

66:5-7. A nation's story

Here is the ground of the final hope just expressed. The crossing of the Red Sea and of the Jordan (6) proved decisively God's power and will to save His people and judge the rebellious (7). By the same token it showed that Israel's calling to be the blessing of the world still held good (*cf.* 8). So the Exodus is no dead letter in the Old Testament (or the New): it is a past event whose repercussions are *for ever* (7), and whose pattern, like that of the cross and resurrection, is reproduced in all God's saving acts. An example of this is probably to be seen in the next stanza.

66:8-12. A nation's trial

As pointed out above, verse 8 reveals the conviction that Israel's fortunes embrace the world, as Abram was promised that they should. This will be put more explicitly in the next psalm. The ordeal which is now referred to is probably not that of the Exodus but something more recent. The biblical habit of seeing the hand of God in all events (*thou . . . thou . . .*, 9-12) makes the suffering as meaningful as the deliverance, since it is seen as a searching scrutiny (*tested*, 10) and a salutary discipline (*tried*, or, as neb, 'refined'). One effect of this experience is already visible in the confession that we enjoy life and security by gift and not by right (9)—a lesson about God the Sustainer which James 4:15 has to reiterate in the New Testament.

11, 12. In the spate of metaphors for the ordeal, the word translated *affliction* is unknown elsewhere, and its meaning uncertain; but it may derive from a root meaning 'to press', an idea familiar to us in our modern metaphorical use of the word 'pressure'. In using the pictures of *fire and . . . water*, Isaiah 43:2 goes a step further than the psalm by promising God's presence *in* the ordeal, as well as His deliverance from it.

The *spacious place* is lit. 'saturation' or 'overflow', the word translated 'runneth over' in 23:5 (AV). If this is the true text, it says rather obscurely what Psalm 23 says plainly, that God's salvation is abundant. But the ancient versions seem to have read 'respite', which may be the right reading.[1]

66:13–15. One man's debt

If this is a strange climax, to have the nation's thanksgiving capped by a single worshipper's, it is a strangeness not unlike the paradox of God's ways, which leave room for the few and the small, who matter to Him as much as the many, and who find themselves, not lose themselves, in His great congregation.

For the paying of vows, see on 22:22–26; with the difference, however, that in the present psalm the offerings are wholly Godward, not of a kind that allowed the worshipper and his friends any share in them. The more usual thank-offerings, which formed the basis of a feast, emphasized the joy of fellowship; these burnt-offerings spoke of total dedication. This suggests a mood of chastened rather than exuberant gratitude, as if to reflect the gravity of the threat that has now been lifted, and the depth of the offerer's debt. The lavishness of the gifts in these verses underlines the point, saying in poetic fashion that the whole gamut of sacrificial beasts would scarcely do the occasion justice.

66:16–20. One man's story

This man's *Come and hear*, addressed to all the godly, corresponds to Israel's *Come and see* (5), addressed to all the world. On the large scale, the church bears witness primarily to the once-for-all acts of God, and calls men to His kingdom (5–7); while at the personal level the individual adds a testimony to His continuing and intimate care. Salvation past and present, corporate and personal, is displayed in proper balance by this double witness.

[1] *I.e.,* r*wāḥâ instead of r*wāyâ.

17, 18. These verses throw incidental light on the practice of prayer, at two points: first, the place of praise in it (17), even when (as verse 14 confirms) it is an urgent cry for help. *Cf.* Jehoshaphat's example in 2 Chronicles 20:12, 21f. Secondly, the requirement of utter sincerity, to which verse 18 gives classical expression, and Joshua 7:11f. the classical illustration.

20. Yet the final word of gratitude is not for the answered request alone, but for what it signifies: an unbroken relationship with God, which is pledged (see on 19.6), personal, and—since it might deservedly have been *removed*—ever a gift of grace.

Psalm 67

The Spreading Circle

If a psalm was ever written round the promises to Abraham, that he would be both blessed and made a blessing, it could well have been such as this. The song begins at home, and returns to pause there a moment before the end; but its thought always flies to the distant peoples and to what awaits them when the blessing that has reached 'us' reaches all.

The only past tense in the whole poem is that of 6a: 'The earth has yielded its increase.' But if the setting of the psalm therefore seems to be a festival of harvest home, it is remarkable (as Weiser points out) how nature is overshadowed by history, and the psalmist stirred by hopes that have no material or self-regarding element. In Psalm 65 the two aspects of God's provision, as meeting our most hidden and most obvious forms of hunger, were held in strict balance (65:4, 5b, 9). Here, nothing matters but man's need of God Himself.

1. If the spirit of the psalm, as already suggested, is that of the Abrahamic hope, its text is the Aaronic Blessing. This verse echoes three of the key words of Numbers 6:24f.; and the *Selah*[1] which follows it, together with the change of person (*his* to *thy*),[2] sets it slightly apart from its sequel. It is as though

---

[1] See Introduction, VI. *c.* 1 (p. 36).
[2] NEB can claim some slight support for reading 'his' in verse 2 (Heb. **3**), but the weight of evidence is against this tidying-up.

the Blessing at the festival lingered in the poet's mind, to germinate in a prayer that explored its possibilities, following them beyond the narrow circle in which he stood and where they might have seemed to terminate.

2. The first overflow from Israel's own blessing will be the spread of life-giving knowledge—a hope wonderfully fulfilled in the writing of the Scriptures, whose twofold work of imparting truth and salvation is summed up not only here (2a, 2b) but in 2 Timothy 3:15f.

3. The point of this refrain, repeated at verse 5, is sadly obscured in AV, PBV, which have 'the people' instead of *the peoples*—as though this were no more than an appeal for hearty singing. It is in fact a prayer of great vision and daring, in which the second line, adding its *all*, clinches its emphasis on God as the Lord whom every tongue must confess.

4. But His reign is joyful, as the repeated calls to *praise*, surrounding this verse, imply. It is fundamentally the joy of perfect fairness, or *equity*, in which the impartiality implied in the word *judge* is partnered by the shepherd-like concern of *guide* (*cf., e.g.*, 23:3; 78:72). The capricious kindliness which makes no moral judgments is as alien to biblical thought as the tyranny that rules without love. See, *e.g.*, Exodus 34:6f.; Isaiah 11:1–9; 42:1–4, for the same marriage of strength and tenderness as here.

6, 7. Only the first line speaks of what is past (see the second introductory paragraph, above); the rest is expectation or prayer, repeating either 'God shall bless us' (AV, RV) or 'Let God bless us' (*cf.* NEB, JB). We can pray this boldly, for He is *our God.* But He is not ours to monopolize, nor will He be any less 'our own God' (PBV) when all His rightful subjects bow to Him. Further, He is no less generous in grace (as we should put it now) than in nature; in the world of men than in the harvest fields. *The earth* with its *increase* can be taken as the promise of still better things to come; perhaps even as a picture of them, as it is in Isaiah 55:10f. and in, *e.g.*, John 4:35; 12:20–24. Let God (the psalm encourages us to pray), who brings much out of little and distributes it in love, bring such blessing on us as to make us, in our turn, the blessing of the world!

Psalm 68

Majesty on High

This rushing cataract of a psalm—one of the most boisterous and exhilarating in the Psalter—may have been composed for David's procession with the ark 'from the house of Obed-Edom to the city of David with rejoicing' (2 Sa. 6:12). It opens with an echo of the words with which the ark set out on all its journeys (Nu. 10:35), and finds its climax in God's ascent of 'the high mount' which He has chosen for His dwelling.

Flanked by the ebullient prologue and epilogue, the two main parts of the psalm celebrate, first, God's victorious march from Egypt, with its culmination at Jerusalem (7–18), and secondly the power and majesty of His régime seen in the ascendancy of His people and the flow of worshippers and vassals to His footstool (19–31).

This history and prophecy of salvation, set out in Israelite terms, is presented in Ephesians 4:7–16 as a miniature of a far greater ascension, in which Christ led captivity captive, to share out better spoils of victory than these, in the gift (and gifts) of the Spirit. *Cf.* also Acts 2:33. Consequently in Christian history this has been from early times a psalm for Pentecost—as indeed it was in the Jewish synagogue for the harvest feast of that name, the Feast of Weeks.

68:1–6. A fanfare of praise

The ancient cry, 'Arise, O Lord . . .', was appointed for the setting out of a procession with the ark (Nu. 10:25); so verse 1 evokes a scene which will be glimpsed again in animated progress in verses 24–27. But it has boldly turned the prayer into praise, although most translations conceal the fact; for in the psalm it runs literally: 'God arises and his enemies are scattered . . .'[1], as in NEB. Here faith is living up to the definition in Hebrews 11:1, with its present grasp of things hoped for, and its conviction of things not seen. The

---

[1] Or, 'God will arise, and his enemies be scattered . . .'. All three verbs of verse 1 are affirmations, present or future. Those of the next two verses therefore continue in this strain, although in isolation they would be translatable as either affirmations or prayers.

enemy is anything but solid (2); the invisible God anything but absent.

4. The middle line of this magnificent verse admits of more than one translation, as RSV mg. indicates, because of the ambiguity of *lift up* (to raise a song or, almost always, a highway, as in, *e.g.*, Is. 57:14) and of *the clouds* (alternatively 'the deserts').[1] It would make good sense in either case, for we are called elsewhere to make a highway in the desert (Is. 40:3); and the heavens of verse 33 would have none of their thunder stolen if verse 3 confined itself to ground level. But both verses probably have the same vision, of the heavenly chariot and its Rider; *cf.* 18:10; 104:3.

5, 6. Protection of the helpless and judgment on the lawless are marks of true kingship, human and divine, even according to the heathen; so these two verses fitly round off the praise of the kingly deliverer. But the ark brings its reminder of the exodus to bear on this as well. That deliverance was the classic provision for the homeless, liberation for the prisoners and chastening for the rebels. In these events, as in the Gospel acts which they foreshadowed, God's pattern of action stands out with special clarity and completeness, and interprets the rest of His ways, which we only partially observe elsewhere.

68:7-18. Royal progress

If this processional psalm was indeed written to escort the ark to the newly won Jerusalem, it celebrated the last stage of a journey begun centuries before at mount Sinai. There the ark had been made, and from there it had led Israel in God's name into the promised land and now at last to the summit of mount Zion. It was a moment of fulfilment.

7-10. The march of God. Now God is praised directly. He is gratefully reminded of His miracles, in a stanza where one scene rapidly coalesces with the next: the exodus march;

---

[1] The title of Baal, 'rider of the clouds' (*rkb 'rpt*), is almost identical with the Heb. expression here, which may be a pointed reminder that only the Lord has a right to it. This close similarity, together with the clear evidence of verse 33, points rather strongly to the translation '. . . who rides upon the clouds'.

the theophany at Sinai; the mighty rainstorm which defeated Sisera (verse 8 quotes the allusion to Sinai[1] from the Song of Deborah, Jdg. 5:4f.); finally the gentler blessings of the rain, year by year,[2] which exhibit His continuing goodness: *cf.* 65:9ff.

11–14. The rout of kings. The Song of Deborah still echoes in these verses, which are a tumble of swift images and excited snatches of description.[3] In the *command* (or simply 'word') of verse 11 we should probably picture a scene such as that of 2 Samuel 18:19ff., where the victorious general releases the news (*cf.* Mt. 28:18ff.), and that of 1 Samuel 18:6f. where the women take it up with songs and dances (the word for *those who bore the tidings*[4] is feminine). The RSV catches the immediacy of the Hebrew: '*they flee, they flee!*'

The scene as the women *divide the spoil* is illuminated by Judges 5:30, where Sisera's mother pictures to herself the rich garments which her son will bring home. (The interjection of 13a[5] picks up Deborah's taunt against Reuben, who chose the woman's role but missed the spoil: Jdg. 5:16.) *The wings of a dove*, flashing *silver* and *gold*, have been taken to refer to Israel basking in prosperity (Delitzsch), to the enemy in flight (Briggs), to the glory of the Lord manifested at the battle (Weiser), or even to a particular trophy seized from the enemy (*cf.* NEB); but could it not depict the women of 12b

---

[1] W. F. Albright (*BASOR* 62 (1936), p. 30) has convinced most modern translators that *yon Sinai* should be rendered 'the One of Sinai', concluding the preceding line. (RSV's second occurrence of *quaked* in this verse is an addition to the Heb. text.) This avoids the somewhat rare construction implied by 'yon Sinai' (but *cf.* 'this Moses', Ex. 32:1,23), though it has to find its support from non-Israelite sources. The line will then run, as in NEB, 'Before God the lord of Sinai, before God the God of Israel'.

[2] In verses 9 and 10 (Heb. 10,11) the verbs *shed abroad* and *provide* should be present or future; *cf.* NEB.

[3] We need not accept the counsel of despair by which T. H. Robinson (following H. Schmidt) likened this to 'a page from the index of a hymn book'—a view of it reached independently by Albright: 'A Catalogue of Early Hebrew Lyric Poems', *HUCA* 23¹ (1950–51), pp. 1–39.

[4] This phrase is a single Heb. word, one of the characteristic verbs of Is. 40ff. Its Greek equivalent has given us the word 'evangelize'.

[5] The PBV, 'Though ye have lien among the pots', adds its own touch of obscurity. 'Lien' means 'lain'. 'Pots' is an unlikely meaning for the rare word which most modern versions give as 'sheepfolds', but K-B as 'pack-saddles'.

preening themselves in their new finery:[1] peacocking around, as we might have put it?

The *snow . . . on Zalmon* (14) is another rapid allusion which we can scarcely catch. There was a mount Zalmon near Shechem (Jdg. 9:48), but it need not have been the only 'Black Mountain' (as the name appears to mean); it may have been a term for Jebel Druze, on the borders of Bashan, as Albright suggests.[2] Whether the rout of kings there was caused by a blizzard, or whether the battlefield was 'snowed' with weapons and garments (or, later, with bones), or the fleeing armies compared to driven snowflakes, we cannot tell.

15-18. The mount of glory. The mention of snow-clad Zalmon leads the mind to the white-capped giants in and beyond Bashan. The *mighty mountain* (lit. 'mountain of God', a way of expressing the superlative) was perhaps Jebel Druze[3] (Zalmon?—see on verse 14, above) within Bashan, or the pre-eminent Hermon further north. In comparison with these, mount Zion is the merest hill; yet Zion, as if to their baleful *envy*,[4] was God's choice. *Cf.* Isaiah 66:1f. It is the kind of paradox that God delights in, like the choice of David himself (to whom the psalm is attributed), and of little Bethlehem; indeed of 'things that are not' (1 Cor. 1:28).

17. While RSV, NEB, JB present substantially the same picture as the Hebrew text, they have slightly emended it by reading *The Lord came from* (*bā' mi-*) instead of 'The Lord is among them' (*bām*), with consequent further adjustments. Weiser gives the truest translation of the first and third lines: 'The chariot[5] of the Lord are the ten thousands . . . the Lord is with them, Sinai is in the holy place.' While other poems picture God sallying forth from His mountains (*e.g.* Dt. 33:2; Jdg. 5:4; Hab. 3:3), this declares that where God is, there is Sinai—and, we might add, every place of revelation or

[1] It is encouraging to find that J. H. Eaton makes a similar suggestion (*Torch Bible Commentary*).
[2] W. F. Albright, *HUCA* 23[1] (1950–51), p. 23.
[3] *Cf.* D. Baly, *The Geography of the Bible* (Lutterworth, 1957), pp. 194, 222.
[4] The old translation, 'Why hop ye so' (PBV; *cf.* AV) is not tenable. But the mountains still 'skip like rams' in 114:6, where it is a different verb. The present verb means 'to watch narrowly', as if in ambush.
[5] More probably 'chariotry'; this singular is often used collectively: *e.g.* 2 Ki. 6:17. But it is possible that the whole angelic host is visualized as the Lord's chariot-throne, as in Ezk. 1.

encounter. The new sanctuary at Zion has not to compete
with Bethel, Sinai or any other spot; it is here that God has
chosen to be found. The thought will be carried still further
in Hebrews 12:18–24.

18. As the ark, the throne of the invisible God, leads the
procession up to its resting place, its progress is a victory
march completing the exodus. Once again the triumph-song
of Deborah supplies the words for it (Jdg. 5:12), although the
ringing phrase 'thou hast led captivity captive' (AV) is somewhat muted in RSV, *etc.*

Who are these captives, and whose are the gifts? The battle
imagery and the echoes of the Song of Deborah indicate
enemy prisoners and enemy reparations. God has won His
war, entered His capital and put *the rebellious* under tribute.
Then verses 19f. show His people sharing the benefits of the
conquest; likewise in Ephesians 4:8 it will be this outcome
that dominates the thought of Paul. In the psalm (as E. E.
Ellis[1] points out) 'God . . . shares with them the booty of His
victory; Paul applies the Psalm . . . to the gifts Christ gives
to the Church after His victory over the "captivity" of death.'[2]

68:19–31. Royal state
With the ascent of 'the high mount' the psalm has reached
its climax. Now it unfolds the consequences.

19–23. Heirs of victory. The key to this stanza is the word
daily (19), or more emphatically, 'day by day', which links
the story of redemption firmly with the present and future.
First, there is God's all-sufficient care, *who daily bears us up.*
The old translation, 'who daily loadeth us (with benefits)'
(AV) is not impossible, since the expression is lit. 'loads-up
for us' (*cf.* the provisions loaded on to the asses of Ne. 13:15);

[1] E. E. Ellis, *Paul's Use of the Old Testament* (Oliver & Boyd, 1957), pp.
138f.; *cf.* p. 144.
[2] Where the MT reads 'received gifts among men' (or perhaps 'consisting
of', or, as in Ugaritic, 'from men'?), Paul has 'gave gifts to men'. This
summarizes rather than contradicts the psalm, whose next concern is with
the blessings God dispenses (19ff., 35). Note however that Paul's 'give'
agrees with the Targum, which could be based on a variant Heb. reading,
i.e., the verb *ḥ-l-q* (share, assign) for *l-ḥ-q* (take), and which incidentally
fits well with the otherwise awkward expression, 'among men'. If this is
the original reading (an admittedly precarious conjecture), the phrase 'even
among the rebellious' will imply a gesture of reinstatement, as in AV.

but God as burden-bearer is perhaps the more likely meaning. It is a metaphor used very tellingly in Isaiah 46:1–4 and 63:9, where His tireless love is contrasted with both the ponderous feebleness of heathenism and the fickleness of those whom He helps.

20. Two words here, *salvation* and *escape*, are plural in the original, which is a way of indicating their repeated occurrences, and probably their richness and range. *Escape* means literally 'exits' or 'goings forth'; and the Christian can reflect with David that, while death is apparently a domain with many entrances and no exit, God has made it one from which 'he brought me forth' (to quote the related verb) 'into a broad place' (Ps. 18:19, Heb. 20).

21. *Enemies* remain, despite the initial conquest and its climax in verse 18. David's psalms are never wholly quit of them. The *hairy crown* may allude to a practice of leaving the locks unshorn in the hope that wholeness and strength would be thereby preserved: *cf.* Deuteronomy 32:42; also perhaps Judges 5:2 (NEB mg., JB).

22. It is hard to say whether God is reminding Israel of the perils He overcame to restore them to the promised land (*cf.* 136:13, 20), or declaring that no hiding place will shelter the fleeing enemy (*cf.* Am. 9:2f.).[1] But the former seems the more likely.

23. The passage reeks of blood, but not so certainly of bloodlust—*i.e.*, of killing for the sake of it. There is undisguised joy of victory, and no pretence that victories are anything but gory; but 21b should not be overlooked. This is judgment, not imperialism. *Cf.* Genesis 15:16.

24–27. Cavalcade of Israel. The various groups that escorted the ark meet us in the narratives of 1 Chronicles 13:8 and 15:16–28, where many individual names are preserved; but here the scene effectively 'comes into view' (NEB) in its order of march. On a point of detail, *the maidens* should be pictured 'surrounding' the singers and minstrels (Weiser; *cf.* RV) rather than interposed between the two groups. Their role with the *timbrels* was time-honoured: *cf.* Miriam, and Jephthah's daughter, and the women who greeted David and Saul. The tribal names are samples of the whole: two each

---

[1] NEB 'Dragon' assumes that Bashan (*b-š-n*) is the equivalent here of Ugaritic *btn*, 'serpent'; *cf.* Am. 9:3 (but a different word).

of the southernmost and of the northernmost. *Benjamin* may
have led the way in memory of the lead it took at Deborah's
battle (Jdg. 5:14) or because Jerusalem was within its borders.

28–31. Homage of the nations. The theme of this stanza
is developed with great power and fullness in Isaiah 60, and
its initial fulfilment is by now a matter of history, as a spiritual
rather than political conquest, in the Gentile influx into the
Kingdom.

29. *Because of thy temple* is lit. 'from thy temple'. Either
meaning is possible. The former agrees well with, *e.g.*, Isaiah
2:2f.; Haggai 2:7f.; while the latter makes sense if it is taken
with the previous verse, as in JB. *Cf.* the prayer 'May he send
you help from the sanctuary' (20:2). In either case the second
line should be translated 'Let kings bear gifts . . .', in view
of the imperatives in the surrounding verses.

30. No translation of this verse can, as yet, be more than
tentative, particularly in the third line. In the opening phrase
'the Beast of the Reeds' (JB) is evidently the crocodile or
hippopotamus, a nickname for Egypt, Israel's traditional
oppressor (*cf.* Ezk. 32:2). The *bulls* and *calves* (or bullocks)
are the hostile *peoples*,[1] great and small, or the leaders and
the led. In the third line, RV is almost completely literal; but
its margin indicates some of the uncertainties, which lead to
two main interpretations. Either God is trampling on the
covetous[2] (RSV), or the enemy is grovelling[3] before Him with
tribute money (AV, JB). In the fourth line the imperative,
scatter, is strongly supported by the ancient versions, against
the MT which reads 'he scattered'. It involves no change of
consonants.

31. *Ethiopia* represents the Hebrew 'Cush', *i.e.*, Nubia or
North Sudan (*cf. NBD*); a telling example of a remote people
seeking God. *Cf.* Isaiah 18; Acts 8:27.

68:32–35. A closing fanfare

If the opening chorus was Israel's alone (1–6), the concluding
one is universal, in keeping with the tribute scene just visual-

---

[1] The 'genitive' in 'bullocks of peoples' is explanatory or appositional
(G-K, 128 l); *cf.* 'a wild ass of a man', Gn. 16:12.

[2] *I.e.*, reading *rōṣê*, 'those who take pleasure in', instead of *raṣṣê*, 'pieces of'.

[3] This 'self-trampling' is attested by Pr. 6:3, mg. But NEB transposes the
consonants of this verb, to read, instead, 'from Pathros' (following a
conjecture by E. Nestle, *JBL* 10 (1891), p. 152).

ized. But while it reasserts the cosmic power of God (33f.; *cf.* 4), it names Him still *the God of Israel*, no diffused and faceless deity. The psalm itself, by its almost uncontainable enthusiasm, bears witness to its grasp of this reality, this union of immense power and intense care, in the God *whose majesty is over Israel* (as verse 34 expresses the latter of these two), *and his power is in the skies*.

Psalm 69
Persecution

This psalm reveals a vulnerable man: one who could not shrug off slander, betrayal or self-accusation (5), as a hard or self-absorbed person might, and whose sense of justice had not been dulled. His prayers and curses both alike spring from this personal and moral sensitivity, and the New Testament sees Christ prefigured in the singer's zeal for God's house and in his sufferings (9; *cf.* 21). But the very juxtaposition of David cursing his tormentors and Jesus praying for His, brings out the gulf between type and antitype, and indeed between accepted attitudes among saints of the Old Testament and the New. This is discussed further in the Introduction, v, pp. 30ff.

The pattern of the psalm can be gathered, to some extent, from the sequence of the headings suggested here for its main divisions. The last stanza, with its collective note, may have been an addition to give the congregation its own part after the individual had finished his declaration, or to re-interpret the whole of this prayer as that of the nation personified.

Title
The title has similarities to those of Psalms 45, 60 and 80, on which see Introduction, VI. *c.* 3, p. 42.

69:1–5. A sea of troubles
This distracted beginning demonstrates the value of putting one's plight into words before God, for David's account of his crisis clarifies and grows more reflective as he prays. The desperate metaphors of inner turmoil and floundering (1, 2)

245

give way to more objective (though still agitated) descriptions of his state and situation (3, 4), and finally to a searching of his conscience (5). Prayer is already doing its work.

4. On our Lord's allusion to *those who hate me without cause*, see on 35:19, where the parallel expression, *those who attack me with lies*, is also found, differently translated. In Hebrew, the question *must I now restore?* is on the face of it a statement, as in the older translations. It is better taken so, for it has no interrogatory prefix and makes good sense as it stands, showing the pressure that David's enemies can put upon him.

5. In using the word *folly* there is no attempt to pass off misdeeds as mere misjudgments. It is a sin against truth, a piece of 'moral insolence',[1] even though it is more thoughtless than deliberate, unlike that of the *nābāl* of 14:1, *etc.*

69:6–12. The sting of insult

A note of concern now mingles with the lament, as the prayer enlarges its circle of vision outwards (6) and upwards (7). What will happen to God's people and His name if a servant of His can be insulted with impunity? To feel the force of this, we may picture the dismay of a devoted ambassador (9a), whose country does nothing to protect him from a campaign of humiliation aimed, as he can see, against its own prestige. The fact that both halves of verse 9 were to find fulfilment in Christ (Jn. 2:17; Rom. 15:3) puts the matter into so new a context that the Christian reader finds it difficult to enter fully into David's bewilderment, as distinct from his pain. The 'weakness of God' now makes sense, for it is redemptive; and 'to suffer dishonour for the name' (Acts 5:41) is, despite its cost, a compliment.

69:13–18. The cry

Although the return of the metaphors of *mire* and *deep waters* (14f.; *cf.* 1f.) shows that the sense of helplessness is still overwhelming, the prayer continues to break new ground. Now for the first time it concentrates on the Lord's goodness and mercy (although He has already been named 'my God' (3), 'Yahweh of hosts' and 'God of Israel' (6), which are strong grounds for encouragement). The divine faithfulness is richly described in verses 13 and 16.

---

[1] See the Tyndale Commentary on *Proverbs*, p. 41.

13. In RSV the phrase, *At an acceptable time*, controls the request, *answer me*. It is a humble admission that however urgently one may cry out 'make haste' (17), one's times are in God's hand (31:15). But the natural division of the verse may imply the conviction that the prayer itself is being offered in a day of grace—perhaps in the context of atonement (*cf.* Lv. 1:4) or of God's call (*cf.* 32:6, mg.; Is. 55:6)—without referring to the time of God's answer.

Faithful help is not quite a strong enough expression: better, 'sure salvation'.

18. *Redeem* is the verb connected with the duty of a man's next-of-kin to stand up for him in trouble: *e.g.* avenging his death (Nu. 35:19), or buying back his land or liberty (Lv. 25:25, 48f.). *Set me free* is better translated 'ransom me' (NEB), to bring out its basic idea of purchase; see on 31:5 (*pāḏâ*). The two verbs are found again side by side in Isaiah 35:9f., where God's people are named 'the redeemed' and 'the ransomed'; but the full implications of this way of speaking come to light only in the New Testament.

69:19–21. The cup

There are few wounds as deep as those expressed in the words *reproach, shame, dishonour*. They have already left their mark repeatedly on verses 6–12. In the close-knit society of the Old Testament, public shame was even more devastating than in our own (*cf.* the revealing remark of Moses in Nu. 12:14); and Hebrews 12:2 singles this factor out in speaking of the cost of the cross. In Handel's *Messiah* it was an apt choice to place the heart-rending words of verse 20[1] after the mocking in the crucifixion narrative.

21. What David was offered in metaphor, Jesus was offered in fact, according to Matthew 27:34, 48, where the Greek words for gall[2] and *vinegar* are those that the LXX uses here. Matthew, however, does not claim this as a prophetic fulfilment, although John 19:28 speaks of Jesus' thirst in such terms.

---

[1] But *Messiah* adopts PBV's insertion of 'Thy' (Thy rebuke), which makes it God's reproach instead of man's, against the sense of the context.

[2] The word translated *poison* is rendered 'gall' in AV, RV, PBV, as in LXX. It is the name of a herb (Ho. 10:4), not certainly identified. In the Old Testament it is often coupled with 'wormwood', for bitterness, but is also used as a poetic term for snake venom (Dt. 32:33; Jb. 20:16).

69:22-28. The curse

Up to this point, Christ and His passion have been so evidently foreshadowed (see on verses 4, 9, 21) that we are almost prepared now for a plea approximating to 'Father, forgive them'. The curse which comes instead is a powerful reminder of the new thing which our Lord did at Calvary. It is not simply an emotional difference. David's anger was fanned by his zeal for justice, which the Old Testament largely exists to keep before us; but Christ came to crown justice with atonement. Zeal for this, now it is accomplished, will stir us differently: cooling anger instead of kindling it; fostering rather than stifling compassion. See also Introduction, v, pp. 30ff.; also comments on 35:7, 8; 109.6ff.

The judgment which David calls down on these persecutors (for such they are, 26; *cf.* Zc. 1:15) enumerates, by contrast, the things that normally make life worth living: at one level, food and fellowship;[1] one's faculties and strength (*eyes . . . loins*); a place to belong to; and more fundamentally, the goodwill of God (*cf.* 24), His clearance from guilt (27), and to be known and accepted by Him (28; *cf.* Ex. 32:32f.). This last need is as basic as any: *cf.* the highest cause for joy according to Luke 10:20, 'that your names are written in heaven'; and the finality of 'I never knew you'.

69:29-33. Praise from the heart

In a sense, verse 29 stands by itself (as in RSV); a final gasp of prayer. But its second line is so positive, asking for more than mere respite, that it links itself to the outburst of praise that follows.

The point that is being made in 30ff. is that personal, explicit praise is more to God's liking (31) and more to man's help (32f.) than the most expensive sacrifice. There is a note of dry amusement in the glance at *horns and hoofs*—how useful to God!—which calls to mind Psalm 50:12ff., where a similar point is sharply driven home.

33. The striking expression, *his own that are in bonds*, lit. 'his prisoners' (RV), reveals what touches God particularly closely

---

[1] *Sacrificial feasts* is the Targ. reading; other ancient versions read 'for requital' (as a parallel expression to *snare* and *trap*). These differ only slightly from the MT, which appears to mean 'for peace (or welfare)' as in AV, RV; or 'for allies' as in 55:20 (Heb. 21). The italics in AV, RV show the slight difficulty of the MT here.

(see on 72:2), and brings out the contrast between Him and the grasping gods of heathendom: namely our relationship to Him, and our need. The NEB rendering of it as 'those bound to his service' seems unsuited to the context; see rather 68:5f.

69:34–36. Praise from the host

On the relation of this corporate praise to the prayer of the individual, see the second introductory paragraph at the head of the psalm. The mention of *Judah* rather than Israel points to a time later than David, and verse 35 would fit the situation of Hezekiah, when Zion was threatened and 'all the fortified cities of Judah' captured (2 Ki. 18:13). Whether this was the occasion or not, the nation's plight was comparable to David's own, long before. It is striking, then, that what is added is not petition but praise; and praise which looks beyond the day of decline and insecurity to the full extent of God's dominion (34) and the perfecting of His people's inheritance. The psalm is yet another reminder that the most desperate of prayers can end, and rightly so, in doxology.

Psalm 70

Be Quick, Lord!

This is practically identical with Psalm 40:13–17. It is helpful to be able to sing this plea either by itself or in conjunction with the praise for past help which dominates the longer psalm. This duplication came about, it would seem, through the compiling of separate collections of psalms (see Introduction, II, for further discussion and examples). See also Psalm 71, which opens with three verses which largely coincide with the beginning of Psalm 31.

For the main comments, therefore, see on 40:13–17. Here it is enough to point out the places at which the two diverge. On the **title,** see on Psalm 38.

In verses 1f. the difference from Psalm 40:13ff. is the greater brevity of this prayer, giving a stronger sense of urgency; then in 3ff. there are a few verbal variants.

1. The opening, *Be pleased,* is not in the Hebrew text here; the translators have borrowed it from 40:13 (Heb. 14). Instead, we have literally 'God, to deliver me, Lord, to my help, hurry!' The older translators were justified in their abrupt opening, 'Make haste'.

2. Here too there is a tightening of the language, speeding the petition where the Hebrew of 40:14 added 'together' after *confusion*, and 'to snatch it away' after *life*.

3. *Be appalled* is rsv's 'correction' of the text to agree with 40:15 (Heb. 16).[1] The standard text reads 'turn back' (NEB 'shrink back'), as at 6:10 (Heb. 11); 56:9 (Heb. 10).

4, 5. *God . . . God . . . Lord* (Yahweh) is a sequence corresponding to 'Lord (Yahweh) . . . Lord (Master) . . . my God' in 40:16f., illustrating the general interchangeability of the terms. *Hasten* (*ḥûšâ*) is found where 'take thought' (*yaḥǎšōḇ*) appears in 40:17 (Heb. 18). Once again the petitions in this form of the psalm emphasize the urgency of the matter. There is not a moment to lose; or so at least it appears at ground-level. On the other dimensions of such a situation see, *e.g.*, Daniel 10:2f., 12f.; John 11:5f.; Isaiah 60:22b.

Psalm 71

A Psalm for Old Age

No author is named for this psalm. There are Davidic expressions (*e.g.* 'my rock and my fortress'; 'my enemies'; 'make haste!'), but as the writer is drawing freely on earlier psalms this tells us little. All that we know, or need to know, is that he is old or ageing, and has seen exceptional trouble (7) which shows no sign of abating. Against his failing strength he now sets a long memory of God's faithfulness and a growing hope in His life-renewing power.

71:1–3. Rock and fortress

These verses are an almost exact quotation of 31:1–3a (Heb. 2–4a), where further comments can be found. The main difference is in the Hebrew of verse 3, which rsv considers to have been miscopied here (see rsv mg.). But as it stands, it reads '. . . a rock of habitation[2] to come to continually (for)

---

[1] A few mss support this, but they are probably influenced by Ps. 40.

[2] Heb. *mā'ôn*, where 31:3 has *mā'ōz* (refuge). These two words are closely alike (*cf.* 90:1, mg.), but the two passages diverge further after this.

thou hast commanded to save me' (*cf.* AV, RV). This is suffi-
ciently distinct from the passage in Psalm 31 to look like a
deliberate variation, to stress the theme—especially dear to
an old man—of what is familiar and habitual, introducing
here the word 'continually', which will recur in verses 6 and
14.

71:4-6. Friend from birth

These thoughts run parallel with those of 22:9ff., though
they are differently expressed. Here the psalmist looks back
to the limits of his memory (5) and beyond (6), to be reassured
by the threefold cord of a relationship that was lifelong, that
had sufficed in other times of frailty, and that was not of his
own devising. On his side there had been filial dependence,
but God had been already at work for him,

> 'Before my infant heart conceived
> From whom these comforts flowed.'[1]

In verse 6, NEB replaces *he who took me* by 'my protector',
following a reading suggested by LXX, Vulg. But 22:9 (Heb.
10), which is probably the background to this verse in different
words, supports the sense given here in RSV.

71:7-11. Failing powers

It seems best to understand *a portent* here in its bad sense of 'a
solemn warning' (NEB), somewhat as in Deuteronomy 28:46
where the disobedient suffer an exemplary fate. With people
drawing the worst and, to them, most gratifying conclusions
from his sufferings, this psalmist resolutely pursues the theme
he has begun in verses 5f., looking to God to see through to a
conclusion the work He began so long ago. So the very fact of
old age and weakness (9) is turned into a strong ground of
appeal. Note, too, the pivotal effect of the phrase *but thou* (7b)
in re-directing his attention from himself and the encircling
enemy (8); an escape *to* reality rather than from it. The
similarly emphatic 'For thou—' of verse 5 had had the same
effect. It is another point of resemblance to Psalm 22, where
see comments on 22:1-21.

---

[1] J. Addison, 'When all Thy mercies, O my God'. The hymn makes a
good partner to the psalm.

71:12-16. Rising hope
This crescendo starts from a mere whisper, and the prayer at first leans on the words of David uttered under similar trials. (Verse 12a echoes 22:11; 12b takes up 70:1b; verse 13 is close to 35:26 and 109:29.) Such praying is enriched by the echoes, other pilgrims, we are reminded, have passed through this valley. Two of our Lord's three prayers on the cross were likewise from the Psalter.

15. The growing volume of praise is nourished by plenty of facts: note in these verses the concentration on what God has done. The concepts expressed by *tell* and *number*[1] are related to each other in Hebrew, as in various other languages (*cf.* the two meanings of our expression 'the full tale'), so that there is at least a glance here at the idea which is taken up in the sound advice of the jingle 'Count your blessings, name them one by one'. With the fact that the blessings are nevertheless innumerable, compare the paradox of Ephesians 3:19.

16. Some MSS have the singular of *mighty deeds*, as in AV's memorable phrase 'I will go in the strength of the Lord God'. Even the plural could express this, as a plural of fullness. But since the verb normally means *come*[2] rather than 'go', the RSV is probably right to see this sentence (like the next) as a resolve to come before God with praise, rather than go out to do exploits.

71:17-21. Late harvest
In taking up the theme of God's lifelong care of him, the singer strikes the same note of mingled confidence and pathos as in verses 5-9, but now with a livelier interest in the future. There is much to be done: he is eager to do it. Once again Psalm 22 seems to prompt his praying: now it is the buoyant ending of it which he makes his own, catching the same eagerness to pass on his story to posterity. *Cf.* 18b with Psalm 22:22, 30f.

19-21. There is more than a hint of the exodus miracle in 19f., with the phrase '*who is like thee?*' from the Song of the

---

[1] NEB ('although I have not the skill of a poet') follows LXX, Vulg. in their interpretation of the rare word for *number* in 15b. As this note of self-deprecation seems out of place and even false, there is little reason to prefer this side of the tell/number equation.

[2] G. R. Driver, *VT* I (1951), p. 249, tentatively suggests the meaning 'enter upon'='commence with'. So NEB, 'I will begin with a tale of great deeds'.

Sea (Ex. 15:11), and with the picture of deliverance from the 'watery depths' (20, NEB; Heb. *tᵉhōmôt*; *cf.* Ex. 15:5). So the troubles of the present are, by faith, put in this great context, in much the same way that Paul teaches us to relate our situation to 'him who raised Jesus from the dead' and who still raises the dead (Rom. 8:11; 2 Cor. 1:9).

It is tempting to read verse 20 as a statement about resurrection, but in the Hebrew text the first two lines speak of 'us' rather than 'me'. Israel, like the psalmist, has seen its disasters, but its revivals too; he can have the same confidence. Pressed to its conclusion, this hope makes little sense if it stops short of resurrection; but the psalmist shows no sign of looking further than a new lease of life. There is nothing here quite comparable to the hope of being in God's immediate presence, which crowns Psalms 16, 17, 49 and 73.

71:22-24. Unremitting praise

The sense of sharing in Israel's redemption while experiencing his own, which was brought out in verse 20 (see comment), reappears in the singer's double invocation of his Lord: the personal cry, *O my God*, and the cry of an Israelite, *O Holy One of Israel* (22). The latter name, moreover (which is a rarity outside Isaiah),[1] is one in which 'unapproachable light' and covenant-love meet together. Appropriately, therefore, the theme of his praise is the partnership of righteousness (*righteous help*, 24) and *faithfulness* (22) in his deliverance and in the silencing of the enemy. This is vindication, not vindictiveness. It will be part of the joy of heaven (*cf.* Rev. 15:3; 18:20).

So, with his name cleared and his faith confirmed, this veteran can set his mind at rest, and his fingers, lips and heart to the praise of God and the telling of his story.

Psalm 72

The Perfect King

This radiant psalm has won itself a special place among English-speaking Christians through two fine hymns: James Montgomery's 'Hail to the Lord's Anointed', and Isaac Watts' 'Jesus shall reign'. Both of them translate the terms of earthly

---

[1] It occurs in 2 Ki. 19:22 (quoting Isaiah); Pss. 71:22; 78:41; 89:19; Je. 50:29; 51:5.

Israelite empire into those of Christ's dominion. The New Testament nowhere quotes it as Messianic, but this picture of the king and his realm is so close to the prophecies of Isaiah 11:1–5 and Isaiah 60–62 that if those passages are Messianic, so is this. Language that would otherwise be no more than courtly extravagance makes sober sense with this reference. This is not to say that it was a purely visionary composition. As a royal psalm it prayed for the reigning king, and was a strong reminder of his high calling; yet it exalted this so far beyond the humanly attainable (*e.g.* in speaking of his reign as endless) as to suggest for its fulfilment no less a person than the Messiah, not only to Christian thinking but to Jewish. The Targum at verse 1 adds the word 'Messiah' to 'the king', and there are rabbinic allusions to the psalm which reveal the same opinion: see footnote to verse 17.

Title

The title ascribes the psalm to Solomon. The AV followed LXX in making it a psalm *for* Solomon, which the Hebrew in itself would allow. But it is the construction regularly translated 'A psalm of' David, *etc.*, and unless those headings are to be rendered 'A psalm *for*' So-and-so,[1] this example must be a genitive like the rest. There is no strong reason against Solomon's authorship: the final verse is rounding off a book or books of the Psalter, in which David is the chief but not the only author. The psalm has a style of its own, and whether it is a prayer of Solomon initially for his own reign (possibly at an anniversary of his accession) or for that of his son, it is apt to his times, when Israel was briefly an empire, and to the ideals of kingship which his prayer at Gibeon expressed (1 Ki. 3:6–9).

72:1–4. Royal righteousness

The king's role as guardian of justice and protector of the poor is emphasized in history—if too often by default: *cf.* Jeremiah 22:15–17—and in Messianic prophecy: *cf.* Isaiah 11:4. In verses 1 and 2[2] the fourfold *thy* goes to the heart of

[1] See Introduction, VI. *b* (p. 33).
[2] The form of the verb which opens verse 2 favours the translation 'he shall judge', introducing a series of prophecies in verses 2–7, rather than prayers (*cf.* AV, RV). But the majority of interpreters follow LXX in translating the verbs as in RSV. Verses 8–10 and 15–17 are introduced by verbs which leave no doubt that they are prayers.

the matter, first in that the ability to deal justly is seen as God-given (as both Solomon's prayer for wisdom in 1 Ki. 3, and the prophecy of the Spirit-filled Messiah in Is. 11 emphasize), and secondly in that even the poor are seen as *God's* poor—a far-reaching concept which will be given its classic expression in Matthew 25:35ff.

Righteousness (1, 2, 3) dominates this opening, since in Scripture it is the first virtue of government, even before compassion (which will be the theme of verses 12–14). This point is made explicitly in the Mosaic law, which forbids partiality in judgment, whether it favours (surprisingly) the poor or the rich (Ex. 23:3, 6).

3. *Prosperity* (Heb. *šālôm*), the harmonious wholeness which includes peace (the word most often used to translate *šālôm*; *cf.* AV, RV here),[1] is also secondary to righteousness, which is the soil or climate in which peace flourishes (*cf.* verse 7 and also Is. 32:17 for the same order of priority). In this verse (3) *righteousness* has something of its wider but related sense of 'proper functioning'; see note on Psalm 24:5.

72:5–7. Endless reign

The prayer, *may he live*, is a reading based on the LXX, whereas our Hebrew text has 'may they fear thee'.[2] But in either case the stanza speaks of an enduring dominion, in the light of verse 7, and introduces what is almost a refrain with its allusion to the life-span of the *sun* and *moon* (5, 7, 17). How little this might mean is obvious from the address, 'O king, live for ever', in the book of Daniel; yet also how much, can be seen from the Messianic prophecies and from the way these were understood in New Testament times.[3]

6, 7. This beautiful simile may have been prompted by 'the last words of David' (2 Sa. 23:1–7), where the just king is like sun and rain to his subjects, creating the conditions in which all that is fresh and good may flourish. It is the other side of kingship to the 'rod of iron' of Psalm 2:9; yet the one is the true complement of the other, as verse 4 has shown already. A further point emerges from the Hebrew text of verse 7, which has 'righteous man' instead of *righteousness*,

---

[1] NEB here translates it by both words together, 'peace and prosperity'.

[2] LXX evidently had a text reading *ya'ᵃrîk*, 'may he continue', as against MT *yîrā'ûkā*, 'may they fear thee'.

[3] *E.g.* Ps. 110:4; Ezk. 37:25; Jn. 12:34; Heb. 7:24f.

drawing attention to the humble counterpart of the righteous king: the individual subject, on whose integrity depends the *peace* or wellbeing (see on 3, above) of the whole. *Cf.* Isaiah 60:21.

72:8–11. Boundless realm

Sea to sea . . . may be a reference to the promised boundaries in Exodus 23:31, 'from the Red Sea to the sea of the Philistines' (*i.e.* to the Palestinian shores of the Mediterranean) 'and from the wilderness to the River' (*i.e.* to the Euphrates, RSV). But if so, verses 10 and 11 make it the nucleus of an empire that is world-wide.

9. RSV unnecessarily 'corrects' the Hebrew to read *his foes*, where the text has 'desert-dwellers'.

> 'Arabia's desert-ranger
> To him shall bow the knee.'[1]

Admittedly the word for 'desert-dwellers' usually denotes non-human creatures; yet not invariably. *Cf.* 74:14, lit., 'to a people, desert-dwellers'.[2]

10. *Tarshish* may have been Tartessus in Spain; it was in any case a name associated with long voyages; likewise *the isles* or 'coastlands' were synonymous with the ends of the earth: see, *e.g.*, Isaiah 42:10.

11, 12. *Sheba and Seba* seem to have been either related peoples in South Arabia, or alternative spellings of the same name, in which case 'and' will have its sense of 'even' (*cf.* the articles on these two names in *NBD*). The Queen of Sheba was but one of many who made such a journey as this 'with gifts' (1 Ki. 10:1ff.; 23ff.), but the psalm looks beyond these tokens of courtesy and culture to 'something greater than Solomon' and to gifts of total homage. It is all the more striking, in view of this, that the first stirrings of this great Gentile movement were greeted by Christ with resolves of self-offering (Jn. 12:20ff.), not with Solomonic self-display.

72:12–14. Compassionate king

Solomon continues to speak more wisely than he was ever to act. His prayers, at his accession and the dedication of the

---

[1] J. Montgomery, 'Hail to the Lord's Anointed'.
[2] For suggested reinterpretations of 74:14, see comments there.

Temple (1 Ki. 3:6ff.; 8: *e.g.* 38ff.), show the sensitivity which he admired in the king whom he describes here; but his people's verdict was that 'he made our yoke heavy'. It was again the opposite of what his greater Son would be known for (Mt. 11:28ff.).

72:15-17. Endless blessing
Many kinds of wealth are touched on here: the *gold* which is won by human daring and skill (*cf.* Jb. 28:1ff.); the *blessings* which are prayed down in love, the wealth of growing things[1] (*the tops of the mountains* are mentioned as the most unpromising of soils) and of teeming cities (the context is not our urban jungles but a land waiting to be used, and defences to be manned); not least, the wealth of honour and happiness[2] of a kind which comes recognizably from the hand of God. The terms of verse 17 are virtually those of the promise to Abram in Genesis 12:2f.[3]

It is a magnificent prayer for a king and his country; for a leader and his enterprise; for *the* King and the consummation of His kingdom, into which 'the kings of the earth shall bring their glory', and 'by (whose) light shall the nations walk' (Rev. 21:24).

72:18-20. Doxology and Conclusion
The doxology rounds off the Second Book of Psalms (42-72), rather than this psalm by itself; but the world-wide vision which has just unfolded lends its colour to the praise, especially in 19b.

20. It seems from this verse that the word *prayers* was the earliest collective term for the Psalms. They are now entitled 'Praises' in the Hebrew Bible. Between them, the two terms bring out the two most characteristic notes of the Psalter.

---

[1] The word translated *abundance* (but AV, RV mg. 'an handful') occurs only here in the Old Testament. G. R. Driver (*VT* 1 (1951), p. 249) sees it as a loan-word meaning 'lot, bit, piece'; hence, 'an allocation, *i.e.*, plenty'. (*Cf.* our colloquial use of the word 'lot'.)

[2] The last word of verse 17 would be better translated 'happy', as in NEB.

[3] *His fame continue* is lit. 'His name be productive' or 'His name have offspring'. A rabbinic tradition treated the verb (*yinnôn*, 'be productive') as a proper noun, making Yinnon one of the names of the Messiah. Artificial as this is, it confirms that this psalm was treated as a Messianic prophecy.